LOS ANGELES IN THE 1970S:

WEIRD SCENES INSIDE THE GOLD MINE

edited by

DAVID KUKOFF

A Barnacle Book | Rare Bird Books
Los Angeles, Calif

THIS IS A GENUINE BARNACLE BOOK

A Barnacle Book | Rare Bird Books
453 South Spring Street, Suite 302
Los Angeles, CA 90013
rarebirdbooks.com

FIRST TRADE PAPERBACK ORIGINAL EDITION

A portion of "It Was Fun While It Lasted" was previously
published in *Los Angeles Magazine.*

Set in Minion Pro
Printed in the United States

10 9 8 7 6 5 4 3 2

Publisher's Cataloging-in-Publication data
Names: Kukoff, David, editor.
Title: Los Angeles in the 1970s : weird scenes inside the gold mine / edited by
David Kukoff.
Description: First Trade Paperback Original Edition | A Barnacle Book | New
York, NY ; Los Angeles, CA: Rare Bird Books, 2016.
Identifiers: ISBN 978-1-942600-71-8
Subjects: LCSH Los Angeles (Calif.)—1970-1979. | Los Angeles (Calif.)—
Civilization—20th century. | Los Angeles (Calif.)—Social conditions—20th
century. | Los Angeles (Calif.)—History—20th century. | Popular culture—Los
Angeles (Calif.)—History—20th century. | BISAC LITERARY COLLECTIONS
/ American / General
Classification: LCC F869.L857 K85 2016 | DDC 979.4/94—dc23

CONTENTS

INTRODUCTION

by David Kukoff

A
S OUR CITY'S POET laureate (and one of our contributors), Luis Rodriguez, says, "To truly love LA you have to see it with different eyes, askew perhaps, beyond the fantasy-induced Hollywood spectacles." That "askew"-ness has all too often been the dominion of the outsider, the eastern media interloper who has painted a portrait of Los Angeles in brush strokes of smog gray and desert beige, all of it whitewashing a monochromatic barometric gauge that rendered us a superficial lot of sun-baked, surfed-out zombies. It felt redolent of what invariably lies at the root of all one-sided rivalries: jealousy, pockmarked by a curious brand of group delusion that willfully spun chronically foul weather and stingily small skies as glorious seasonal change, the exaltation of which always smacked to me of Stockholm syndrome.

Like most of my native peers, I spent years bristling at Woody Allen's dismissal of our city's cultural offerings. Especially given that when *Annie Hall* was released, I was all of nine years old and had no idea how liberating it was to come upon a red light and realize that, depending on your lane and direction, it had no power to impede your progress. In time, I would come to appreciate the symbology behind this and realize that Woody had, in assessing LA's ostensible sole cultural perk, unknowingly identified one of the great virtues our city bestows upon its citizens: the ability to grasp the fluidity behind life's red lights.

I wrote my novel, *Children of the Canyon,* for many reasons, but among them was my desire to add a dimension to the countercultural terrain Joan Didion and Joni Mitchell had so vividly conferred upon the cultural canon. Here, now, these women were finally making their voices heard…and yet there was still something missing from the filmy residue of the flower children's experience: namely, the experience of the actual children. I had attended school with several kids whose parents were part of this world, and it occurred to me that we had never seen it depicted through their eyes. The more I wrote, the more I realized that there was more to the story than a series of local episodes at the hands of our opposite-of-helicopter parents. That while the seventies were single-handedly responsible for more nostalgia among my contemporaries than all the other decades of their existences combined, it was a decade that also represented a tectonic, seemingly permanent shift in the country's psyche. At some point in those ten years, America went from the "we're all in this together" mentality of the Great Society Sixties to the "greed is good" ethos of the Reagan Eighties, an ethos that still reverberates in the sociopolitical landscape today. And Los Angeles—the second-rate beach town, the Hollywood fluff-factory—had, fittingly enough, been an actor that had played a crucial part in that shift; not only had so much of the most visible counterculture taken place right in our own backyard, but the solution to the perceived failure of the sixties idealism—Ronald Reagan—was also something of a local product. It occurred to me, long after I'd finished writing *Children,* that while a great swath of Los Angeles's history (certainly anything to do with corruption and our indigenous juxtaposition of sunshine and noir) had been covered in print and film, the 1970s remained something of a dark decade in the city's recorded history. And so, under the stewardship of Tyson Cornell of Rare Bird Books, I decided to ask some of the city's citizens to tell their stories.

I soon realized that the Los Angeles of the 1970s might, on the surface, have looked like a cultural desert—complete with all the requisite mirage metaphors—but it was also a thirsty, parched terrain at the edge of Big Sky territory where smarts, hustle, and more than a little chutzpah could turn a half-assed dream into a full-fledged reality.

It was a landscape fashioned on *Brady Bunch*–worthy Astroturf, but one on which, in reality, preteens challenged—with more than a little complicity from the lax sexual ethics of the era—the threshold that, in generations prior, had so inviolably separated them from full-fledged adulthood. It was a metropolis in which racial discrimination had seemingly never before been so forcibly challenged, yet at the same time remained so business-end-of-a-police-baton as usual. It was postwar (two, if you count Vietnam) and pre-Olympics, which is the event most Angelenos identify as the origin point of Los Angeles's current status as not only a world-class, but perhaps America's most important, city. It was still, put simply, very much the Wild West, the last decade in which Los Angeles bore some resemblance to the frontier town it had once been—the unchartered, "anything goes" fertilized soil that had granted so many repressed, cast-off souls a shot not only at redemption (there was plenty of that, too, but redemption is cheap and hardly region-specific), but at something far greater: reinvention. Which—as anyone who's ever sailed right through an intersection that, by New York's rules, would stop them dead in their tracks, knows—is why the demography continues to favor the East to West migratory pattern, and not vice versa.

Here, then, are some of the most colorful tales, some of the most— per the words of contributor John Densmore's famous Angeleno band—"weird scenes inside the gold mine" that was Los Angeles in the 1970s. What's inside said gold mine? A kidnap/murder involving the proprietors of a private sex club. An officially-sanctioned, alternative school that practiced Scientology and est. The Johnny Wadd origin story. Anthony Davis, the USC running back who followed in O. J. Simpson's cleats. Feminist art installations. The Z Channel and Dr. Demento. Densmore waxing on putting L.A. Woman on wax. Geza X on his strange journey from Gong Show reject ("Would you gong Jesus? Would you gong Moses? WOULD YOU GONG IDI AMIN???") to Dead Kennedys' and Germs' producer. Pieces from LA poet laureate, Luis Rodriguez, and acclaimed authors Matthew Specktor, Deanne Stillman, Steve Hodel, Chip Jacobs, Bruce Ferber, Joel Drucker, Dana Johnson, Sam Geimer, and Jeremy Rosenberg. Original essays from award-winning film and television luminaries

Jillian Franklyn, Ken Levine, Howard Gewirtz, and Michael Lazarou. Observations from academics Debra Wacks and Erica Cohen Lyons, as well as from journalists, social impresarios, and art scenesters Mitch Schneider, Joe Donnelly, Lynne Friedman, and Del Zamora. Poetry from Library Girl founder Susan Hayden and Beyond Baroque legend Jim Natal. And more…and more. If it was breathtaking, groundbreaking, exciting, or just flat out…well, weird, and took place in LA in the 1970s, chances are it's in this book.

My most heartfelt gratitude goes out to Tyson Cornell, Alice Marsh-Elmer, Julia Callahan, and Winona Leon at Rare Bird for their endless enthusiasm, guidance, and patience. I also have to add that, if I make it sound as though opportunity waned post-seventies, that memo hasn't been received by the literary world of Los Angeles, the members of which accepted me as one of their own and couldn't possibly have been more inclusive and supportive of this project at every turn. On the personal front, my love and life partner, Julie Jennings, gave me everything from editorial advice to the operational backup I so desperately need every time I read, attend an event, or attempt to leave the house without my head screwed on. Lastly, a huge thank you to my parents, Ben and Lydia Kukoff, who, deliberately or not, raised me in the city I have come to love, and blessed me with the foundation that made this book possible.

L.A. WOMAN REDUX

by John Densmore

O N A RECORDING BREAK one afternoon, Jim and Robby went across the street to Monaco Liquors to get some beers for themselves and cigarettes and apple juice for Ray and me.

"Do you know what 'Hyacinth House' means, Ray?" I asked while Jim was gone.

"No, but I see the bathroom is clear."

"Yeah, that's a funny line. It's almost pathetic in its paranoia. I love the feel, though. Folk rock is fun for me to play on drums…as a change of pace. It's loping and technically easy."

> *What are they doing in the Hyacinth House?*
> *To please the lions this day*
> *I need a brand new friend who doesn't bother me.*
> *I need someone, yeah, who doesn't need me.*
> *I see the bathroom is clear,*
> *I think somebody's near.*
> *I'm sure that someone is following me, oh yeah.*
> *Why did you throw the Jack of Hearts away?*
> *It was the only card in the deck that I had left to play.*
> *And I'll say it again, I need a brand new friend.*

Edith Hamilton's book on Greek mythology illuminated the Hyacinth myth for me. She helped me realize that Jim's song "Hyacinth House" was possibly the saddest one he ever wrote. Hamilton wrote:

> *Another flower that came into being through the death of a beautiful youth was the hyacinth.*

...

> *The festival of Hyacinths.*
> *That lasts throughout the tranquil night.*
> *In a contest with Apollo.*
> *He was slain.*
> *Discus throwing they competed,*
> *And the god's swift cast*
> *Sped beyond the goal he aimed at*

> *and struck Hyacinthus full in the forehead, a terrible wound. He had been Apollo's dearest companion. There was no rivalry between them when they tried which could throw the discus the farthest; they were only playing a game. The god was horror-struck to see the blood gush forth and the lad, deathly pale, fall to the ground. He turned as pale himself as he caught him in his arms and tried to stanch the wound. But it was too late. When he held him, the boy's head fell back as a flower does when its stem is broken. He was dead and Apollo, kneeling beside him, wept for him, dying so young, so beautiful. He had killed him, although through no fault of his, and he cried, "Oh, if I could give my life for yours, or die for you." Even as he spoke, the bloodstained grass turned green again and there bloomed forth the wondrous flower that would make the lad's name forever known.*

***

IN THE SPRING OF 1971, the low-budget concept on the *L.A. Woman* album paid off. Our previous record had been a comeback for us, but there'd been no hit singles. Elektra prez, Jac Holzman, called a meeting to confer with us on picking a song to be released off what was to become our last album.

I was leaning against the Spanish fireplace in Jac's office, Jim and Ray were sitting in the green velvet, reupholstered antique chairs, when Jac made his pitch.

"I have a hunch about 'Love Her Madly.'"

I did, too.

"Nah, it's too commercial," Robby responded quickly from the corner of the room.

It staggered me. Robby had written the song; didn't he want another shot at the big time ("Light My Fire" being his previous monster)?

"Isn't that what a single is supposed to be?" Jac retorted.

"Yeah…well," Robby said, walking up to the fireplace. "How about 'Riders' or 'Changeling'?"

"'Riders' is too long, Robby," Ray chimed in.

Jim seemed ambivalent.

"I'd love to release 'L.A. Woman,'" I added, "but it would have to be cut at seven minutes, and I don't know where."

"'Love Her Madly' is a top-five record," Jac negotiated. "Let's go with it, and if we get some action, then we can have a second single. 'Riders On The Storm' will get more FM airplay than any record in history. If 'Love Her Madly' is a hit first, then we release 'Riders.'"

"That sounds okay," I said, looking at Robby for approval. Ray and Jim nodded, and Robby reluctantly confirmed. He knew that Jac had verbally committed to spending the money to release a second single. I still couldn't get over the fact that Robby was so protective of his version of the bad-boy Doors image that he would sacrifice having one of his babies on the air.

***

SONG BY SONG, JAC Holtzman predicted exactly what happened. On April 24, 1971, "Love Her Madly" went to number four, and we were back on AM radio, hot and heavy. I didn't know yet that the lyrics predicted what was to come in my relationship with Julia.

Don't you love her madly
Want to be her daddy
Don't you love her face
Don't you love her as
She's walkin' out the door

They aptly described my shaky inner world to come and our outer public life, which was getting increasingly strong. Meanwhile, "Riders On The Storm" was receiving heavy FM airplay, as was the single "Love Her Madly," and the pressure was on to put "Riders" out and get it to chart. But it was six minutes long and nobody knew how to cut it down.

Except me.

With my jazz background, I heard several sections in Ray's piano solo that could be lifted out, without sacrificing any soul. I called up Bruce Botnick, went over to his house, and we did the surgery. The piano solo still built methodically and logically, but it was condensed, and Bruce and I were very proud when Ray couldn't tell where the cuts were in the edited version.

Despite this, there was no escaping the fact that huge success had befallen us four lads from Venice, California, and there was no time for the original gestation period of a song. Gone was the time for the womb-like incubation we liked giving to each of our creations. Jim had suggested moving to an island and starting all over. He alluded to that idea in our song, "Strange Days," saying that our old way of making music was being destroyed and we should find a new town. He was trying to get back to renew that elusive quality that was with us in the rock and roll garage many years before; but it, like so much other Hyacinthine beauty that had been there along the way, had left us. Soon, Jim would, too, and years later we would find ourselves in court, fighting tooth and nail over the integrity of our name and our music.

***

JAC RELEASED "RIDERS" ON the heels of "Love Her Madly." Despite being our least commercial rock song, it, too, climbed the charts. (Little did I know that its popularity would lead to it being licensed for a tire commercial in England. When asked why I had allowed it, when we'd had a strict policy against our music and commercials, I said, "I guess I felt bad saying no all the time. That was the only time we permitted use of our music for a commercial, and I felt like I was betraying Jim so I gave my portion of the proceeds to charity.")

The Sunset Strip was now studded with billboards advertising record albums, a trend Holzman started with our first record. He forked out the bucks for our second billboard, with an image from the inner sleeve of the record jacket. It was a startling shot of a woman crucified to a telephone pole: the L.A. Woman.

> *Drivin' down your freeway*
> *Midnight alleys roam*
> *Cops in cars, the topless bars*
> *Never saw a woman so alone*
> *So alone, so alone, so*
> *Alone…*

What Jac didn't know was how prophetic it would prove to be. None of us knew. The sign was at the foot of the entrance to Laurel Canyon, facing the billboard, where we'd had our first ad for the first record four years before. The entrance to Laurel was like a shrine to me. Where Jim, Robby, and I had lived. Bookends to our career. *The Doors*, our first album billboard, faced east—the rising sun, our occidental, a land we conquered. The *L.A. Woman* billboard for our last record faced west—the setting sun, the end of Western civilization, and the end of our public life as a group.

> *Weird scenes inside the gold mine*
> *Ride the king's highway west, baby*
> *The west is the best*
> *Get here and we'll do the rest…*

John Densmore *was the drummer for the legendary Doors, whom he joined with guitarist Robby Krieger after the two were recruited out of a band called the Psychedelic Rangers. Although Densmore was perhaps the least visible member of the group, his jazz training provided subtle rhythmic shifts away from the rock norm, furthering the band's unique sound. After The Doors' dissolution, Densmore was fairly quiet; he worked with Robby Krieger off and on, both on Krieger's solo albums and with the Butts Band. In more recent years, Densmore penned the acclaimed* Riders on the Storm: My Life With Jim Morrison and the Doors, *an account of the band's rise and fall from his own perspective, as well as* The Doors Unhinged, *about his legal battles over The Doors' licensing legacy.*

WHAT NEEDED SCREWING GOT SCREWED

by Luis J. Rodriguez

Any good craftsman carries his tools.
Years ago they were always at the ready.
In a car. In a knapsack.
Claw hammers, crisscrossed heads,
thirty-two ouncers. Wrenches in all sizes,
sometimes with oil caked on the teeth.
Screwdrivers with multicolored plastic handles
(what needed screwing got screwed).
I had specialty types: allen wrenches,
torpedo levels, taps, and dies.
A trusty tape measure.
Maybe a chalk line…

IN THE 1970s, I labored within industrial Los Angeles—in a steel mill, a foundry, a paper mill, a chemical refinery, and in construction. I had skills: truck driving, mechanics, welding, carpentry, smelting, piping, down, and dirty. When people think of the city, they generally don't conjure up steel mills or auto plants. The images tend toward Hollywood. Glittering lights. Marquees. Sunset Strip. More like beaches.

Los Angeles is that, but it's also the country's largest manufacturing center. Today it leads in aerospace, defense, and the so-called creative economy—movies, music, fashion, design. It has the largest commercial port in the US: the Los Angeles/Long Beach harbors.

I'm now part of that creative economy, the current official poet laureate of the city with fifteen books in poetry, children's books, fiction, memoir, and nonfiction. I cofounded and help run a cultural space, bookstore, and small press called Tia Chucha's Cultural Center in the northeast San Fernando Valley.

But in the 1970s I was an unlikely working class hero (I was more likely a working class fool). When union-negotiated consent decrees in the 1970s brought African-Americans, Mexicans, Native Americans, and women into the higher-paid skilled jobs, previously dominated by white males, the Bethlehem Steel Plant in southeast Los Angeles hired me for their "repair gang." Prior to this I labored in unskilled drudgery. The year was 1974. I had just married my "high school sweetheart," who received her diploma only two months before the wedding. Less then a year after, we had our first child.

I recall donning my hard hat, safety glasses, steel-toed shoes, and mechanic's uniform, and staring at the mirror. I felt as if my life had purpose, direction, longevity. This job had rotating shifts, including "graveyard," often double shifts (sixteen-hour days), and great pay, particularly with overtime.

The plant's nineteenth-century equipment was brought over from back east around World War II, when LA also boasted fabrication, assembly, or refinery work in auto, tires, garments, canneries, shipbuilding, aerospace, meatpacking, oil, and more. We had GM and Ford plants, Firestone and Michelin, Boeing and Lockheed. This industry drew workers of all ethnicities from the South, the Midwest, the Northeast, the Southwest, and Mexico for what were largely well-paid, mostly union jobs with pensions, health benefits, and a taste of blue-collar stability.

Despite being miles removed from the industrial powerhouses of Chicago, Detroit, Pittsburgh, Cleveland, and the like, in LA you could follow much of this industry from the northeast San Fernando Valley, to the Alameda Corridor north of downtown, down to the Harbor. Whole towns with names like Commerce and Industry thrived.

But in the mid-1970s, deindustrialization began to hit throughout the country, picking up steam in the 1980s, mostly due to advanced technology, including robotics. Labor-saving devices became labor-replacing. Major industries also sought cheaper labor markets in the South, Mexico, Central America, Southeast Asia, and such— impoverished areas with little or no regulation, down to dollar-a-day wages, and low living standards. Then during the first Reagan administration, the worst recession since the Great Depression exploded in 1981–82 and the unemployment rate went to double digits. Only the 2008 recession cut deeper.

Homelessness became a permanent feature of American life.

We all know about the Rust Belt that traversed through states like New York, New Jersey, Pennsylvania, Illinois, Michigan, and Ohio. Los Angeles may not be considered part of the Rust Belt, but the impact was the same. As plants closed, the two most industrial cities—Los Angeles and Chicago—were known as the "gang capitals" of the world when drugs, guns, and gangs became key to a new, largely illicit economy.

Mass incarceration, which heightened in the 1990s, turned into its own "industry" arising from the crisis. In California alone, the state went from 15 prisons with 15,000 people in the early 1970s to a height of 34 prisons and up to 175,000 prisoners in the 2000s.

The places I worked at during the height of industrial might in the 1970s went down—Bethlehem Steel in 1981, and at St. Regis Paper Company, National Lead Foundry, Chevron Chemical Refinery at various times… I can go on and on. Some three hundred big mills and plants were gone by the mid-1980s. Forever. And with it, any illusion of stability.

What needed screwing got screwed…but only figuratively. In the literal sense, it was far less constructive.

I don't want people to forget the City of Angels as a City of Workers. My decade or so in that time, that industry, were extremely meaningful to me. At the same time, we can't go back fully to that kind of work. Instead the city, the country, and the world is crying out for something new and momentous—aligning our governance, our economy, our environment, and our culture to the possibilities of the new technology as well as the creative potential in every person, family, and community.

And, again, Los Angeles leads the way...

I often met other travelers, their tools in tow,
and I'd say: "Go ahead, take my stereo and TV.
Take my car. Take my toys of leisure.
Just leave the tools."
Nowadays, I don't haul these mechanical implements.
But I still make sure to carry the tools
of my trade: words and ideas,
the kind no one can take away.
So there may not be any work today,
but when there is, I'll be ready.
I got my tools.

Luis J. Rodriguez *is a former gang member, drug user, and occupant of multiple jails in and around East Los Angeles, including juvenile hall and two adult facilities before leaving that life by age twenty. He then worked as a truck driver, bus driver, carpenter, foundry smelter, mechanic, welder, paper mill worker, and more, including four years in a Los Angeles–area steel mill. Determined to be a writer, Luis attended community college at night, received a journalist certificate one summer at the University of California, Berkeley, and worked in weekly newspapers in East LA, a daily newspaper in San Bernardino, and as a radio news writer, among other jobs in the field. He covered stories in Mexico and Central America and also wrote poetry, short stories, and essays. He edited a literary arts magazine and later wrote for a community-based political newspaper as well as an all-news radio station in Chicago. Today Luis has fifteen books in all genres, including the best-selling memoir* Always Running, La Vida Loca, *and* Gang Days in L.A. *Now back in LA, he is the founding editor of Tia Chucha Press and cofounder of Tia Chucha's Cultural Center & Bookstore, both in the San Fernando Valley. From 2014 to 2016, Luis served as the official poet laureate of Los Angeles.*

VENICE BOHEMIA: FROM ABBOT KINNEY TO THE Z-BOYS

by Joe Donnelly

A S MAJOR EVENTS GO, this one may not rank up there with Alaskan statehood, the advent of NASA, or even that April fifteenth day when twenty-three thousand plus fans packed Seals Stadium to see the erstwhile Brooklyn Dodgers take on the erstwhile New York Giants in the first major league baseball game played on the West Coast. Even so, it was not without consequence when, in 1958, Skip Engblom's mom finally gave into the boy's badgering and moved the family to Ennis Place, behind Venice Circle.

Those were good times in the good ol' US of A. The Cold War was still cold enough, and at the midpoint of the American Century we were happily turning away from Old World entanglements while embracing everything *new*! Los Angeles, of course, was the capital of the new. By 1958, the city's can-do spirit was fueled by aerospace- and defense-industry prosperity, Hollywood's rising entertainment hegemony, and a suburban development boom. It all added up to a uniquely sun-and-fun-flavored Space Age optimism perhaps best captured in the local proliferation of whimsical Googie architecture and design.

Skipper Boy, as Engblom would be called for years to come, saw many things sprout from the seeds of the mid-century's seemingly limitless possibilities. The aforementioned Dodgers came to town. Downtown Los Angeles grew skyscrapers on Bunker Hill. Freeways were starting to connect the vast region. CalTech and Jet Propulsion Laboratories were rocketing toward space. UCLA, Otis Arts Institute, Chouinard (cum-CalArts), and the Ferus Gallery were already setting loose on the world artists such as Billy Al Bengston, Ed Ruscha, Ed Moses, Noah Purifoy, and John Baldisseri who would define a muscular, new west avant-garde.

It was a heady time, and while Engblom saw a lot, nothing moved him quite like what he saw that day when he kept pedaling his bike past the old farmer's market, where his mother worked, until he finally reached the place where the cement met the sand. There, at the end of the road, Santa Monica Boulevard, the terminus of old Route 66, he found a little stand from which he could rent an inflatable raft and venture into the ocean. Bobbing around in the breakers, he saw a guy stand up on a surfboard and ride a wave.

"I completely flipped out," Engblom recalled. "It was probably the defining moment of my existence. I knew it was all I ever wanted to do. I needed to do that more than anything."

That need is what propelled Engblom and his family to Venice Beach where, years later, he, Craig Stecyk, and Jeff Ho would join forces to capture a little cultural lightning in a bottle known as the Zephyr Skate Team. The Z-boys were what was left over after the sweet dreams of Abbot Kinney and Kennedy's Camelot died violent deaths side by side at the end of the road. And the kids skated like they knew it, sparking a sea of change in youth culture that established them as the last gasp of bohemian Venice and, perhaps, its enduring legacy.

***

FIRST, THOUGH, LET'S GO back to 1958, when Skipper Boy arrived in Venice.

At the time, the Venice West Cafe and Gas House coffee shop scenes were in full swing. Lawrence Lipton, the controversial scenester/

impresario/journalist/screenwriter and Beat-poet-wannabe, had just published *The Holy Barbarians*. The book, though sometimes derided as the work of a cultural climber, is as responsible as anything for codifying the public image of the hopped-up, beret-wearing, bearded Beatnik weirdo. Though Lipton never quite earned the respect as a poet he strived for, he had his consolations. For one, his son, James Lipton, the erstwhile procurer of Parisian prostitutes, would grow up to be the oddly charismatic and slyly hilarious host of *Inside The Actors Studio*. And Lawrence himself did land a role as the "King of the Beatniks" in the 1960 B-movie *The Hypnotic Eye*.

Barbarians brought unwanted attention to the Beats and artists who lived and worked on the cheap in the "Appalachia by the Sea," (as Venice and the Ocean Park neighborhood of Santa Monica had come to be known.) Before long, lurkers and opportunists, some less savory than others, had overtaken the scene, instigating a campaign by more civic-minded (or property-values-minded) citizens to stamp out the latest outbreak of Venetian bohemianism.

The Beat era, though, may have been the closest Abbot Kinney's dream of Venice By The Sea as a catalyst for an American cultural renaissance ever came to fruition. Though Venice By The Sea would take a turn for the tacky, at first Kinney had more high-minded literary and intellectual aspirations for his burg.

Kinney's long and winding journey west is a Bunyan-sized tale itself, but to make a long story short, the sickly and insomniac scion of a powerful New Jersey family who made millions in tobacco found a place he could get a good night's sleep and breathe a little easier near the marshy lands around what is now the border of Santa Monica and Venice. He founded Ocean Park with partner Francis G. Ryan in the late 1880s. When Ryan died, his widow married Thomas Dudley who became Kinney's new partner in coastal real estate speculation. The two didn't get along, and Kinney turned his sights toward the swamps south of Ocean Park.

Here, Kinney started digging out his dream, literally—canals, colonnaded architecture, highbrow cultural events at the Venice Assembly modeled on the Chautauqua programs in upstate New York. He even imported gondoliers from Italy. Kinney's vision made Venice, even if it never quite became what he envisioned. How earnest he was about it all, or how much of it was a hustle to reel Midwesterners in from the cold, wasn't entirely clear when Venice of America opened up in 1905.

Regardless, what Kinney wrought was staggering in scale and mind-blowing in detail. From Windward Avenue to the bathhouse to the canals to the swimming lagoon, the Midway Plaisance, the miniature railroad, the Ship Hotel, the Venice Pier, and, yes, the beach itself—even the skeptics, who'd taken to calling the project Kinney's Folly, were impressed.

But almost from the start, Kinney's lofty ideals, sincere or not, competed with the lowbrow and sometimes illicit underbelly of the area's main draw—the handful of amusement piers that sprouted in the sand and jutted out into the sea along this short stretch of coast, each trying to outdo the other in a turf war of attractions.

After a fire in 1908, Kinney rebuilt his amusement pier in 1913 to compete with Alexander Fraser's new "Million Dollar" Pier and the Pickering Pier, both in Ocean Park. Sunset Pier (at what is now North Venice Boulevard) opened on July 4, 1921, tripling the values of beachfront lots. The Lick Pier, adjacent to Fraser's pier on the Venice side of the sand off Navy Street, opened that following September. Mere sun, surf, and sand apparently weren't enough, and soon the landscape was blotted by flying circuses, aerials, multiple rollercoasters, racing derbies, speedboats, carousels, games of chance, theaters, dance halls, and, inevitably, brothels.

The piers drew hundreds of thousands of tourists every weekend. Complicit in Venice and Ocean Park's turn toward the tawdry were the city of Los Angeles's Victorian-era restrictions on public dancing. To get their kicks, denizens of the big city flocked to the Wild West seaside where folks could pursue the ancient rites free from persecution.

A major problem with the piers, though, was that they were always catching on fire. Abbot Kinney's Venice Pier burned first in 1908, and again just a month after he died on November 14, 1920. The Frasier Pier (aka Ocean Park Pier) burned in 1912 and 1915. The Pickering and Lick Piers burned in 1924. Each time a pier burned, it grew more expensive and unwieldy to rebuild. Most were in disuse by the 1940s.

Kinney's grand vision may have had some checkered incarnations, but he himself lived longer, bigger, and more imaginatively than he probably dreamed possible when he was growing up as an asthmatic, sleepless boy back in New Jersey. In that way, he is a prototypical Angeleno. Even so, he probably turned over in his grave when his increasingly overextended Venetians voted 3,130 to 2,216 for annexation to Los Angeles over Santa Monica, thereby turning Venice of America into Venice Beach, a suburb of the big city seventeen miles to the east.

Perhaps fittingly, famed Los Angeles evangelist Aimee Semple McPherson waded into the Venice Beach surf six months later and disappeared. McPherson had been lobbying against Sunday dances, and it was rumored a hit had been put out on her by business interests. A massive search turned up nothing, though a lifeguard drowned looking for McPherson. A distraught mourner committed suicide when it appeared McPherson had perished. A month after her disappearance, Venice Beach hosted a memorial and flowers filled the sea. Two days after the memorial, however, McPherson turned up outside Douglas, Arizona, telling of kidnap, torture, and escape. The tall tale didn't quite add up and charges were filed and later dropped.

It felt like the end of an era and, even it if was all a holy con, it had been one hell of a ride.

The Depression put a damper on Venice and Ocean Park's carnival days and the crowds started thinning. When the Ohio Oil Company struck oil in 1929, the area had a new economic imperative that littered the area with wells and clogged the waterways, all but choking the remaining vestiges of Kinney's dream. Los Angeles filled in the canals, and master plans called for the eventual dismantling of piers and widening of beaches. Venice and environs lay fallow throughout the war and after, as the local oil boom subsided and Los Angeles's attention went elsewhere. Property values dropped, rents were cheap, and the bohemians, artists, Beats, and bums filed into the slum by the sea.

***

SKIP ENGBLOM HAS PROBABLY been called one or all of these things at various times in his life. His pedigree is eclectic enough to fit the bill. Engblom's father was an innovator of modern pro wrestling. He wrote characters and storylines featuring the likes of Haystacks Calhoun, the giant who wore a chain around his neck with a horseshoe dangling from it and was a frequent household guest of the Engbloms. Skip's 1958 arrival in Venice was just in time to see the specter of Abbot Kinney rise once more from Davey Jones's locker—this time, in the form of Pacific Ocean Park, affectionately referred to by locals as POP.

Pacific Ocean Park was a $10 million investment in both the past *and* a starry-eyed vision of the future. Its primary benefactors were CBS and the Los Angeles Turf Club, aka Santa Anita Park, which was founded by the charismatic "Dentist with the Golden Drill" Charles "Doc" Strub. POP rose from the charred husks of the former Ocean Park Pier ("The Playground of the West") and its next-door neighbor, The Lick Pier, home of the famed Aragon Ballroom. It opened in July 1958, three years after Disneyland, with which it was meant to compete as a destination.

The park attempted to mix the carnival heritage of the area's legacy piers with a family-friendly, nautical-themed modernism. You could go on a Flight To Mars, or visit Neptune's Kingdom, take a ride on the Ocean Skyway, enjoy kitschy diversions such as the Enchanted Forest and Mystic Isles, or simply opt for amusement park stalwarts, like the rollercoasters. In retrospect, the entire enterprise feels like one final burst of damn-the-torpedoes whimsy before Los Angeles got serious. And it did just fine at first, it even outperformed the Magic Kingdom for a few years. But air conditioning, television, backyard pools, and the increasingly derelict environs surrounding POP took their toll on the attraction.

The park, in constant need of reinvestment to keep up with the powerhouse to the south, eventually reached the point of diminishing returns and closed down for good on October 6, 1967, the tail end of the Summer of Love. For the next half a dozen years or so, POP loomed forlornly over the borderland between Venice and Ocean Park, an area that artist, photographer, and cultural historian Craig Stecyk would dub Dogtown. During these years, as the sixties hardened into the early seventies, POP regularly caught fire (or was torched in acts of arson) and crumbled into the sea. Hollywood picked over its carcass, using the eerie setting for films such as *The Fugitive* and *They Shoot Horses, Don't They?* It remained a favorite set for cop shows until it was finally torn down. Meanwhile, POP offered a jurisdictional safe haven for hippies, surfers, hustlers, addicts, and artists who set up both workshop and home there and thrived in its skeletal remains.

In 1967, the Aragon Ballroom became the Cheetah Club and Lawrence Welk gave way to all the great bands of the day—The Doors, Buffalo Springfield, The Byrds, Pink Floyd, Jimi Hendrix, the Grateful Dead, and house band Nazz (soon to be Alice Cooper). William Wegman and John Baldessari had studios behind what would become the Zephyr surf shop on Bay Street and Main. Artists Wayne Holwick and Dana Woolfe put murals up on vacant buildings. Vato graffiti and the custom-car and pinstriping movements took cues from each other while the legacy of former residents David Alfaro Siqueiros and Stanton MacDonald-Wright hung in the air.

"We were exposed to art and culture continuously," Engblom said.

They were also exposed to something else. By the late sixties, the area's more than four hundred oil derricks were down to a handful of survivors. The carcass of POP, the vacant storefronts, the disappearing oil derricks, and filled-in canals were constant reminders that they were living in a sort of failed state. Venice locals The Doors were painting the psychedelic sounds of the Summer of Love in a darker hue, singing about this being the end, and the music being over. Someone said the sixties died here when Robert Kennedy was gunned down up the road.

"Nero fiddled while Rome burned. We surfed while America went down the tubes," Engblom told me some years ago. "Robert Kennedy (before he got assassinated that day), I walked out of my apartment on Venice Boulevard and he wave[d] at me and my mom and he was dead a couple hours later. Starting with all that—John F. Kennedy, then Martin Luther King, and then the brother—you just knew something bad was happening. Any sense that good things were going to follow pretty much died at that moment."

Did any neighborhood encapsulate the burned-out nature of the times better than Venice? The kids coming-of-age here in the seventies were latchkey kids, many of them from broken homes that didn't survive the sixties haze. These kids were survivors, hardened against the soft naïveté of their flower-power parents. Dogtown was ripe for something new, something more aggressive in the 1970s.

It happened in a surf shop. Actually, it happened first in the surf.

By now, Skip Engblom made it through the crucible of localism—which included the grommet's standard rites of passage of getting chased away, beaten up, and thrown in a dumpster—to become one of the regulars in the lineup at the Cove. The Cove was a break whose waves formed amid the pilings of a section of the old POP that went by the same name. Surfers would actually surf through the pilings when the waves broke through them. The fierce localism was partly protective—it was just too dangerous out there for kooks—and partly territorial: when you don't have much, you hold onto what you've got.

Engblom and Stecyk met in 1966 at a festival in Pismo Beach, where they ran into each other one morning and got to talking. Each thought he'd lure the other to a local breakfast joint and then step out on the tab. When they both ended up on street at the same time, an enduring friendship was formed.

Jeff Ho, Stecyk, and Engblom all went through a version of *Big Wednesday* during the late sixties. Dogtown youth tended to be 1-A eligible, and these guys did what they could to avoid the war. "I grew up in Venice around Black people, Mexicans, and Asians," Engblom explained. "The idea that I was going to go over and shoot Asians was totally repugnant to me."

Engblom joined the merchant marines, Stecyk went for student deferments, and Ho fudged his physicals. Each eventually made it back in one piece to the beach, where Engblom and Stecyk met Ho on a winter day in 1970. It had been raining for the better part of the week, and Engblom and Stecyk were parked at the beach, waiting out the tail of a storm in Engblom's Cadillac. When the rain cleared, he and Stecyk realized they were parked next to a 1948 Chevy truck—

the classic surfer's ride. This one also happened to double as Jeff Ho's sleeping quarters since his recent breakup with a well-to-do debutante.

Ho had already earned a reputation for shaping high-performance boards designed for the quick turns necessary to dodge POP pilings and other assorted wreckage at the Cove. Engblom had helped Larry Stevenson, a Venice Beach lifeguard, USC grad, and kick-tail innovator, with his fledgling Makaha skateboards. All three guys had surfboard shaping experience and backgrounds with lowrider and hot rod customizing, and were early skateboard adaptors.

Stecyk had also been painting totemic, streetwise cultural references to his environs on custom surfboard art for years (a 1966 Dave Sweet model he painted is on permanent display at the Smithsonian). "Stecyk invented the airbrushed surfboard," Engblom insisted. "I don't care what anybody else is telling you, he was making airbrushed surfboards a year or two before anybody was putting them on the market."

Stecyk also suggested that some of the money Skip had accrued in the merchant marines went toward financing a business focused on manufacturing the types of boards they wanted to ride. Jeff Ho Surfboards and Zephyr Productions opened in 1971 on the southeast corner of Bay Street and Main in Santa Monica, across from the Sunrise Mission, and next to Star Liquor on the northern edge of Dogtown. Despite the grand dreams of Abbot Kinney, Lawrence Lipton, the Dentist with the Golden Drill, and many others floating through the firmament of Venice history, this surf shop is probably responsible for the neighborhood's most enduring legacy.

***

SEVERAL YEARS BEFORE THE Zephyr shop opened, a towheaded little grommet paddled up to an older dude who was ripping it up at the Cove and said, "Man, that was a really good ride. Who are you?" It was a bold move for a seven-year-old, but even then Jay Adams was known for his bold moves.

"I'm Jeff Ho," the guy answered.

"You make surfboards, don't you?"

"I do."

"I wish I could have one of your boards."

"Maybe you will," replied Ho.

In time, Jay Adams was riding one of Ho's boards as part of the Zephyr shop's junior surf team. Among the other junior team members were Tony Alva, Stacy Peralta, Bob Biniak, Wentzle Ruml, Shogo Kubo, and Jim Muir. To get on the team, these guys, and girl—the pioneering Peggy Oki was an original Z-boy—had to prove themselves in the surf at the Cove. When the waves weren't breaking, they'd take the radical maneuvers honed at the Cove onto the concrete playground of Dogtown and its vicinity.

The shop and the team were part savvy marketing (it was a badge of honor to be seen wearing the colors of the renegade Zephyr team) and part clubhouse for the area's feral youth. Engblom said that the Zephyr team gave them a sense of family and empowerment at a time and in a place when it took some determination to generate as much. "We had an us-against-them mentality. It was so much more than just a business."

It's hard to precisely put into words how much more than a business it became. For a lot of these kids, who were constantly being reminded they existed on the margins, what little positive reinforcement they got came from the Zephyr shop. Earning a Zephyr T-shirt "was the one thing we could make our mark with, so we all wanted to do that," said original Z-Boy, and eventual world champion skateboarder, Stacy Peralta.

The opportunity to prove that they were as good as anyone else, despite hailing from the slum by the sea, came in the spring of 1975 at the Del Mar Nationals skateboarding competition. Del Mar, a polite, affluent community just north of San Diego that the turbulence of the sixties and early seventies seemed to have passed over, was everything Dogtown wasn't.

"We had to work these people over," said Engblom. "We had to validate our existence."

Self-determination came on the heels of innovation. By 1975, Cadillac Wheels had introduced urethane wheels into skateboarding, which, at the time, had a mostly tame, upright style. The new wheels meant that the Z-boys, who had been outperforming their equipment for years, finally had something that could fully accommodate their low-slung, slashing style—a style that looked more like radical surfing than the combo of roller and figure skating most skateboarding resembled at the time.

Peggy Oki finished first in the women's junior freestyle at the Del Mar Nationals, and Jay Adams and Tony Alva finished third and fourth in the men's juniors. The judges didn't even know what they'd just seen, let alone how to judge it. Adams and Alva, in particular, blew minds and even outraged folks with their audacity. But the kids knew what they were doing—they were claiming the future.

Much has been said, written, and filmed about what followed. The Z-boys legend is well told by now—the world championships, Stecyk's "Dogtown Chronicles" for *Skateboarder Magazine*, the documentaries, the Hollywood feature. But even now, it's hard to appreciate fully how the human flotsam and detritus of Abbot Kinney's folly changed the vernacular of popular culture and remade it in their image. Glen E. Friedman, Spike Jonze, Shepard Fairey, Vans, Volcom, the Beautiful Losers…it all goes back to this. There may not have been an American Renaissance by the sea, but if you're a kid with even a hint of cool, no matter what your age, you're probably living in some version of 1970s Dogtown.

Of course, now, it mostly lives in cultural and commercial appropriations. In the seventies, you could buy a corner lot home in Venice for $30,000. These days, probably, $3 million would get the conversation started. Bohemia gives way to bourgeois—the dull, homogenizing effect upscale gentrification has certainly had with Dogtown as with much of Los Angeles. It's a safe bet nothing as radical as POP or the Z-boys will sprout from these environs anytime soon.

Fittingly, in 2007, the former Z-boys headquarters was slated to be demolished. An application to preserve it as a historic landmark and to pay homage to the Z-boys' legacy was filed in response. It was quickly approved. Now, it's the home of Dogtown Coffee, "a café with a surfer-skater vibe serving local coffee blends plus vegan & gluten-free menu choices." At the entrance is a surfboard with an imitative graffiti scrawl on it that says, *No Kooks*.

Joe Donnelly *is an award-winning journalist, writer, and editor. He is currently Visiting Assistant Professor of English and Journalism at Whittier College. His short story "Bonus Baby" was recently selected for the 2016 O. Henry Prize Collection, as one of the twenty best short stories of 2015. "50 Minutes," a short story he coauthored with Harry Shannon, was selected for* The Best American Mystery Stories 2012.

References:
1. "The Ghosts of Dogtown," Joe Donnelly, *L.A. Weekly*, August 22, 2001.
2. "Father of the Now: Surf, skate and street-art legend Craig Stecyk spawned the 'extreme generation,' but these days he's an absentee dad," Joe Donnelly, *New Times Los Angeles*, September 12, 2002.
3. *Fantasy by the Sea: A Visual History of the American Venice*, Tom Moran and Tom Sewell, 1979, Peace Press, Inc.
4. *Pacific Ocean Park: The Rise and Fall of Los Angeles' Space-Age Nautical Pleasure Pier*, Christopher Merritt and Domenic Priore, 2014, Process Media.
5. Venice History Site, www.westland.net/venicehistory.

SNAKE VS. WOLF

by Chip Jacobs

VERYBODY, IT SEEMS, WAS watching the little white house on Bollinger Drive: pretty divorcées and kids on bikes, electronics whizzes and the Westside LAPD. Everybody was keeping a lookout for suspicious activity at the request of the owner, a feather-haired lawyer sleeping with a shotgun by his bed after the creepy sect he helped expose threatened to pay him a visit. Sure, it sounded melodramatic—killers skulking about a coastal town of rustic stores and quiet streets. And still there was that lurking, green Plymouth carrying two men up front and three friends in the trunk.

A real estate appraiser, who'd just stopped at a nearby corner market for a frosty drink, was the first to be flummoxed by it. Here he was, idling behind the sedan at a Pacific Palisades red light, unable to decipher its newfangled vanity license plate: 27 IVC. What narcissistic gloat could that represent? *At twenty-seven I varoomed to California?* Something about Ventura County? His puzzle-solving brain worked the variations. Then, by looking closer, Les Rahymer knew.

This wasn't cutesy, aluminum-engraved conceit. This was deception. Lamely applied blue tape—tape the same ubiquitous hue as the plates' background—concealed a "4" before the "27" and blurred the "G" into a "C". Rahymer, a dark-haired thirty-something, sat in his black Datsun 280Z, prickled with goose bumps. What was he supposed to do when the Plymouth motored nonchalantly down

Baylor Avenue: tail it like a real-life Jim Rockford (whose series filmed blocks away)? No, he was supposed to glimpse into his rearview mirror, where, by sheer happenstance, a Los Angeles Police Department patrol car was whipping left onto Sunset Boulevard like him.

"Did you see that car with the altered license plates?" Rahymer blurted, after waving the officer over. "Write down these numbers before I forget them." David Ybarro jotted as told and even sketched passengers' likenesses from the good samaritan's account. It was a wickedly hot October afternoon, a day before the World Series opened at Dodger Stadium amid bunting and beer commercials.

Wait! Did he say a drab, early-seventies-model Plymouth Executive? If so, Ybarro himself had noticed the car earlier while serving an unrelated subpoena, figuring it for an undercover narcotics vehicle pursuing stoners and snow-white tans. Dispatch reported the car was registered to the group Synanon at its Marin County outpost.

Shazbot, as the kids said: not good. Especially after the dude in the Japanese import took off before Ybarro learned the driver's name.

Ybarro, who walked a beat in this sun-glistened suburb a few minutes from Will Rogers State Beach, whistled for backup. Two LAPD colleagues, who arrived to hear him out, left, apparently unconcerned. Another pair drove past the lawyer's range-style home on Bollinger with bougainvillea out back, observing nothing afoul. But Ybarro couldn't shake the eerie butterflies. A few minutes later *he* was on Bollinger, telling a bike-riding boy to holler if he spotted the Plymouth. At shift's end, he logged his experience.

Only the next day would the report surface—in a department trash can, ignored.

***

CHARLES DEDERICH, SYNANON'S BEARDED, pear-shaped leader, was about the last demagogue you wanted to rile in 1978 Los Angeles. A decade earlier, he'd been a kind of pied piper of clean living, transforming a dingy Santa Monica club that sobered people up through acerbic group therapy into a multimillion-dollar alternative society legitimized by Hollywood and recognized by the courts.

"Today is the first day of the rest of your life," he told the desperate, pollinating, gruff messiah with Hallmark pitchman. Now, he seemed unrecognizable, spewing so much paranoid bombast at anyone critical of the sexual control, vendettas, and other excesses he demanded from his minions that you expected the FBI to commission his sketch. And of all the threats to his precarious reign, no one's threat surpassed the pretty boy do-gooder half his age on Bollinger Drive. That's why they'd packaged an exotic delivery for him.

A dissolute planet needed reminding: some New Age movements are best defended in Old Testament fashion.

***

AT 3:15 P.M., THE gas-guzzler with the bogus plate flashed by California Highway Patrolman Donald Growe, then en route to get his car washed. *Ping.* He followed the car up the California Incline, the steep access road connecting Pacific Coast Highway with Santa Monica, and toggled his siren. Protocol next: wary approach, boots crunching asphalt, fingers above revolver.

"You, out of the car!"

The driver, Lance Kenton, twenty, was lean, blond, and compliant. Joseph Musico, his older, presumptuous buddy, went to join him until Growe ordered him to freeze. The patrolman made Kenton pop the trunk. Nothing much there, aside from a plain canvas bag. Growe, too, radioed in the plate—the real one—though he heard nothing about Synanon's vendetta (which the LAPD itself had only recently been made aware of).

"Some people must have done this so we would be stopped," Kenton volunteered about the taped plate. Without asking, he started peeling the adhesive off one of the plates while Musico disembarked to work on the other. As the pieces fluttered around in the Santa Anas, Growe weighed his options. While the car's registration was expired and its plate doctored—both of which were illegal—neither passenger was acting jumpy. Checking warrants and inquiring what the men were doing felt excessive. As far as he was concerned, this tape horseshit really could've been a practical joke—and juvenile

pranks don't necessitate handcuffs. So he wrote nothing on his pad
and freed them.

***

PAUL MORANTZ, WHO RESEMBLED Mark Spitz and wouldn't have
minded playing Geraldo Rivera, was bored. Thirteen months before
that magic Plymouth stalked him, he was leading a perfectly normal
life, perfectly uninspired. Could he really have plateaued at thirty-one?

Legal crusading had twice thrust him into the spotlight, but that
had receded into nostalgia land. Another lifetime ago, he'd been a
campus celebrity at the University of Southern Californian, studying
journalism and whooping it up one merry semester at a time. As sports
editor of the *Daily Trojan* during the late sixties, Morantz enjoyed
VIP access to John McKay—the wry, cigar-gnashing, championship
football coach—and star players alike. Nicknamed "The Wolf" after
one sarcastic column, Morantz was an outlier, whether it was nailing
the first local interview of O. J. Simpson or getting a McKay assistant
in dutch for blustering that they'd travel to Cal Berkeley to "burn their
barns and rape their women." The *Los Angeles Times*, predictably,
offered him a job. His girlfriend, however, thought law school a better
alternative, as did his middle-class parents. Three more years at USC,
delaying reality in a topsy-turvy America, it was! Besides, everyone
knew journalists earned chump money next to billable hours.
Writing—his sacred passion—was something he could moonlight.

Bar exam passed, Morantz was rejected for a starter job at the
district attorney's office, which suggested his tanned, blow-dried style
was better suited for "defending the bad guys." Hence, a year before he
lost his hero—his father, a compassionate meatpacking executive—
he joined the public defender's office. Representing poor, mostly
guilty folks, even so, wasn't exactly like Atticus Finch. Thankfully,
Judge Noel Cannon invigorated the joint. As Morantz himself wrote,
"She decorated her office in pink to match her endless array of pink
outfits and summoned select defendants for impromptu sermons
by her personal preacher…" Cannon, just the same, was more than
a platinum-tinted showboat. She was also a tyrant, habitually jailing

public defenders who contested her rulings, including Morantz. Their bickering evolved into bona fide courthouse theater. Then one day she imprisoned a client of his previously arrested for assault and battery, this *after* the victim recanted and the DA dropped charges. Morantz, the happy-go-lucky SoCal native, could tolerate eccentricity, just not official misconduct. When not handling cases, he compiled evidence against Cannon and bundled it off to authorities. The response: crickets.

There had to be something better, and when his boss reprimanded him for freelancing a magazine piece about the murder of a fellow public defender without prior approval, he quit. He joined his older brother, Lewis, in private practice. During off hours he womanized and wrote, both adroitly. Film interest in his article teased literary fantasies. A year later, the California Supreme Court, aided by his evidence and testimony, removed Cannon from the bench. The boyish lawyer, who idolized Serpico and Davy Crockett, was jubilant while it lasted, because litigating ho-hum fender-benders and business squabbles was as un-chivalrous as it got. Back to his Remington typewriter he went for excitement, tapping out a story about a catering truck driver framed for robbery. Again, a movie producer acquired the rights. On its heels came *Rolling Stone*, which published his feature about Jan and Dean, the kings of sixties surf rock. CBS even planned to adapt into a TV movie of the week. *Bang*: that was trajectory.

Out of nowhere, a cold call tip from a liquor store owner redirected that path toward downtown's Skid Row. T. J. Renfroe, a sixty-ish alcoholic released from county jail for public intoxication, the man said, had been kidnapped and "sold" to a Burbank mental-health nursing center. Over the next weeks, acting on spec, Morantz smuggled out documents, posed as a patient's relative, and preserved the incriminating records. Afterward, his skepticism about human trafficking at retail prices hardened into Woodward-esque realization. Crooked nursing homes were paying $125 per person to middlemen who would deliver them alcoholics in a scam to bilk Medi-Cal for treatment of fabricated mental disorders. Lest they resist, the "patients" were sedated with Thorazine, a potent anti-schizophrenia drug. Morantz submitted the incriminating evidence to the Los Angeles County Board of Supervisors. They launched a massive investigation and credited the sleuthing lawyer, who basked in another gratifying puff of local fame.

Two years later, in June 1977, living in a beachside home financed with his cut from the class action suit he'd filed, the lawyer who wasn't sure he wanted to be one found himself flirting with domesticity. Stability could be all his for the price of a diamond ring. Marying Trudy—the heart-melting, Cheryl Tiegs–*esque* with kids from a previous relationship—would produce an instant family. Better yet, he could still play weekend beach volleyball and write when the law made him yawn. Another mystery abduction that surfaced, even so, provided what none of those could: the further opportunity for endorphins slaying hometown injustice.

***

CHARLES DEDERICH ENTERED A world that was always abandoning him.

By eight, he'd lost his dad to a car wreck, his brother to influenza, and would soon lose his mother, who was to wed a second husband young Charles reviled. The bright, tortured boy made liquor his panacea. He flunked out of Notre Dame, USC's historic archrival, and let alcohol trash his first marriage. A bout of meningitis next ravaged his appearance, causing the right side of his face to droop and twitch. Migrating to Santa Monica, the disfigured wanderer went homeless in his fresh start town. He straightened up enough up to lasso a new wife and job, only to have alcohol torpedo both. Discovered conked out on his kitchen floor, he was told the obvious: without treatment, he'd die before he'd lived.

Bottomed out at forty-three, Dederich began attending Alcoholic Anonymous meetings and devouring Emerson's *Self-Reliance,* and similar works. In 1956, he volunteered for a government-backed LSD experiment at UCLA. Epiphanies cascaded, with Dederich soon preaching about the enormity of human potential and his own newfound purpose. He'd get people sober without psychiatry or other traditional methods. Before long, drunks cluttered into his shabby apartment to eat soup and listen to his self-help sermons. His next move would be more seminal. He cashed a thirty-three dollar unemployment check and chartered an AA splinter group from a Venice storefront. Synanon, named by linguistic mash-up of "symposium" and "seminar," was on to something.

Synanon became a grassroots phenomenon. Connecticut Senator Thomas Dodd glamorized it as a "miracle by the beach." A *LIFE* magazine spread functioned more as an early-day infomercial than a piece of objective journalism. Appearances by Jane Fonda, Ben Gazzarra, Charlton Heston, Cesar Chavez, and Tim Leary confirmed it as a celebrity pet cause, though some glitterati merely wanted to meet heroin-addicted jazz musicians. Reporters were left starry-eyed by its ascent, parroting claims that Synanon had saved thousands. So what if Dederich, the Machiavellian reformer, had weeded out the original alcoholics and made drug fiends more the focus?

AA revolved around God and the twelve-step philosophy. The linchpin here was the "Game," where group participants verbally unloaded on new "Synanites" by rubbing their faces in the consequences of their destructive behaviors. Other than forbidding physical violence in the cold turkey detox, all bets were off. People berated for hours and, deprived of sleep, invariably collapsed into sobbing, semi-psychotic heaps. Once their "dirty brains" were cleansed, the freshly converted experienced temporary clarity in their exhaustion. The objective of this mishmash psychotherapy, breakdown, ritual, and shaming was, Dederich said, "to get you loaded without acid." In the taxonomy were witches (robed ceremonial guides), headsuckers (caring Synanon mothers), trippers (non-addicts seeking enlightenment), and splittees (loathed defectors). Dederich's knack for proselytizing surprised even admittedly bigheaded him. "When I sit down and start to talk," he observed, "people start gathering." Crime, narcotics, and delinquency, to him, shared a common weakness: an "addiction to stupidity."

The group, richer by the day, expanded into the vintage Club Casa del Mar and primped for its star treatment. Columbia Pictures' 1965 release *Synanon*, a stark, black-and-white depiction of the "Game" featuring Edmond O'Brien and Chuck Connors, was a global legitimizer. Privately, however, Dederich knew a bombshell that lay at odds with his fame: statistically, his methods cured addiction no better than AA.

Consequently, around 1967, influenced by the increasing number of communal living and dropout experimentations, "Big Daddy" redrew the conception. Synanon would phase into an alternative lifestyle commune free of society's narcotic distractions and head north to freer spaces and fewer hassles. At Tomales Bay, north of San Francisco, the movement spread out over thousands of acres. At a second location in Tulare County, a rural expanse between Bakersfield and Fresno, it inhabited buildings, an airstrip, and a dump. The state chipped in without asking the right questions, donating an empty San Francisco warehouse. A handful of affiliates from New York to Malaysia began to debut, too, all in an arc resembling pre–Tom Cruise Scientology.

Synanon was in its heyday as Americans wrestled with Vietnam, Watergate, and the ulcers of early-seventies disenchantment. Ringing its sites were services at the ready: libraries, offices, a movie theater, sewage plants, medical clinics, barbershops, and hundreds of cars, planes, and boats. Tomales Bay residents accessed horseback riding, swimming, tennis, and bathhouses. Jitneys zipped between settlements. A one-legged DJ emceed a closed-circuit radio station, KSYN. Its fire department collaborated with the state during emergencies. Among its ranks were bankers, architects, attorneys, and professors, some of them credentialed from Stanford, UCLA, and the *Los Angeles Times*. These weren't society's dregs.

Dederich's genius for improvisation was rivaled only by his talent for generating cash streams. Thirty million dollars in assets (the equivalent of roughly $133 million in 2015) didn't lie. Red-blooded believers such as Reliable Mortgage's Ed Siegel donated nearly a million in stock; another deep-pocketed believer handed over the title to his accounting firm. Supplementing benefactors' gifts like these and member-paid room and board was a line of promotional items (pens, key chains, lighters), gas stations, and philanthropic/subsidy arrangements with much of the Fortune 500. *The Hollywood Reporter*, *Billboard* magazine, and others anted up free ad space. Many government types even regarded Synanon's tough-love treatment as an innovative drug-fighting weapon.

"We spend so much on mace, helicopters, clubs, and other devices when money could be spent on programs like this," articulated San Francisco Sheriff Richard Hongisto.

Dederich sometimes ridiculed his very kingdom, donning a Hawaiian shirt and crown harnessed from popsicle sticks. Yet there was truth in satire of an aging emperor projecting new battles with old demons—namely fear of desertion—onto his subjects. A 1972 *San Francisco Examiner* exposé accusing Synanon of being the "racket of the century" precipitated no soul searching by him. Rather, it ignited a culture of xenophobic overreaction. Addicts were soon prohibited from "graduating" to an outside world scorned as evil. Families were consolidated in Marin County; Synanite mothers were restricted from visiting their newborns. The overall trend line was ominous: an off-the-grid utopia of good-hearted, if misled, people were under the thumb of an unhinged ruler dictating their lives by his inner obsessions. When Dederich stopped smoking, his flock had to. When his wife, Betty, dieted, sayonara to everyone's fatty foods. Zealots once shaved their heads to punctuate their loyalty. Young filmmaker George Lucas cast some as extras in his futuristic *THX 1138*, now that Manson Family bald chic was mandatory.

Synanon further mutated from its roots in 1974 with its reclassification as a tax-exempt "religion." Its secular god, two years later, unveiled an Orwellian population control blueprint that would define it. All men (except Dederich) were required to undergo vasectomies, and any pregnant women, abortions; one had the procedure in the second trimester. Several hundred acquiesced, yet, tellingly, almost as many bolted over it—Dederich's brother, William, among them. "I'll give you my life, Chuck, but not my balls," one former Synanite wrote in his book. Any lingering doubt that a commune was fast warping into a sect vanished when Betty died of lung cancer in 1977. Dederich, having lost the only person able to restrain his other megalomaniacal impulses, licensed group libido to compensate. He remarried an acolyte and decreed that *all* married couples needed to disband every three years to pair with new mates. What sociologists called swinging, Dederich termed "love matches." Some were teamed through randy auctions.

Since little of this leaked out publicly, judges and parents continued entrusting Synanon to rehabilitate wayward children, unaware that some were being slammed into buildings or beaten, especially if they attempted escape. Outwardly, Dederich remained the "Great Hope," his followers regarded as patriotic humanitarians. And many were— redistributing food, clothing, and whatnot to charities in sync with government agencies. Los Angeles Mayor Tom Bradley was duly impressed, naming a day after Betty Dederich upon her passing. Which was why a December 1977 *TIME* magazine feature portraying Synanon as a powder keg cult hiding in the mainstream marked an ominous crossroads for everyone. In addition to publicizing Dederich's sexual preoccupations and generous salary, it revealed his group's plunging membership (down one-third to about twelve hundred) and a Marin County grand jury child abuse probe. Dederich, wearing a hat reading, "I'M THE MEANEST S.O.B. IN THE VALLEY," believed he'd charmed reporters via folksy self-deprecation. "A lot of guys," he said, "could do this from an old Ford roadster. They're holy men. I'm not. I need a...Cadillac." Cue the sound of a massive backfire.

TV viewers watching Dederich erupt over *TIME*'s "contemptible hatchet job" must've cringed with déjà vu about another messianic circus bubbling. In a January 1978 interview with CBS Los Angeles's Connie Chung—whom, privately, Dederich considered a fox—he threatened journalists attacking "religious freedoms," grumbling that he wanted them "as nervous about the safety of their children and their grandchildren" as he was about his. Looking like a malevolent Burl Ives, he next told Jess Marlow of Los Angeles's NBC affiliate that, "Bombs could be thrown at...some of [*TIME*'s] clowns." He then compared his misunderstood persona to Jesus, who "ran with a bunch of smugglers, drunks, and crooks." Of course, Jesus never spoke like him. After the California Health Department announced it would visit the grounds, Dederich barked that his followers would "surround" inspectors with guys "twice their size" and explore which of them practiced sodomy or bestiality. His band of lawyers were equally truculent, filing $400 million in libel and slander suits against *TIME*, the health department (for likening Dederich's threats to Nazism),

San Francisco's ABC affiliate (for a segment alleging Synanon guards "terrorized" neighbors in Badger), *Reader's Digest,* and others. Despite this emphasis on lawyers, guns, and money that better channeled Warren Zevon than a sober paradise, Dederich still hoped to be a Nobel Prize candidate. You didn't have to be an oddsmaker (or swami) to see a bloody confrontation between his world and the outside one looming on the horizon. Which was the precise time a man distraught about his wife decided to dial a Pacific Palisades wolf.

***

FRANCES WINN WAS A depressed, young homemaker who, in June of 1977, went to a Venice health clinic for a tranquilizer. Instead of prescribing her medication, they referred her to Synanon's Santa Monica reception facility. After she formally requested help there, she found herself sucked into Dederich's rabbit hole. Her welcoming party mowed her hair with electric scissors and locked her in a basement. The next day, against her wishes, she was transported to Tomales Bay and jettisoned into a tent. Ed Winn tried fetching his wife repeatedly, but her captors notified him their marriage was over. Winn wrote to reporters, politicians, even President Carter for attention. Offhand, an acquaintance mentioned an ex-neighbor of his—the lawyer who had rescued the shanghaied alcoholics—to the frazzled spouse. Contacted by Winn, Paul Morantz barely hesitated.

Synanon didn't care. It could afford to be hostile to outsiders, exempted as it was from state licensing for drug rehabs and mental health providers. Morantz, unfamiliar with the gray-area turf, negotiated a compromise phone call between the Winns, which climaxed in Frances' reassertion that she wanted out. Synanon, keen to ditch problem clients as the heat against it rose, demanded a waiver first, so Morantz typed up a hollow document that the organization swallowed. Once Frances was safe, Morantz said farewell to her former caretakers with a raised middle finger.

At a foothill ranch outside Visalia three months later, Dederich held court about his movement's encroaching enemies. While acolytes dined, the Ohioan with the low, froggy voice spoke into "The Wire," the organization's internal broadcast system. Anyone there afraid of the "Holy War" they were waging should leave, because the "sound of cracking bones" was fundamental to their survival. "Don't mess with us," he snarled. "You can get killed. Physically dead…" His Imperial Marines, a private militia expected to grow to two hundred well-trained soldiers, tolerated no resistance. Who knew the Hells Angels could have competition?

Indeed, blood had spilled earlier that year when two seventeen-year-old surfers parked near Synanon's Santa Monica building—famous for its black sign—and one of them committed the unthinkable: he peed outdoors. A mob of *Deliverance*-ish shitkickers in overalls and blue shirts joyfully thumped them in a teeth-flying, body-dragging scrum. "This is not the type of place Synanon is," protested a female devotee trying to halt the pasting. Actually, it was now. Up near Fresno, around Thanksgiving, a redneck trucker named Ron Eidson, who had refused to apologize for a traffic miscue, could have benefitted from Billy Jack's services as four Imperial Marines brandishing sawed-off shotguns appeared at his property. In front of his terrified wife and three children, they pounded and pistol-whipped Eidson into a coma. To confuse him about his assailants at a later police lineup, the marines sent in lookalikes. Ex-heroin, LSD, and barbiturate addicts dropping by for visits, or to express their dismay about the organization's violent bent, were greeted similarly. They were bound to poles, interrogated as spies, belittled as "scumbag" defectors, and thrashed with steel-toed boots. Others had their fingers snapped one by one, or were chased into ditches before beatings, and had their lives threatened to ensure they wouldn't sue or report it.

The organization was considerably sweeter to firearms dealers arming it with a virtual munitions depot. Roughly $300,000 worth of rifles, Colt .45 handguns, and automatic pistols, as well as pallets of ammunition that included armor-piercing bullets, stocked its cache by early '78. Only the bazooka the boss wanted was missing. The US Bureau of Alcohol, Tobacco, Firearms, and Explosives inquired why a religion needed those bulk purchases. Synanon was hot to answer: the weapons, it said, were self-defense against trespassers, bullies, and other troublemakers emboldened by the sensationalizing media.

***

BACK IN HIS SMALL Brentwood law office near Hamburger Hamlet, our lawyer fielded calls from exasperated parents asking him to liberate their offspring from Dederich's clutches. When not working those angles, Morantz immersed himself into the Kool-Aid–tinged waters, reading Mao, Mazlov, B. F. Skinner, and Werner Erhard. He'd had his own brushes with cults that made this all seem more than coincidental, starting with his boozy 1963 high school graduation party in Santa Monica. There, ironically right under the bluff housing Synanon's old base at the National Guard Armory, he'd stumbled away from the crowd and right toward the mortifying shrieks of newbies being lambasted during the "Game." Time passed before he met a conservative, tie-tearing Texan at a part-time job during college selling women's hairpieces at Contessa Creations at Melrose and La Cienega. Morantz delighted in escorting his Southern friend around after work to the big city's bounteous supermarket of sex, drugs, and rock and roll. Later he realized his horror. The buddy he'd known as Charles Watson was the killer the world knew as "Tex" Watson, a Manson lieutenant in the 1969 Tate-LaBianca murders.

He still could have walked away from these degrees of separation and into the arms of Trudy, who was anxious about him poking at the crazies. His place on Bollinger—two bedrooms, red brick barbecue, bay windows—was all teed up to be their Shangri-la. In spring of 1978, she illuminated her affection, hosting a dinner to celebrate CBS's broadcast of *Dead Man's Curve*, the Jan and Dean movie inspired by his *Rolling Stone* article. Ordinary legal work—a film deal or two— could have bankrolled a cushy life knitted around such times. Except that scenario wasn't enough, not for a restless spirit like Morantz who, inexorably, needed the thrill of a fresh hunt to keep sane. Trudy soon said her peace on the subject—just about the time Morantz helped convince Daryl Gates' assistants to discontinue LAPD "est" seminars, citing what he'd learned about infiltrating brainwashers. They were at a now-forgotten Washington Boulevard restaurant when she announced she couldn't marry someone more obsessed with unearthing wrongdoing than burrowing into commitment. Morantz felt clobbered; his Skid Row theatrics brought him a death threat. Trudy's breakup was a living death.

Deep inside, he knew it was for the best. Who'd want a spouse telling confidantes, "They're coming to kill me"? Because that was Morantz's refrain to many after hearing about splittee Phil Ritter.

The Greenpeace's anti-nuclear activist never wanted a bitter goodbye. He had logged eight years at Synanon, some of them quite pleasurably as its transportation czar. It was Dederich's unstable behavior and coterie of toadies and thugs that disillusioned him into leaving. Out, Ritter cajoled authorities to step in—effectively to save Synanon from itself—while petitioning for custody of his son from its clutches. His former cohorts never forgot his disloyalty. Entering his Berkeley home one night, knuckle draggers started bashing in his skull. Neighbors running toward his screams chased the assailants away before they murdered him. Ritter, astoundingly, recovered from his payback-fueled thrashing.

But that was as far as it went.

No collective outrage percolated over his attempted homicide, or the dozens of other Holy War thrashings. Local detectives, meantime, were busier than plastic surgeons, grappling with a record murder rate and elusive serial killers, as well as a bumper crop of hitmen targeting abusive husbands, debonair embezzlers, and others. For the most part, officials reacted indifferently, as if Synanon beatings were little more than overheated misunderstandings. Generally, they dropped charges, reduced them to misdemeanors, or sentenced the offenders to community service and probation. Between its scrappy reputation for helping lost souls and the era's dalliance with pop psychology solutions, the group was a trusted brand. Doubting it was like doubting Monty Hall or Sears. Contesting the organization without a badge, hence, was not just perilous, but, crusade-wise, isolating.

Not that Morantz was cowering. Indeed, just about the time that the Plymouth set out on its lethal trip to the house on Bollinger Drive, he won a $300,000 judgment against Dederich and company for what a judge deemed Winn's "unpardonable" treatment. San Francisco cops, due largely to his efforts, had by then surrounded a house to free three adolescent members. But his last action against it was a neutron bomb. At the solicitation of two Marin County Supervisors—up-and-comers Dianne Feinstein and Barbara Boxer—he lobbied against state legislation that would have perpetuated the group's golden ticket: its waiver from licensing regulations. The bill lost by a single vote.

In the ensuing days, he lived fidgety with the shadows, cognizant that Synanon threats were rarely empty bluster. Fun times peering under his Volvo hatchback before starting it, or fretting about his border collies, Tommy and Devon, knowing an ex-Synanite's dog was found hanged. Sure enough, Dederich had his public enemy number one. "When is someone," he vented over "The Wire", "going to be brave enough to get Morantz?" An outside hitman priced the job for ten large. Leadership opted to do it in-house.

Meanwhile, a stressed-out Morantz indulged in some R&R in Hawaii, where the marines didn't venture. Stateside again and still missing Trudy, he hyperventilated while watching USC nip Alabama. On October 5, at a recording studio, he met another dream girl, Australian singer/actress/eye-candy Olivia Newton-John. After letting her know he was the genius behind the Jan and Dean movie, flirtatious embers smoldered. Still, who would date a marked man?

On Tuesday, October 10, Morantz gulped coffee and drove to work like any other day. Around 2:00 p.m., a pair of LAPD intelligence officers and a suit from the California Attorney General's criminal investigative branch settled into his conference room. Morantz, recapping the fatwa he gleaned from his sources against him, requested bodyguards. Shouldn't be a problem, they said, once they conducted a threat analysis. Morantz, incongruously cocky and cautious, measuring any coming darkness in days, not hours, said fine.

***

DEDERICH'S GOONS KENTON AND Musico, who were circling his house just then, weren't the most compatible of killers. Young Kenton approached tasks with Eagle Scout verve, determined to excel in Synanon academics, karate, and outdoor activities. (His father, admired composer Stan Kenton, had entrusted Dederich to keep his boy drug-free while he toured.) Musico, a tough ex–New Yorker and

Vietnam vet, was just looking to avoid incarceration; the military had dishonorably discharged him after his stint overseas, where he bragged about fragging prick sergeants and stringing necklaces from "gook ears." Mayhem continued in civilian life, until his mother interceded. She persuaded the courts to ship him out for rehabilitation at Synanon. There, Musico actually fit in for a change, women weak-kneed for his rugged good looks and men drawn to his storytelling bluster. But Dederich's militarization stunted that growth, reawakening a sadistic flair that initially resulted in a proposition to assassinate Morantz with a shotgun blast on the freeway. The vendetta against the man their leader caricatured as a hunched-over ambulance chaser divided the would-be killers. Kenton wanted to shelf it after the CHP stopped them, and Musico and he might've exchanged punches. Nonetheless, they soldiered on.

An eleven-year-old boy was outside pedaling his bike as the sedan looped Bollinger on a half-dozen passes. Each time it rumbled past Morantz's place, it slowed disturbingly. The frightened kid, whose brother Morantz sometimes paid to walk his dogs, ran to his mother. She told him to relax; the car was probably an unmarked police vehicle checking up on the house. Edie Ditmars, on the other hand, remained in the spooked category. The attractive woman, fresh from a divorce, was chummy with her next-door neighbor, so when she heard Morantz's dogs bark, she beelined to her kitchen window. How peculiar. A strange car was parked in his driveway. Now a clean-cut lad in a sports coat and tie was marching toward the front door. Ditmars hurried to her living room window for a better view. Fatefully, the angle obstructed her sight line.

Next thing she knew, Morantz's mailbox lid, the one chiseled into his stucco front wall, slapped closed. *Phew.* Ditmars sighed in relief, assuming it a routine delivery. A nine-year-old girl across the street also noticed the Plymouth. Remembering the heads-up for vigilance, she crept outside, feeling self-conscious, and ducked beneath a bush to spy the license plate. But then the Plymouth blazed away.

The main attraction pulled up around 5:30, with Vin Scully's catchphrase on the brain: "time for Dodger baseball." His dogs, as was custom, gave him a friendly mauling once he entered, loping outside next to frolic on the lawn. He was in his signature button-down shirt, slacks, and cowboy boots. Dorky eyeglasses should have hung from his ears, but his vanity objected and the hipper pair he ordered hadn't yet arrived. He plopped the Synanon evidence files on his green-tile kitchen counter. All that lay between him and the first pitch was a menial task: retrieving the mail from his shoebox-sized chute. *Odd.* Blurry vision notwithstanding, he could see an elongated object stuffed in there. *Must be a scarf someone assumed was his.*

His right hand popped the tin cover. His left hand plunged in. But it didn't grab silk. It grabbed something alive.

***

THE FOUR-AND-A-HALF FOOT WESTERN diamondback rattlesnake now in his left hand was unhappy with its confinement. "Little Chuck," as the police would tab it, lunged forward with its V-shaped head, sinking its fangs into his wrist. *Fuuuucck!* Little did Morantz know, as he stood there in agony, that had his mailbox been larger, Kenton would have deposited all three snakes from the canvas bag in there. The marines had been collecting Badger-area diamondbacks for months to condition them for this. Isolation had bred extra aggressiveness around foreign heat sources. None, though, could give advance warning before striking, not with their cicada-sounding rattles surgically removed for stealth.

"Bastards," cursed Morantz. "They'd really done it." Why hadn't he noticed his dogs' claw marks on the mail canister, where the serpent slithered in wait? All those cops and a block full of observers and this got under the wire in plain daylight. All those warnings of an imminent attack by Dave Mitchell, editor of *The Point Reyes Light*, a small Tomales Bay weekly that would earn the Pulitzer for its Synanon coverage, and he was staring at a scaly grim reaper at thirty-three. Waiting for the LAPD threat analysis.

He dropped the checkered, grayish-brown reptile onto his hardwood floor, where it coiled near his ankles, forked tongue curling, eyes glaring. The *Crotalus atrox* was scared, poising itself for another defensive strike. His boyhood fascination in herpetology quickly washed back; he'd trapped garter snakes as a kid. He knew he needed ice on his wound and had to keep his heart rate down to slow the neurotoxins before traumatic shock overtook him. Another crisis brewed, too. From the corner of his eye he saw his dogs galloping toward the house after he'd yelped. In seconds, they'd be tangling with the thing, perhaps to their death. There'd be three corpses then. Morantz's head juked one way, causing the snake to follow, and in one fluid stroke he stretched his right arm diagonally over it to slam the door closed. Carefully, he edged away.

A moment later he was through his kitchen, pitching toward Ditmar's house, delirious in the sunshine. Shouting for ice. Crashing his right shoulder into her door, smashing it off a hinge. Beseeching someone to call the police, an ambulance! His hand felt as if a vice was pulverizing it. Neighbors raced toward the hullabaloo. Irv Moskowitz, a Caltech electronics supervisor, home early for Yom Kippur and knowledgeable about snakebites after finishing a CPR course on the subject that day, yanked the resistant victim to the ground. He tore off his shirt and wrapped Morantz's left arm in a makeshift tourniquet while someone piled ice over the fang marks. A jacket was laid over him despite the Indian summer swelter.

Inside his entryway, two firemen eyeballed the biggest snake they'd ever seen. One distracted it while the other pinned its writhing, muscular body, as thick in spots as Steve Garvey's bat, with a shovel. Decapitating it through that carbon-fiber-like skin necessitated numerous whacks. After Little Chuck's head was severed, they flushed it down Morantz's toilet without contemplating that it could be felony evidence. An LAPD officer, who later saw the animal's formidable corpse, remembered the squad briefings about Synanon. "He should've had protection," he muttered.

Morantz arrived at what's now UCLA Medical Center in Santa Monica in blinding pain, before it got Kafkaesque. The hearing-impaired nurse who did his intake needed his insurance information, and the cotton-mouthed patient with the swollen left side and tingling extremities could hardly speak, other than imploring her for drugs. Was he really sure, doctors inquired, it was a rattlesnake? Word by now was spreading at light speed. His friend Nicki, with whom he was supposed to have dinner that night, raced to the ER, where she had a nurse slide a magnet bracelet over Morantz's wrist for cosmic healing. He was then administered eleven vials of anti-venom and the morphine-like Demerol, which ferried his mind from watching the tail end of the World Series game (which the Dodgers won 11-5) to a hallucinated shoreline.

He was transported to USC County General hospital three hours later for its snakebite expertise. The *LA Times*' Narda Zacchino, one of the few local reporters to write about the true Synanon, squiggled past security. She pecked him on the cheek and said forget she'd been there or Synanon would manipulate it. By far the best face over him the day wasn't a journalist or doctor. It was Trudy, whom he'd asked the LAPD to contact. When the doctor ordered everyone to leave, she refused, plunking herself into a bedside chair. When he awoke the next morning, the girl of his dreams was still there.

The same day Angelenos learned their city would host the 1984 Summer Olympics, the globe learned that reptiles can be weaponized. Walter Cronkite harrumphed about a "bizarre event," even by cult standards. Chevy Chase on *Saturday Night Live*'s Weekend Update hyped Synanon's sale of pre-Christmas rattlesnakes. In this tizzy, a detective working the Hillside Strangler serial killer investigation was assigned to the case that actually wasn't much of a whodunit. Splittees phoned in tips, ratting out Musico and Kenton, and they were soon arrested up north. Donald Growe, eager for atonement, confirmed they were the two men he'd stopped, but not detained. Ybarro contributed, too. Both wanted another chance at that witchy sedan that had converted so many sharp-eyed people into mushy spectators.

Morantz, a few days later, was rolled out in his bed for a jam-packed hospital press conference reminiscent of John and Yoko's 1969 "Bed-in for Peace." A man normally covetous of public adulation appeared overwhelmed, less modern Sir Lancelot than someone with goldfish eyes. He told journalists what he'd stressed to film producers and cops earlier: dangerous cults were everywhere. But when asked if Synanon specifically planted the snake, Morantz hesitated, saying he'd only been told he was on an "enemies list." You never knew if

Synanon's "long ears" were present. The group's lawyer/spokesman
Dan Garrett denied any connection, characterizing Synanon as "law-
abiding" in its quest to solve social problems and character disorders.
Stories to the contrary were "inflammatory and irresponsible."
Translation: beware.

***

SIX DAYS OF HOSPITALIZATION later, Morantz returned home as LA's
"Reluctant Crusader," with the media ravenous to interview him as
cult fascination revived. Weeks later, after the Dodgers blew the series,
another messiah flexed his muscle to ruin lives on an unthinkable
scale. Over nine hundred members of the People's Temple lay sprawled
in Jonestown, Guyana, in a macabre quilt after drinking cyanide-
laced punch—a mass suicide orchestrated by the embattled Reverend
Jim Jones. Morantz shivered, thinking, *I could've been there.* And in a
way he was. Among those murdered by Jones' gunmen were two NBC
journalists who had been at his hospital press conference. They'd flown
with a California congressman down there to uncover the truth.

Here were *his* truth-seeking perks: sheriff's department officers
living in his house for *months* while Dederich's Imperial Marines
taunted him into paranoia mode. They inquired about where he
socialized and made sure he knew they knew his mother's address.
They harassed him with midnight phone calls about what they could
see inside his house with binoculars. His inability to play volleyball
made them giggle. They also promised "another snake" was coming.
And it might.

People continued asking when he'd get back to "normal."
Morantz, who now stashed a gun in his Volvo, couldn't tell them.
He was psychologically whiplashed, relieved to have survived a
Synanon kill shot and lost about what'd come next. Early December
became the second full month of his new discombobulated life as
his wrist improved and his determination to resume his fight against
brainwashing started nicking his consciousness. He'd stay with it,
which naturally—and decisively—spelled of the end of his brief
reconciliation with Trudy. More death.

He limped back to Hawaii to grieve, and while he was there, the other shoe dropped. A battalion of cops raided Synanon's million-dollar hideaway in Arizona's Lake Havasu. Sitting inside, staring ahead in a stupor, was America's most famous "reformed alcoholic," plastered after draining a bottle of Chivas Regal. Dederich required two hospitalizations to recover before arraignment. "Even though he's drinking now, we have to remember all the good things he's done," one acolyte rationalized. Apparently, he'd restarted his addiction on a trip to Italy that summer—the same European trip where Synanon had opened secret bank accounts and Dederich had sanctioned the hit.

Kenton and Musico stared death rays at Morantz during their preliminary hearing. He had too much invested to let it silence him, and placed an *LA Times* ad seeking the identity of the 280Z driver to buttress the prosecution. Because of it, a gas station owner soon recognized the car, and Rahymer testified about crossing paths with that slippery Plymouth. The marines ultimately pled no contest, and Morantz acted again, albeit from the opposite direction: he urged the judge to show his would-be killers leniency as Dederich's mind-manipulated *victims*. It'd be a theme. Both were sentenced to a year in prison. Big Daddy, then in failing health, also pled no contest and was given five years probation, a $5,000 fine, and the stipulation he no longer associate with his former utopia. Things worked out differently for his marines. A star actor with a flamboyant affection for cocaine and buxom women hired Kenton. Musico was thrown to his death off a roof in a "pimp-dope" turf war.

But the ghost of Little Chuck loomed larger than any human because the unsuccessful assassination pretty much guaranteed the movement's collapse. New leadership dropped lawsuits, circled the wagons, and tried ingratiating itself in Washington, DC, yet found no takers. In 1991, with the FBI on Synanon's scent and the IRS's revocation of its nonprofit status, the curtain dropped. A reclusive Dederich died in 1997.

For Morantz, those fang marks were his baptism into a club he'd never leave. Over the decades, they'd galvanize him to become, arguably, California's top legal cult expert. He would press muckraking suits against the Church of Scientology and the Moonies. He would challenge the Center for Feeling Therapy (where doctors beat patients or had sex with them) and Bhagwan Rajneesh (whose followers poisoned the salad bars of ten Oregon restaurants). His quest to be somebody not coasting on fumes calcified into a more humble existence, where former cultists were his new friends and a failed marriage gave him a wondrous son unfamiliar with his suffering. He'd gone from hero to newsmaker to historical D-list as "the guy bitten by the snake" in a city that often forgot him.

At a New Year's Eve party in the dwindling hours of 1978, before he intuited what the stars intended for him, Morantz shambled outside, a broken hero with fading teeth marks on his wrist. Trudy, literary stardom, the remotest definition of normalcy: he'd relinquished them all to tilt against the decade's brainwashing craze. Tears poured down his face and dread blanketed him like an x-ray vest. That's when he heard *the* voice he never heard speak before, a voice louder than Dederich's loony threats.

"Stop crying," it said. "This is who you are."

What's a wolf to do but oblige?

Chip Jacobs *is a Los Angeles-area author and journalist. His most recent book is* Strange As It Seems: the Impossible Life of Gordon Zahler, *the updated biography of a Hollywood dreamer-schemer who lived outrageously in a ticking time bomb of a body.* Publishers Weekly, *in its review, called Jacobs an "exceptional storyteller" and said the "extraordinary life" being told was a "peculiar page-turner" rendered with an "imaginative" touch. His other books include the environmental social histories* The People's Republic of Chemicals *and the bestselling* Smogtown: The Lung-Burning History of Pollution in Los Angeles *(both with William J. Kelly); the* Fargo-*esque true crime tale* The Ascension of Jerry: Murder, Hitmen and the Making of L.A. Muckraker Jerry Schneiderman; *a collection of articles* The Vicodin Thieves: Biopsying L.A.'s Grifters, Gloryhounds, and Goliaths; *and the privately issued biography* Black Wednesday Boys. *His profile of Los Angeles political figure Richard Alatorre appears in two Greenwood Publication anthologies.*

Sources:

The Los Angeles Times; the New York Times; Gizmodo; Escape: From Miracle to Madness: The True Story of Charles Dederich and Synanon (Cresta Publications: 2015); *My Lifelong War Against Cults* (Cresta Publications: 2013); paulmorantz.com, Paul Morantz interview September 2015; *People; TIME.*

MARCH 1974

by Dana Johnson

I'M ALMOST EIGHT AND everybody's been talking about the burned up people in that house on Fifty-Fourth Street. That rich white girl caught up in all that mess with those crazy hippies or whatever they're supposed to be, that's what Mama says. But Miss Mary, she says, "Nuh uh, Honey. Everybody knows that girl is just Cinque's girlfriend, that's why she involved in the first place." Mama and our neighbor Miss Mary are talking about all kinds of other stuff they don't think I'm listening to or understanding because I'm a child. They speak without filter. So I know all about who's "stepping out" in the building and who doesn't keep her apartment clean enough for Miss Mary or Mama and who don't know how to dress right since she's somebody's mama now. It's true I don't understand this time, this place, and these people like I will, least of all a white heiress feared dead in the crawl space underneath a house on Fifty-Fourth Street, but still alive, after all. It is told the house caught on fire because of all the ammunition inside, but Miss Mary says you know the cops are behind it, burning up folks on purpose. Those were the times. Cops kicking in your door, like the time Daddy's friend got shot in bed during a raid, for just standing up in surprise. Shot dead.

"That's how it is, man," Daddy says. "The police," he says, shaking his head. "Uh. They're the only thing wrong with the neighborhood."

The neighborhood is good. That's why we moved, that's what Daddy says. He and Mama and my brother moved to Eightieth Street from Watts because it was clean and safe, and rent, when they first moved to Eightieth, was fifty dollars a month. Later, Daddy will laugh when he tells the story. "They thought I was crazy for paying fifty dollars a month for rent. Thought I was crazy for blowing my money like that!"

But he is right about the neighborhood. We know everybody. Mama and I are next door, in Miss Mary's apartment, like we always are, in apartment nine, to watch Niecy and her friends practice their routine for the talent show they're going to be in. They have been doing it for days and will be doing it all night, practicing to Blue Magic, and they're trying to get their steps tight and right, like The Temptations, like The Spinners, but one of the girls is always out of step, and Niecy is throwing a fit, asking her over and over, "What are you doing? Why you messing up my routine? You need to count right! Why you not counting right!" And her mama, Miss Mary, just keep smoking her cigarettes and laughing, telling them to stop and start over, but telling them they're good, too. "Y'all are too cute," she says. "You going to win. I know you going to win," and I think they will, too, those five girls look like grown movie stars to me, even though they are just fifteen.

Niecy, she is wearing a blue polka dot halter top and jean shorts that my mother thinks are too short, and brown platforms that lace up in the front. Her hair is dyed a copper color, just like her mother. But that is it, nothing else like her mother. No lipstick, not yet. She is not allowed to be too grown. None of us are allowed to be too grown or mess up. Miss Mary yelled at me one time to get out of the streets and she isn't even my mama. Anybody who's grown could tell me what to do and Mama would say, "That's right. You better listen."

I'm sitting next to the record player, wanting so bad to get in the line and hold an invisible microphone in my hand. If I was the sixth girl, I would be in step and my hand would extend out to the audience, the same time I'm bowing, and I would sing for real and sound just as good as the lead singer in Blue Magic, my voice not like the voice of a little kid who doesn't know anything about life, but like the voice of a people who sang songs since they came to America, every moment of that journey that led us to 1974 layered in my voice and in the smoothness of the gesture of my hand extended out to you.

But for now, Miss Mary puts me in charge of the record. Every time they finally get through the song or even if they're in the middle, mid step, maybe even at the very beginning, where the man says *Trouble sleeping, dreaming of you,* she tilts her head toward the record player, points her cigarette, and that means that I need to go lift the needle and put it back at the beginning of the record.

***

THAT NIGHT, WE ARE still waiting for one more girl, the girl who should be the star, prettier than all the rest. But Niecy is not going to have it. It's her steps that everybody's doing. She's the choreographer. She's the one with the talent and looks—some of the looks that the other girl has. The other girl, her cousin, has light skin and light eyes—green—so everyone automatically picks her as the prettiest, without thinking. We wait—I wait and watch the dancing—but she never shows up, because her mother calls to say that, with all that's going on, she doesn't believe she needs to be in the streets with her daughter. "Girl, that's all right," Miss Mary says. "They need to keep practicing, anyway. They probably still going to be trying to get this dance right into next week."

And the music keeps playing and I always want the routine to get better and better so that they can get to the end more often, so I can hear Blue Magic's high voice singing *Must have put a spell on my mind, must have put a spell on my mind…*But Niecy is laughing and yelling at the same time. "We need to get through this, y'all! Stop playing!" she says, and then she shoves the girl next to her, the girl with octagon glasses that are wire, her afro high and round and fire red. I put the needle on the record one more time. And nobody, still, is tired of that song.

***

MUSIC IS WHY DADDY says we were bad tenants, March 1974, and every month and year we live on Eightieth street. The apartment manager, he lives downstairs, a tall man with bushy sideburns and plastic covers on all his furniture. His daughter is in private school. I don't like her because she thinks she's better, the kind of girl who doesn't share. He's always calling up to tell Mama and Daddy, "Your music is too loud up there. It's just too loud." But music, that's the thing that's got strangers knocking on our unlocked apartment door Friday and Saturday nights after Daddy is home from work at Goodyear and just wants to have fun.

It's the music that makes you turn the doorknob to somebody else's apartment door, just stepping in like you're home. A lot of times, we don't even know who the people are. They just hear Marvin Gaye or The Stylistics or Millie Jackson and here they come with a bottle in their hand. Millie is singing *There's no price for happiness, there's no price for love.* And there's a stack of records on the table or a barstool or laid out on the floor with green shag carpet poking up between the album covers like grass. And sometimes, I can make a request. I can ask Daddy to put on the Chi-Lites asking "Have you seen her?" if the party is winding down and I'm supposed to be in bed but I'm not. In all the parties, the only time he draws the line is at Captain & Tennille. One time I asked after we moved in 1977, even though he's the one that bought the album for me, because whenever the radio played "Love Will Keep Us Together" Daddy told me I sang that song like I wrote it.

***

DADDY WILL TELL ME, one of these days when I'm older, that those were the times when no one locked their doors. Those were the times when going from one apartment to the other was like leaving one room and going into another. The only thing to fear was the police. But still, the times were strange, hippies killing people in the hills, fake Black Panthers getting real brothers killed, and a rich white girl on the run that other white people are giving away, that's what Daddy says. They don't want her anymore, white people. He had a theory, years later. "No way would they shoot up the house and make it blow up if they cared about her. Take that chance on blowing up a white girl. The brothers, they were killing us every day. But by then she was already one of us, running around with a black man, so that was that. If she burn up, she burn up."

***

THE STRANGEST THING OF all, when I'm almost eight and the whole country is looking for Patty Hearst, is that I walk around the neighborhood all by myself. Mama and Daddy, they both let me. Mama will tell me not to go too far off and Daddy will say, "Where you going again? Don't go no farther than Harry and Maynail's house."

It's true I'm just a child, but the neighborhood is mine. I can put my transistor radio at the bottom of the stairs and Hula-Hoop, with Mama upstairs talking to Miss Mary. Or I can jump rope with Cassandra, who always wants me to watch her jump rope. "Watch me! Watch me!" She says, her pink barrettes bouncing all around her head, and she always messes up early. The rope always slaps her legs. Or I can just go. I don't have to be playing with anybody. As long as I say where I'm going, nobody will look for me. I take my radio with me, wrapped around my wrist, and I walk, music always with me. The Chi-Lites sing, *For Gods sake, you got to give more power to the people.* I go to my favorite tree, a kumquat tree that I just pick from and eat as much as I want. It's in the neighbor's yard, but they don't care. They don't care if anybody picks them. They're for everybody, and I love the waxy feel of the skin on my tongue and that tart sweetness when I bite down. I go into people's houses. I sit down. I watch what they're watching on TV. I listen to what they're playing on the stereo and watch them dance and snap their fingers. They ask me about Mama and Daddy. Sometimes they give me an orange or a cookie or peppermint and tell me to be safe. But I always am. I always come back home like I am supposed to. Nobody kidnaps me. I just walk up and down my street singing songs.

***

I DON'T REMEMBER HOW it comes to be that Mama and I are riding in Miss Mary's car, the radio playing on the way to see the burned out house, LaBelle singing *Hey sista go sista soul sista go sista*... People are coming from everywhere and far away, that's what Mama and Miss Mary say, but we don't have to drive far at all. I sit in the back seat, my face barely reaching over the car door to see outside. I have to stretch my body to look. I know that we have gotten to where we are supposed to be because of all the people. We park the car and Mama takes my hand and we walk until we are across the street from the house. Nobody is talking. It's quiet, except for a radio. There's a man next to the radio, standing, painting a picture. I can hear low voices and the clicks of cameras. The day is fresh. Clear and crisp and bright. Across the street, the house, what's left of the house, is black. I have been listening, so I know: people died underneath that house. But that can't be the whole story of why people would come from all over just to look. It's the strange case, the case of a white girl and other white people led by a black man into South Central Los Angeles, to find themselves underneath a house. Symbionese, that's what they are, and it sounds like Siamese. People joined together. Later, I will also know: the story is complicated. She is kidnapped, she is raped. She begins to think the way she did to survive. But no, the prosecution will say, the prosecution and some people. She wasn't raped at all. She was a loose woman getting some free love. She's guilty of robbing a bank. She is rebellious and turned revolutionary out of nowhere. Fists in the air, machine gun pointed. More power to the people. *How*? people will wonder. *How has it come to this*? Running around with a black convict that calls himself Cinque? That is why, Daddy says, the white people gave her away, gave the white Symbionese away, too, and took their chances with her maybe underneath the house.

That's what people come to look at. The *how* of it. From wealth and power to *this* and *these* people. From wealth and power to *being* one of the people. Next month, she'll tell everybody, "I am a soldier in the people's army."

So Mama and Miss Mary and I are standing on the street, with so many other people, looking at the house, what's left of the house. Miss Mary says, "I guess the police made their point, didn't they? You want a revolution? Not in LA, you don't."

Mama says, "They just shot all around the place, didn't they? You see what we worth?"

They stand there talking to each other, but I want to go look at what the man is painting and listen to his radio playing. *La la la la la la la la la means I love you.* I dance while I watch him paint and sing along to the *la la la*'s as pretty as I can, but my voice doesn't sound beautiful like the voices coming out of the radio. He looks down at me, brush in hand, and smiles, and I like his cornrows and his big medallion hanging on his neck. "You sound all right, little sister," he says. And he's putting polka dots on the blue dress of a woman in his picture.

I ask him. "Who's that?"

"Don't you see her, little sister?" he says. "She standing right over there." He points with his brush, and I remember that woman now, somebody I didn't know, remember her standing on the sidewalk in March 1974. Maybe she lived in my neighborhood. She had on a blue dress that billowed in the wind, with white polka dots. And she was wearing a big blue church hat with a giant white ribbon. I remember her, and the painting looked just like she looked. He painted her the way she really was.

Dana Johnson *is the author of the short story collection* In the Not Quite Dark, *available from Counterpoint. She is also the author of* Break Any Woman Down, *winner of the Flannery O'Connor Award for Short Fiction, and the novel* Elsewhere, California. *Both books were nominees for the Hurston/Wright Legacy Award. Her work has appeared in* The Paris Review, Callaloo, The Iowa Review, *and* Huizache, *among others, and was anthologized in* Watchlist: 32 Stories by Persons of Interest, Shaking the Tree: A Collection of New Fiction and Memoir by Black Women, *and* California Uncovered: Stories for the 21st Century. *Born and raised in and around Los Angeles, she is a professor of English at the University of Southern California.*

FROM THE DESERT TO THE SEA: FIRST ENCOUNTERS WITH LOS ANGELES

by Deanne Stillman

M Y FIRST EXPERIENCES IN Los Angeles were in the 1970s, and, initially, these all had to do with work. I was living in New York, but would visit LA to work on projects I was cowriting with close friends who were also writing for the brand new television show *Saturday Night Live*.

Sometimes we would head out to Desert Hot Springs for a few days, where we would stay at Two Bunch Palms, the rustic hipster retreat that, although expensive, had not yet gone corporate and was a haunt for creative types from New York and LA who needed to get out of town. My friends and I would sit in the springs and simmer and then emerge and write, return to the springs, perhaps the cold one this time, then quickly head to the warm, simmer again, emerge, pick up our notepads and continue writing. Later, we would get a massage from one of the very fine bodyworkers who were well-versed in helping tightly-wrapped movie industry folk stop talking or thinking or reacting, if only for a little while, and then we might have dinner and drinks on the patio, or back in our rooms (when available, we stayed in the spacious Al Capone house—he had once stayed there, went the story.) The following day and the day after that, we would repeat the scene, returning to New York a week or two later with part of a script or pages for a book in hand.

When not at Two Bunch Palms, sometimes we stayed at the Chateau Marmont in LA or with friends, and had classic local experiences—eating at the organic restaurant on Sunset called The Source (the one where Woody Allen backs out of the driveway with his convertible top stuck in the half-way up or down position in *Annie Hall*), driving our own convertible from Rent-a-Wreck, having meetings at the studios with executives who chattered in the industry shorthand—"red-eye," "turn-around," "A-list," and on it went.

For me and many of my friends at that time, Los Angeles was an extension of New York, and we constantly made comparisons. I have long since realized how unsettling this endless NY-LA triangulating must have been for people who grew up here, especially other writers who had to endure wave after wave of NY-LA jokes, most famous of which, perhaps, was Woody Allen's line that "the only cultural advantage to LA is right turn on red." I, too, succumbed to these comparisons. (How could I not? It was what I knew at the time, although I did often feel like taking a shower afterward, for they made me feel shabby and as if I had committed some sort of betrayal— more than that I could not explain.) I guess I was on autopilot, even writing my own such pieces, including "The Last LA-NY Article," published in the *LA Times* sometime later. I don't remember what I said and can't find the piece. (The paper wasn't buying electronic rights then because there was no such thing, so it's not online, and I have a physical copy somewhere, but exactly where I don't know.) But of one thing I am sure: it really wasn't the last LA-NY article; I've seen many since, not with that title, but each in the same vein, and some very funny, but not really, because in the end, the comparison is a false one. Yet I was not able to take LA in on its own terms during my first visits. I didn't know what I was taking in, exactly. For my whole life, I was accustomed to reacting, and having wanted to be a writer since I was a little girl, by the time the 1970s rolled around, I had made a practice of it. My father had taught me to write as a child, first by way of his favorite writers, including Edgar Allan Poe, whose poem "Eldorado" became a signpost and a passport in my life. I would enter the poem as he read aloud, traveling with the gallant knight into sunshine and shadow, which for me became the wide-open spaces of the primordial West, tales of which I began to read on my own. Yet my father was also a wiseacre, and his favorite writers, favorite people I should say, also included comedians—all of the Borscht Belt greats, and those who came later. During the years that he was teaching me to write, he would read the works of Ring Lardner and other *New Yorker* writers out loud, and at some point we subscribed to *Mad* magazine and we would invent characters and write sketches and scenes and short stories together, and I started submitting pieces there—as an eight-year-old!—soon receiving notices in the mail that said *not right for us.* To this day, if I get one, I remember all of that, me as a little girl racing to the mailbox, hoping for good news, only to receive something so perfunctory and impersonal. WTF *Mad* magazine! That wasn't very funny!

But seriously, by the time I had moved from my land of origin, Ohio, to New York to begin my writing career, I had refined my comedy skills very well. You see, my parents got divorced around the time that I was submitting pieces to *Mad,* and for some time, my father disappeared from my life. Yet I had my survival kit—being funny—and I knew how to use all of the tools. Rather than admit to myself that I was in pain, I became accustomed to holding it down and channeling it into my writing, which took the form of humorous pieces about whatever struck my fancy. I sold many of these pieces to the major publications of the day and was becoming known as a writer of humor—or, as my friends and I called it, we were "funny for money," a line that although witty, also reflected, for me at least, the dilemma in which I was mired: it was a cute reaction to a life devoted to reacting and although I was becoming known and celebrated for making people laugh, I didn't like it one bit.

Living in New York reinforced the thing that I was doing, or perhaps I should say that it was the right place for me at the time. It was fast, witty, and unforgiving. But more to the point, I simply did not know how to express my pain—or even realize how deep it went—and so suppressed were my feelings that I was not able to fully accept the main man in my life at the time, someone with whom I lived for twelve years. The success being offered for my being funny was glamorous and shining, like my father the handsome wiseacre, and my boyfriend, too (also a ladies' man, but there were oh-so-many rivers beneath that surface). If relationships are for helping two people heal, I was only able to do that up to a point, and as he began to show me his own vulnerability, he came to represent not my father, but my mother, which is to say I began to see him as a loving, reliable person waiting for me at home in New York when I was in LA and I hated it and was in excruciating pain because of it, pretending, of course, that everything was fine—funny even!—hopping into my car and shutting the world out on the freeway, where I would get lost in the endless whirlpool, emerging for accolades here and there and love substitutes with a parade of boyfriends. At one point there was even a succession of fellows with the same first name, and I came to refer to this part of my life as "some like it Larry."

But the joke was on me, because this was a life I could not maintain, not even with the mountains of cocaine that were readily available at any party, the expensive champagne that followed to level it out, and all of the soaking at Desert Hot Springs. Throughout my life, I've had dreams that have been trail markers, very palpable ones, and if there's one thing that I've done without equivocation, it's taking them at their word. Back then, there came a nightmare, the worst I've ever had, in which I was strapped to a gurney and being embalmed while I was still alive. I woke up in terror and dialed a psychiatrist. That was the beginning of years of therapy, during which I began to peel back the layers of pain. Shortly after that, or maybe it was just before, I came down with walking pneumonia while writing for a network comedy series in Los Angeles, some time after I had permanently moved to LA from New York. It would be the last of several such jobs; although being "funny for money" had gotten me a lifelong membership in the Writers Guild, it was killing me and I had to stop.

During my years of therapy, I had also begun to wander the desert, especially the sands of Joshua Tree National Park. Having lived inside the poem "Eldorado" as a little girl, and also attended the

University of New Mexico where I hiked through Pleistocene canyons and rode the red rock mesas atop a pony, it was not an unfamiliar place to me. But now I needed it more than ever, and, as always, it was there waiting. The deeper I got into it, the more I realized that the whole comedy thing was slipping away like a skin. The terrain of Joshua Tree National Park was all about listening, and my non-stop reacting, a New York style that went well with my need to conceal the pain of my childhood in Ohio, didn't have a home there—and I liked it. I liked being able to see things, listen, feel them, and not respond to an urge to comment or start translating the experience into a funny piece that I could sell. Although here I must confess: my "Rocks in the Shape of Billy Martin" piece, which I wrote later, about what became an annual pilgrimage to Joshua Tree for the aforementioned rocks, has been oft-reprinted and is one of my own personal favorites; better yet, years later, when I was writing about the park for the *New York Times* travel section, I used that line in the piece, and the *Times* fact-checker called and asked where the rocks were, lest a *Times* reader actually try to find them and die of thirst in the process. I told her they were two arroyos down from Lou Piniella Arch, or maybe it was Sandy Koufax Wash, I can't remember which line I used, but she said okay and then we moved on to the next question. To this day, that remains my best fact-checking anecdote, and my weirdest *New York Times* experience. Anyway, as you see, I may have let my own pain come forth, but sometimes, a gal just has to laugh.

One day back in Los Angeles, I was on assignment for a local weekly newspaper, asked to write about "the shaman of Beverly Hills." As I've written in my essay, "Ohio Girl: How I Travelled the NY-LA Fault Line and Got Home," I decided to do something that life in New York would have completely precluded; I decided to take this shaman at face value—at worst, I'd come away with a magazine article and a free weekend at the Airport Hyatt with complimentary Cobb salad and garment bags. The first day of the weekend journey was unproductive for me; unlike the others who had meditated and found their power animal, I was unable to find mine—and was disappointed, as I love animals. But on the second day, everything changed.

Once again, the lights were dimmed, incense was lit, and the low drone of aboriginal music began to pulse through the room. Again came the instruction: "I want you all to lie on your backs, breathe deeply in and out, that's right, in and out, really get comfortable, and then we'll begin." After a few moments, we were told to visualize a port of entry into the earth, crawl in, and follow the path to a primeval setting. I knew from my years of wandering the deserts of the Southwest that this is a traditional visualization used by native cultures here and around the globe, not just those in Beverly Hills. My port of entry was a familiar spot in Joshua Tree National Park, which I had been exploring for years prior to this weekend. "Now," said the shaman, "find something you need from someone who has it... At some point you will come to an altar and that's where it will be...something you need from someone who has it." Lulled by the keening of the ecstatic Navajo voice, I proceeded on my journey with great dispatch to a port of entry leading to my own secret world, down into the earth until I found my barely perceptible desert path, marked by a flourish of ocotillo and creosote and signaled by the prolonged cry of a raven. A tortoise crossed my path as I wandered along the trail under the sharp light of the afternoon sun, a pocket of time in the desert when what you see is exactly what you get, but won't be when the raven cries again. As the road runners and jack rabbits and butterflies moved as if frozen in the heat, a tranquilized tableau of zoology, I continued on at a fairly deliberate pace, through a grove of ancient fan palms and up a rocky path to a higher elevation capped by a giant Joshua tree in full bloom. It must have been a hundred feet tall. Could this be the altar? I wondered, and looked around for clues.

There was no such information—no mantel piece, no burning candles, no statues of tortured martyrs. Suddenly from behind the branches of this grotesquely beautiful tree appeared my maternal grandmother. Although she had died long ago, clutching a letter that I had mailed from the desert in New Mexico—my grandmother lived on in the family's memory with her oft-uttered observance that "life is funny, oh dear, oh dear," kind of a metaphysical bumper sticker, which explains everything from who really wrote Shakespeare to Billy Martin's mysterious death in a drunk driving accident. Many times

I have dreamt of my grandmother over the years (and occasionally Billy Martin), yet, as far as I know, have never actually left this realm for a visit. Perhaps the distant hum of departing 747s had fueled my spiritual wanderlust, perhaps the shaman of Beverly Hills had guided me to some sort of cross-dimensional reunion, perhaps it was because my personal apple cart had been upset recently and I knew I could no longer pretend that everything was fine, perhaps it was because I had skipped lunch that day, perhaps it was all of these factors and more. Whatever was operating, there I was, under a Joshua tree in the desert, about to receive something I needed from someone I knew. I was ready.

The sun glinted off a small vial of what I took to be water that my grandmother held in her hand. She stepped toward me, offering the vial. I took it. My grandmother was instantly reclaimed by the desert. As she vanished behind the tree, I knew then that it was not a vial of water, but of tears, my tears, tears which I had not been able to shed since I was a little girl, had not shed during that wrenching moment with my father that had transpired years later. These were the tears of a lifetime's worth of pain. Tears that I had withheld because I was fine, I could handle anything. Since my parents' divorce, I could bear pain no more, so I didn't, at least not as far as the world was concerned. My grandmother, always quick to spot a half-truth, knew the whole story. And so my tears had been stored for me in the land of little rain—as the writer Mary Austin had called it—the land which writhes silently in pain, silently in ecstasy, and now it was time for me to have them. "Sometimes life isn't so funny, oh dear, oh dear."

From that point on, as I've often told friends, the desert became my church, my temple, my turkey tetrazzini. But a new problem of sorts arose. Actually, "problem" is not the right word; something I needed to figure out was now on the horizon. That the identity I had been putting forth for years was false, I now accepted. The person who was always quick with a riposte, a witticism, a reaction, was, yes, hurting on the inside, but I didn't have to keep this under wraps any more; in fact, the New York in me, to use a shorthand, was no longer calling the shots. Los Angeles had taken over, and my life—and writing—called me in a new direction. But how could I make a living telling this new truth as I now saw it? I had spent years laying a foundation in the opposite direction. I found the answer in the desert (of course!), returning to New Mexico on an urge and visiting an old friend, also a writer, who introduced me to an agent who was staying at her house for a conference. It turned out she understood exactly what I was going through, represented others whose work I admired, and said she could help me walk away from the professional persona for which I was known, and start anew. Soon, she began explaining to editors that I was no longer writing comedy—and, more urgently, that someone should fund a most un-funny story about what I wanted to write next: the tale of two girls who were killed by a marine after the Gulf War in Twentynine Palms, which I first heard about after hiking in Joshua Tree National Park and heading into a bar for a drink. That story became my book, *Twentynine Palms*, and part of the work in getting there was convincing editors that I could write it, for many were firm in their view that I was funny and how could I possibly make such a transition? As my agent said, "it was a case of mistaken identity"—not just for me, but for everyone who was with me up to that point, and there were many who could not come along with me in the next phase of my life because they just didn't get it.

Or as a friend of mine put it at the time, "people fall in love with you as one thing and when you change, sometimes it's just too painful."

The particular agent I met in New Mexico did indeed help me shed the last of my molting skin, and after many notes from publishers that said "not right for me," we got a yes. "All it takes is one," the agent said, and I was able to head down my new path. A long and winding one it was, but I emerged ten years later, manuscript in hand, and desert baptism in full effect.

Once I had officially moved to Los Angeles, I would find solace on the freeway, an LA icon that was a punchline in and of itself. I had liked it when I first arrived, perhaps because I had grown-up in Ohio, where sneaking out at night with my mother's Thunderbird and cruising on remote two-lanes under the stars was an escape, if only for an hour or two. As I settled in, there were certain things that began to make me feel like a local, cultural markers which I now understood on a personal level. No matter where you lived, you could always count on Johnny Carson (whom I loved) for a good freeway joke, whether it was something about the exit ramp where "they cut off your Slauson" or ending up in Barstow—hi-yo!!!—I laughed every time Johnny said these things and it all became part of some strange LA mantra that was shaping up for me. When I was on the 10 or the 405, I would think of those lines as I saw related signs and now that I could experience his jokes in a physical way, engaging with a Johnny Carson monologue in the material world, I felt that I was becoming kind of a local.

On the freeway, I began to think of myself as the anti-Maria of *Play It As It Lays*, Joan Didion's popular book of that era in which a character named Maria Wyeth drives aimlessly on the six- and eight-lane thoroughfares of Los Angeles and through the desert wastes, seeking oblivion. I found the opposite; there was much pleasure in entering the freeway whirlpool, something bordering on ecstasy as I merged with traffic coming off of certain on-ramps, and I liked giving myself over and getting lost. For it was inside that moment of stop-time that I felt connected; once again, there was no need to react and somehow I had become part of an American zen.

En route (to anywhere and nowhere), other bits of language floated into my scriptures. There were terms such as "Sig alert" and "lane closure"—yes, call me crazy—but I really liked hearing them. And my fascination didn't stop there. I like to know the origin of words and phrases and I looked up "Sig" and learned that it came from Loyd C. "Sig" Sigmon, a World War II veteran who was in the Army Signal Corps, and developed a system to alert radio engineers of communications problems. Later it was picked up by the LAPD and then it was adapted for traffic in Los Angeles and, well, if you have spent any driving here, you know the rest. For me, once I knew the history of that sonorous term, I was drawn even further into the LA landscape, the language of the freeway, a thing that seemed to emanate from a higher frequency and trigger a kind of silent ecstasy and grounding.

And then there were all of the on and off ramps. I knew which ones were prettier than others, which were a smoother or sexier drive. I admired the landscaping on some of them, and when I exited, I liked the way certain gas stations at the intersection had little gardens, some with benches or rocks that you could sit on, and to this day I am touched when I see carefully tended patches of flowers at a Chevron. *Who has thought to do this?* I think when I see a profusion of poppies and lavender in a triangle of ground next to pump number twelve. *Who has decided on this arrangement?* Perhaps they have the kind of temperament that would permit them to have no desire for recognition or communion with those who are affected by their endeavors, or maybe they wonder if anyone notices their work and what is surely their love. As I pull out of a gas station that has provided such beauty, I say thank you to the unseen caretakers of the road, thank you for providing these little kindnesses of the day. *Do you know you are necessary?*

At some point, I found myself thinking in a similar way about Caltrans workers. By the way, "Caltrans" is another great freeway term; it's fun and satisfying to say and is such an insider term that it's beyond exclusive. During my early driving experiences in LA, I would wonder about them as I drove past in my Rent-a-Wreck amid the stream of big rigs and Mercedes and pick-ups and other assorted vehicles. Unlike the gardeners at the gas station, they were visible, and they, too, were engaged in a beautiful task, laying down the asphalt that curved around foothills and took us through mountains and into the desert. Their occupational forebears had forged historic overpasses and lovely retaining walls with glyphs of Indians and dolphins and mission bells and such roadside sights were a comfort and a lesson and I again uttered my thanks as the whirlpool sucked me along.

Years later I read an item about a Caltrans worker who was removing a dead coyote from the road, and as he did so, he was hit by a car and killed. *Some kind of saint he was*, I remember thinking, and I wanted to write about him but I lost track of the story. Nevertheless, I knew what it was and I still do and it's this: two living things—a two- and a four-legged—run down by vehicles, flung to the side of the road, never to be remembered…except that maybe in our hearts we do remember, we have an ancient memory, it's of this pair, man and wolf in the wilderness, and the wolf becomes a dog for we need his protection in our little and farflung villages and he needs us because we provide food and sometimes, companionship, and sometimes we used to hunt together until there came a day when such a thing was no longer needed and the road forked and we went our separate ways. When I drive the freeways of Los Angeles, I sometimes recall that image—the coyote and the Caltrans worker—and yes, it's so very sad, but is it not also a testament, beautiful in its own way, to the Fates that bind us?

***

Just for the record, I no longer travel the freeways like I used to. Like a million other things, they've changed. They're too crowded and there are too many lane closures. And I don't have to get away from myself, or things, the way I used to. I like it fine just where I am, which is right near the beach. When the weather is right, or wrong for that matter, I'm on the bike path or the sands. I'm ten minutes from the PCH—one of my favorite highways—and I get to drive the California Incline all of the time. Except for when it's closed, like it has been for the past two years! I don't know about you, but I can't wait for it to open. It's the best on-ramp in the world.

Sometimes when I'm down on the beach, I think of my very first trip to Los Angeles, a cross-country drive with two friends from New Mexico. We were excited to get to the beach after heading across the 10 in a sweltering car for what seemed like days. We parked at the Santa Monica pier and ran down to the surf. My friends plunged right in, but I stopped at the edge and didn't even take off my shoes. I was frightened! I had grown up on the edge of Lake Erie, but my God! The Pacific! It was huge and it stopped me in my tracks.

Of course I pretended that nothing bothered me and I probably turned it into some sort of joke. Oh how I had wanted to join my friends. But I was frozen and could not do such a thing. And now here I am where the desert meets the sea and I'm not going anywhere, except into the water when the temperature is right, and onto the road if it calls. "Life is funny," as my grandmother used to say. "Oh dear, oh dear."

Deanne Stillman's *latest book is* Desert Reckoning, *based on a* Rolling Stone *piece, winner of the Spur and* LA Press Club *Awards for Best Nonfiction, a Southwest Book of the Year, an Amazon Editors' Pick, and praised in the* LA Review of Books, Newsweek, Denver Post, Tucson Weekly, *and elsewhere. She also wrote* Mustang, *an* LA Times *"best book of the year," winner of the California Book Award silver medal, and praised in* The Atlantic, NPR, Economist, Texas Monthly, *and many other places. The audio edition is available from Rare Bird Books, featuring Anjelica Huston, Frances Fisher, Wendie Malick, John Densmore, Richard Portnow, and James Morrison. In addition, Deanne is the author of the cult classic* Twentynine Palms, *an* LA Times *"best book of the year" which Hunter S. Thompson called "a strange and brilliant story by an important American writer." The new edition (Angel City Press) includes a foreword by T. Jefferson Parker and a preface by Charles Bowden. She is currently writing* Blood Brothers, *about the strange friendship between Sitting Bull and Buffalo Bill, for Simon & Schuster. She writes the "Letter from the West" column for the* LA Review of Books, *and is a member of the core faculty at the UC Riverside-Palm Desert MFA Low Residency Creative Writing Program.*

HAMBURGERS, HEMORRHAGES, AND HAUTE CUISINE

by Lynne Friedman

USC Hospital, Central Los Angeles.

"Where are you, Hal?"

"I'm with a pretty nurse."

That's how I knew my dad was "with it" in the wee hours of January 14, 2016, after he suffered a brain hemorrhage that put him into emergency surgery.

The surgery had gone well, but sedating an eighty-four-year-old has its risks and it took him a long time to come out of it. He was agitated and fighting to get up, so they had to sedate him again, just for the follow-up CT scan. This last dose of sedative took away his ability to speak or respond for close to twenty-four hours. And that was scary for me, his only child.

When he opened his eyes, the staff tried to evaluate him. They asked him questions about where he was and what year it was. Blank stare. But I knew how we would get a response:

"Do you like Tommy's chiliburgers or hot dogs better?"

"Hot dogs."

"Dad, what's your favorite pie? Apple or rhubarb?"

"Rhubarb," he said.

Then, he looked straight at me. "Will you make me a rhubarb pie?"

And the answer was yes, absolutely yes. I am a chef who cooks upscale international cuisine, but getting that rhubarb pie exactly right for the man who has been my most forthright critic meant more to me than any praise I might get elsewhere. And I hoped I would get to go to Tommy's with him again. I could have a chiliburger while he eats his hot dog, passionately insisting that it is even better than the chiliburger I was eating. I'll take that—and a root beer, too.

***

THE LARGE TOMMY'S SIGN—SQUARE-SHAPED and red, with a bright border of flashing yellow lights—turned 'round and 'round, like a lighthouse beacon, calling people to the corner of Rampart and Beverly Boulevards. The surrounding neighborhood was not particularly walkable at night, but people stood in line under the bright lights at the pearly gates of this fast food heaven, twenty-four-seven.

It was the chili. Not the kind that was served in a bowl, but a proprietary chili specifically formulated with the right mixture of flour and water so it would stick to a burger properly. Outside the shack the restaurant's namesake bought in 1946, students, local artists, gangsters, actors, and tourists stood next to each other, united in a common mission known far and wide to Angelenos everywhere as a Tommy's Run.

By the 1970s, it was not uncommon to see limos parked any hour of the night with a celebrity or two waiting at one of the two Tommy's serving stations that now took up the entire corner. Everybody wanted his or her fix. And that night in early 1972 my dad drove me, his small girl-child, thirty minutes from our home in the suburban West San Fernando Valley to break me into this tradition. Sure, there had been a few other Tommy's locations popping up around town, but this was the original, the only one worthy of "Tommy's Run" distinction. Our black 1965 Buick LeSabre took its place in the parking lot full of cars—big cars, dreamboats, with and without good paint jobs. As we stood at the thin wooden counters (no seats, per true burger shack tradition) and ate our burgers slathered with the unique mortar-like chili, my dad told me how he and his friends used to come here as teens from their homes in South Central, where he had moved in early 1947, back when this simple shack had been the new burger joint in town. I doubt he imagined that, long after he drove out of the lot, long after I fell asleep sans seatbelt while inhaling the leather-scented fumes of the Buick's back seat, I would, as a college student, often drive to make this very same run with my friends.

∗∗∗

TEN DAYS AFTER MY dad's initial surgery, I drove him home from the hospital. Though disoriented and off-balance, he was in good spirits and so was I. I had spent the better part of the last ten days at my dad's bedside convincing him, sometimes physically and almost unsuccessfully, that he couldn't simply get his keys and drive out of the hospital lot. Home would be good.

My parents had always kept their house in decent order, but there was still that room—the room that accumulates stuff. In the not-too-distant future, that room would very likely be housing a caregiver. Opening the door, I looked down and spied a small bit of the green shag carpet that, unlike the rest of the house carpeting, had never been changed. Years of paper, books, newspapers, and other assorted ephemera greeted my eyes, every one of which would require me to determine whether was it part of my parents' soul, and thus in need of preservation, or, say, an expired oil change coupon clipped in 1989. It was almost too much for me to take in, and I considered putting it off for another day…that is, until I noticed all the newspaper articles and books on restaurants. And menus.

A lot of menus.

I sat down and started flipping through them, each one prompting memories—personal, regional, even historical—of a life spent reading between the culinary lines.

∗∗∗

"WHEN I GROW UP, I want to be a waitress."

My ambitious declaration was inspired by our server at the Hamburger Hamlet that night in 1973. Her beehive hairdo, black skirt, and white, frilly apron and cap appeared nothing short of spectacular to my six-year-old self. *She's so friendly and smiley*, I thought, *that she must be the one of the happiest people on earth.*

At Hamburger Hamlet, the burger had taken a walk on the fancy side. Marilyn and Harry Lewis, a married couple who worked as a costume designer and actor, respectively, had founded Hamburger Hamlet back in 1950 as a hangout for their entertainer compatriots. "The Hamlet" had given the burger a new dress: it could be presented on an oak plank, or swathed in mushrooms, avocado, bacon, or bleu cheese. It could attend a Hollywood party escorted by glamorous side, such as lobster bisque, onion soup fondue, shrimp cocktail, and "those potatoes"—fried crispy and layered alternately with sour cream and scallions.

"Would you all like dessert?" asked the spectacular waitress as she peered out from behind her cat-eye reading glasses. The sound of her words was sweet and smooth, like the milkshake I was about to order. Her name tag said "Lovenia" and she was African-American, like most of the other waitstaff. Unlike many restaurateurs in the fifties, sixties, and seventies, the Lewises had made a point of hiring African-Americans, so much so that they were eventually slapped with a reverse-discrimination lawsuit. When they expanded to Orange County in the 1970s, the African-American staff there was escorted to and from their cars by the Costa Mesa police, as the neighborhood white supremacists had threatened death to a chain that dare employ diversity in their homogenous neighborhood.

The milkshake, topped with a mountain of whipped cream, arrived in a shapely, tall glass. (I try to recall, was that glass tinted amber like so many glasses in the seventies? Did the amber color make glasses more groovy? Perhaps…) I enjoyed every drop of it in our high-backed red leather-ish booth in the midst of this dark wood–paneled restaurant.

The Hamburger Hamlet had several locations then and they moved with the times. At one point in the seventies the Hamlet even embraced the disco craze and was asylum to dancing polyester-clad, gold chain–sporting patrons, many of whom spent more time in the bathroom booths hoovering up cocaine than they did in the Hamlet's booths, hoovering up red meat 'n' taters. Trends, however, would change, and as LA's burgers moved into fast-casual territory, the Hamlet fell out of vogue, its equivocation over its dressed-up or stripped-down identity very much echoing the ambivalence of its Shakespearian namesake, whose most-famous quotes adorned its menu pages.

***

"Words, words, words."—Shakespeare's *Hamlet*

Now, post–brain surgery, my dad would often struggle with words as I tried to pry out names of restaurants and stories from his life. Finding the right word to describe what was in his memory about the things we did together was difficult for him. His face showed the emotion of what he was thinking about, but sometimes the exact words refused to bubble up to the surface.

My dad also struggled with writing. In fact, his inability to handwrite easily had been the stroke tip off that sent us to the hospital in the first place. As a young man, my dad had been a professional graphic artist, and, although he switched in 1963 to the bright, shiny new field of computer programming, his artistic vision still peeked through in the birthday cards that he used to make for my mother and me.

A couple days after he came home, it was again my birthday. And, for the first time, my dad was unable to make me a card. Maybe there were a few cards from years past in "that room." But I didn't find a card, I found a menu from Chasen's, where we had celebrated my birthday years before. This year, we would celebrate it at my childhood dining room table. My father was home, and that was my greatest gift.

***

Onetta Johnson, the Chasen's restaurant ladies' room attendant, was tired. After a mad rush (business ebbs and flows in a ladies' room), they finally left her alone for a moment—just enough for her to realize that she was entirely exhausted. She worked two jobs and she was operating on very little sleep.

"I wish all these people would just go home," she said aloud to herself as she dropped her head into her hands. Or, was she only speaking to herself? Donna Summer had walked in the door from the hubbub of Julio Iglesias' Grammy party, just in time to overhear her complaining.

"I'm sorry, Ms. Summer."

"Oh, that's alright," Summer said. "You work hard for the money."

A portal to the heavens opened in the ladies' room that night and the light of creativity shone down on Summer. Pulling a pen from her purse, she wrote the lyrics to what became an early eighties mega-hit on toilet paper in this institution of a restaurant.

Ladies' room attendants weren't always *de rigueur* in Los Angeles eating establishments, but this was Chasen's. Dave Chasen opened a chili joint in 1936 to serve Hollywood actors and it morphed into a full-scale, upscale restaurant where Washington power dined with Hollywood power—literally. In the seventies, conservative President Nixon could be seen dining with Paul Keyes, famed producer of the psychedelic comedy television show *Laugh-In*. The Reagans were engaged there decades back, during their Hollywood days, and they continued to dine there often, even well into their Washington power years. Frank Sinatra, Orson Welles, Lucile Ball, and a number of other notables had booths there. Your position in life could be determined by your seat's power status at Chasen's.

It's important to remember that, for most of the 1970s, going out for fancy food in Los Angeles meant continental cuisine—rich, brown, sweet, and flaming continental cuisine. At Chasen's, tuxedo-uniformed career waiters carted chafing dishes to your table and seared steaks in butter—a lot of butter—just to your liking. The waiter already knew how you wanted it cooked because he knew you. And if he didn't know you, he could make a pretty good guess at how you liked your food based on how you looked or where you were from. The waitstaff studied that stuff as they worked, and many of them had worked there for decades. Bartender Pepe Ruiz joked with celebrities as he lit orange peels on fire with trademark flair, infusing the sherry inside his specialty Flame of Love cocktail. Everything was on fire here; Steak Diane, Crêpe Suzette, and the careers of the Hollywood glitterati who were there to eat, drink, and be seen. But people still came for the chili. Nixon had had the chili delivered to San Clemente so he could enjoy some with Henry Kissenger. A decade before, Liz Taylor famously flew the chili out to Rome during the filming of *Cleopatra,* and she continued to enjoy it on a regular basis with two-time husband Richard Burton. It wasn't on the menu, but it was very much in the hearts and minds of the cognoscenti of Los Angeles high society.

For my birthday, we were invariably seated somewhere between Siberia and the ladies' room, but no matter; they plied me with their infamous banana shortcake. The menu, found under mounds of paper in "that room," memorialized this rich experience, but there was one place where my parents regularly dined for which they had no menu.

***

"Not for five million dollars."

This was the answer Sam Kovich gave a prospective patron when he telephoned and asked, "Would it be alright if my wife wears a fancy pantsuit to your restaurant instead of a dress?"

Kovich, proprietor of The Coolibah, was annoyed, and he meant what he said. You couldn't hand him $5 million to put up with a female patron who didn't wear a dress or a male patron who didn't don a jacket and tie.

The curious customer-to-be was a lawyer, and a good one, so he had to ask another question. "What is on the menu that evening?"

"There is no menu!" Kovich said. "We are not a restaurant, we are a dining room! And, since you asked, it will be hamburgers!"

Click.

But it wasn't going to be hamburgers. It was to be chateaubriand, along with seven other elaborate courses including smoked pheasant soup, shrimp canapés, and lamb noisettes. Until 1977, The Coolibah sat tucked away in a corner shopping mall in the far reaches of the

San Fernando Valley. Despite its location somewhere north of off-the-grid, people came, and Sam Kovich had his rules. It didn't matter who the hell you were: no tie, no dinner.

Kovich also didn't care how far you drove to get there. If you showed up five minutes late, banging on the closed door, he would not let you in. If you were early, and you chose to have a beer at the bar next door, that beer would be the death knell for your dinner plans. Urban legend had it that the brother of President Johnson was denied entry for that very reason. But if you played by the rules, Kovich welcomed you. Appearing at the door, he handed you a glass of sparkling wine and gave you a tour of the kitchen.

"Never trust a place that won't show you its kitchen," he said.

It was spotless. How the hell were they going to spew forth eight magnificent courses from a kitchen that, other than one pot of soup on the stove, did not have a speck of food on its counters? But they did, and the food was world class. Flowers, almonds, Hollywood-esque candelabras, and goblets sat atop the crisp white tablecloths of The Coolibah's diminutive dining room. A red rose for each female guest lay on place settings awash with multitudes of silver forks and knives that marked each course. Sitting next to your date, however, was considered bad manners at a table, and Sam Kovich would not hesitate to come out and say something to that very effect should you make that mistake during dinner. Kiss your date, and you likely wouldn't make it to the next course.

Was all this fussiness worth it? Yes. Celebrities, politicians, gourmets, and gourmands vied to get a table at the The Coolibah. And my dad was a gourmand. Whether it be a downscale, inexpensive meal or a grandiose, costly extravagance, it was all about the food. He would endure anything to consume the best, and a lot of it.

At the end of the meal, there was no bill. You simply left your table and walked up to his little desk behind a screen in the corner where Kovich gave you a number, and you paid it. It was a surprisingly small number—perhaps twelve to fifteen dollars per person—for what you had just been served. Kovich wanted to provide his guests with an unforgettable dining experience, and he held you captive with his food. He never advertised. You had to know his place by word of mouth.

∗∗∗

SUNDAYS IN THE 1970s, Elmer Dills' voice blared from the AM band of our receiver. There was no Internet, no Yelp, no way to punch a few buttons and get a full restaurant rundown with eighty-five smartphone-snapped pictures of menu items. If you wanted to find a good place to eat, you had to listen to what people said. And the man we listened to was Elmer Dills.

"And this week, we are going to talk about Northern Italian," Dills, upbeat voice beckoned people to call into his show and share their dining experiences all over Southern California.

The other voices we listened to were from the *Los Angeles Times*. Instead of saying grace, my dad often read aloud the words of food writers Lois Dwan or Colman Andrews at the dinner table, while my mom invariably produced something good from the kitchen.

My mother was and is an excellent cook. Born in Burma, with her youth spent in India, her curries were perfection. But she loved all international cooking and was never bound by meat and potatoes as were so many 1970s moms. Nor was she a health food enthusiast—a movement in the seventies that produced restaurants like The Good Earth and The Source.

Although it wasn't our scene, The Source restaurant on Sunset Boulevard is worthy of mention in any account of 1970s Los Angeles…or, for that matter, any account of Los Angeles, period. Founded by Rolls Royce–driving, white suit–wearing, cult leader Father Yod, its very existence and patronage by celebrities like John Lennon and Marlon Brando financially funded the spirituality of sex, drugs, and rock and roll for a couple hundred of Yod's cult devotees in a Hollywood Hills mansion. The plentiful revenue from restaurant menu favorites like the "Aware Salad" and the "Magic Mushroom" stopped abruptly in 1974 when run-ins with authorities had the group relocating to the shores of Hawaii. There, Father Yod stepped off a 1,300-foot cliff, his first and only attempt at hang gliding, and crash-landed his way into his next incarnation.

Due to the oil crisis and inflation in the 1970s, our economy crashed as well. Continental cuisine, just like the continent for which it was named, followed suit. And after a recession is served up, lower overhead costs often allow culinary innovation to be the next course.

***

NEXT TO AN OLD mattress store (an old, used mattress store) in a decaying part of Santa Monica, Michael McCarty found the ground that would sprout a Los Angeles culinary revolution.

Back in '75, McCarty came to Los Angeles, a town that, only one decade before, had finally built its own major concert hall. Most of the venerable founders whose names graced the donor walls of LA's Music Center were still hanging out at its concerts. Los Angeles haute culture was in its seedling state.

McCarty brought his own seeds from France, where he had studied at Le Cordon Bleu and École Hôtelière. He could now facilitate the growing of fresh vegetables and herbs for cooking in Southern California. With the exception of earthy-crunchy health food sandwich places, fresh didn't happen that much in 1970s dining. Even culinary education cookbooks in the early seventies said things like, "Open a number ten can..."

And then McCarty opened a can of culinary whoop-ass. At the tail end of the decade, in '79, Michael's restaurant threw wide its doors and its menu to some pretty new stuff.

"The old way was brown, mushy, and sweet," Michael said. "The new way is green, crunchy, and acidic."

Menu collaborations with chefs like Wolfgang Puck, then of Ma Maison, Jean Bertranou of L'Ermitage, and others from the just-materializing American Institute of Food and Wine created new dishes. Many of them incorporated the freshness of southern French or Italian cooking as a starting point and added a twist—a twist inspired by the Latin cuisine of the men who washed the dishes or by the Japanese culinary students who studied alongside McCarty in France. McCarty and his chefs learned from everyone. No longer were white-gloved servers pouring heavy sauces over rich, braised, meaty dishes. Here, at Michael's, you could eat mesquite-grilled quail with jalapeño lime salsa or raw (imagine!) diver scallops with heirloom beet purée and olive oil mâche.

New art came to the kitchen, and a lot of art came to the walls of Michael's. McCarty's wife, Kim, a painter, was entrenched in the art community. At Michael's, artists came and traded art for cuisine, creating a veritable gallery inside the restaurant. And, instead of the piped-in mu*sac* common in seventies restaurants, Michael's played jazz—apropos for a restaurant that "riffed" on traditional food.

The outdoor garden dining area was an ironic rarity in a city known for its good weather. Young movie execs like Steven Spielberg, Jeffrey Katzenberg, and Michael Eisner weren't so tied to old Hollywood or Beverly Hills money. They could be seen eating here at this Westside indoor-outdoor haven where young chefs like Jonathan Waxman and Mark Peel put their creations in front of the new, budding Los Angeles culturati.

Now, in 2016, I found myself dining at Michael's with a friend who was editing a book on Los Angeles in the 1970s. During our dinner, I reflected on my father and on all of the food experiences that he gave me as a kid in seventies. LA food had changed so much at the very place in which we were eating. Los Angeles had flexed its own regional culinary muscles, creating a veritable groundbreaking earthquake that, to this day, is still referred to as California Cuisine. It was the first New American cuisine, and Los Angeles, by the end of the 1970s, had morphed into a new American city.

***

RIFFLING THROUGH "THAT ROOM," I found a newspaper clipping from the seventies with a picture of my dad. I could only assume that it was a company newspaper. Working in Downtown LA as a computer programmer for Transamerica Occidental Life Insurance, he was the unofficial restaurant expert in his office. The picture on the clipping showed my dad smiling as he lifted a fork to his mouth. For a while, after the hemorrhagic stroke, my dad could no longer engage in this simple task. And he still has some trouble remembering the names of streets and restaurants. And yet, on the way back from a follow-up appointment at USC Hospital, as we drove through Central Los Angeles, he pointed excitedly out the window.

"That's the Chinese restaurant where I used to take your mom when we were first married," he said. "We would go there after boating in Echo Park."

My dad was a "foodie" long before the term made its way into our vernacular. As I placed the clipping and menus off to the side, to be catalogued for another time, I still wasn't sure what was at the end of the fork in the picture, but now, three months after his stroke, I was thrilled that he could pick up a fork and enjoy himself once again. Then it struck me. It was time for another Tommy's Run. And, soon after, we stood, father and daughter, more than four decades later, at the narrow wooden counter, enjoying our hot dog and chiliburger, respectively.

Lynne Friedman, *a native Angeleno, has contributed to, among other publications, the* Los Angeles Times *and the* Malibu Times Magazine. *A UCLA graduate in mathematics, her diverse career, spanning from CPA to chef, has brought her to live in Moscow, Manhattan, and Copenhagen, but she will always call Los Angeles home.*

THE MAKING OF A (TENNIS) PLAYER

by Joel Drucker

"YOU LIKE THE FEEL of that, don't you?" she asked. "It's very comfortable to slip into."

It was February 1975. The blonde might have been nineteen, or twenty-three, perhaps twenty-seven, not likely thirty-two. Recalling the movie I'd recently seen, *Shampoo*, I compared her to Goldie Hawn and Julie Christie.

The location was the tennis department of The Summit, a ski and tennis shop on San Vicente Boulevard in Brentwood, located a block from the apartment I lived in on the corner of Bundy and Montana.

Was she flirting? How could that be? After all, I was fourteen years old, in the throes of orthodontic and dermatological hell. Certainly something was going on. My fingers caressed a new product made by Adidas: the first warm-up suit that was slick, smooth, and, if the blonde's manner was to be believed, sensual. Besides its lush, textured feel—satin sheets?—the outfit was canary yellow, sunburst in a way quite different from the austere gray, navy, and white sweats that had occupied these shops as recently as five years prior. It was nothing like the furry acrylic jacket and pants I had on. And it also cost seventy dollars, more than twice the price of mine. But then again, in a decade when tennis captured the sporting soul of Los Angeles, seventy dollars could sure take a player many places.

Tennis had long enjoyed a following in Los Angeles. While most of the country confined itself to a compressed tennis season, year-round sunshine gave Southern California zealots the chance to play every day. The Los Angeles Tennis Club (LATC), located on Cahuenga south of Melrose, was the most tennis-rich club in the world. Great champions such as Bill Tilden, Ellsworth Vines, Don Budge, Jack Kramer, Pancho Gonzales, and Stan Smith had either been members or competed there frequently. Ditto for the two participants in the 1973 "Battle of the Sexes" match, Billie Jean King and Bobby Riggs. Blue bloods in Pasadena and Hollywood folk enjoyed their own special clubs and private courts. Los Angeles was also dotted with hundreds of courts at public parks—Griffith, Exposition, and Rancho among the most active. Still, for most of the twentieth century, tennis was peripheral, regarded as everything from an exclusionary garden party to an effete sissy sport.

By the early seventies, though, the tennis population soared. Political shifts within the sport had opened the floodgates for increased exposure. Pro matches, including a men's circuit funded by millionaire Lamar Hunt, aired regularly on NBC, CBS, and PBS. There was also the newly formed Virginia Slims women's tour, its marquee player the Long Beach–raised King.

Among the masses, an individual's sport like tennis was the athletic personification of a period dubbed "The Me Decade." Along with jogging, tennis was one of the first sports of the fitness boom, an outgrowth of that hippie saying, "do your own thing." In new ways, never to be repeated, tennis in the seventies pervaded American culture. In one of the decade's signature movies, *Annie Hall*, Woody Allen and Diane Keaton first met playing tennis. President Jimmy Carter played, so engrossed in the sport that he personally supervised reservations on the White House court. Celebrity tennis aficionados such as actor Charlton Heston, *Chinatown* producer Robert Evans, and *Playboy Magazine* founder Hugh Hefner added sparkle. Those Hollywood folk, long-barred from exclusive WASP venues like the LATC, lit out for the territory at such nearby nouveau riche hot spots as Caesars

Palace in Las Vegas (where comedian Alan King created a pro event) and, near San Diego, a venue allegedly owned by the Mafia, La Costa Resort & Spa.

Tennis began for my family shortly after we moved to Los Angeles from St. Louis in 1970. My mother, delighted to shake off the snow, figured that everyone in California played tennis, so she trekked to Stoner Park, just south of Santa Monica Boulevard and Barrington Avenue, and took lessons. My eleventh birthday present was a Spalding Pancho Gonzales racket.

It was the perfect sport for my loner persona. It didn't require teammates, or a coach who thought you were good enough, or one who decreed you should play a certain position, or the approval of the Nazi-like PE teacher at Paul Revere Junior High who called me "four-eyes." Tennis demanded you shape your own destiny. Places like St. Louis and my birthplace, New York, placed a heavy emphasis on fitting in. LA was for solo acts.

On a typical Saturday in 1974, I would take the number three Santa Monica Blue Bus (the bus company The Doors wanted to meet you in back of when singing "The End") to Lincoln Park for a match in Santa Monica Teen Tennis, a coed league run by future Tennis Hall of Famer Dorothy "Dodo" Cheney. With the match over by ten thirty, I would head east on Wilshire on the number two bus to Westwood to browse bookstores and see a movie. It didn't matter that all day I carried my sleek, silver Arthur Ashe Head Competition racket. No longer was tennis marginalized. I may not have been cool, but my choice in athletic endeavors sure was. How cool was it, after all, to have purchased that best-selling Farrah Fawcett poster and then see her in attendance at the tournament I was playing in Santa Monica?

"Are you sure you don't want it?" the blonde asked.

It was hard to say no, but the answer was clear. My Jewish, liberal parents were as likely to spend seventy dollars on a warm-up suit as they were to vote for Richard Nixon. We lived in a three-bedroom condo located inside a fifty-unit building. Call my family a member of the Westside's lower-upper-middle class: comfortable, but scarcely lavish. In 1973, my father, head of the jewelry department at Zody's (a now-vanished chain store akin to Target in its day), earned $34,000.

But beginning in 1972, for four straight summers, my parents paid $500 and sent me to Ojai to attend Tony Trabert Tennis Camp. Trabert had been number one in the world in 1955, lived a half-mile from me, and was in attendance at his camp every day. During my years at the camp, he became America's Davis Cup captain—and, perhaps even more importantly, CBS's lead tennis analyst, most visibly during the US Open. It was remarkable to hear Tony on a summer morning tell me to "serve wide in the ad court" or "hit that passing shot with topspin" and then, a month later, make the same comments to the whole country about such titans as Rod Laver.

Trabert, though, was but one of many tennis stars that populated LA's glittering tennis galaxy. Just east of the 405 and Sunset sat the most important man in tennis history, Jack Kramer, another former world number one. Kramer had led the pro tennis tour for decades. His name adorned the number one-selling Wilson frame. Further east, the tennis director at the Beverly Hills Hotel was '59 Wimbledon champ Alex Olmedo.

Beyond those three, LA teemed with superb players—USC and UCLA lettermen, many of whom had played at Wimbledon and the US Open, and dozens more who'd excelled throughout Southern California. But for those of us growing up in LA in the seventies, there was one resident who stood out from the rest, one icon who by 1974 had reached the top and along the way turned the acoustic garden party into an electric jungle.

Per the notion that the right man arrives at the right time, Jimmy Connors moved from St. Louis to LA in the summer of 1968. His mother Gloria, his lifelong coach, had decided it was time for the boy to sharpen his game under the tutelage of Pancho Segura, a superb player back in the fifties who by the mid-sixties had become head pro at the Beverly Hills Tennis Club (BHTC).

All throughout Connors' childhood, his mother and grandmother, Bertha, had infused him with a combative sensibility, fueled by the belief that the Connors family was from the other side of the tracks and that tennis would be a way to show up those snobby rich kids. Just before he arrived in LA, Connors won the US Nationals sixteen-and-under championship. But even then, he was underestimated; his slight frame and baseline game were considered less robust than the net-rushers who were then dominating tennis.

The BHTC would become Connors' doctoral program. Segura was the professor; the court, his classroom; the cocktail napkin, his chalkboard. Under Segura's eye, Connors went from boy to man, from patient foot soldier to balls-out bombardier.

But take an ambitious adolescent from the austere, understated Midwest, bring him to the fame, fortune, and hedonism of Beverly Hills of the late sixties and observe how lessons were learned outside the lines. As Connors witnessed all the rewards extant in places like Beverly Hills, Bel Air, and beyond, as the game concurrently went from black-and-white to Technicolor, his soul absorbed how tennis was building a wave he could ride and perhaps even shape. "My entrée to everything was tennis," Connors said years later. "And in my own eyes, I couldn't just see it as being a little tennis. It had to be great tennis, top-of-the-pile tennis."

While Connors pounded the little ball, the bigger ball spun as it never had: LA at the dawn of a new decade. Three blocks from the UCLA campus Connors started to attend in September 1970, Hare Krishnas sang in the streets. Midway between the LATC and the BHTC, The Doors, led by their own UCLA-educated Jimbo, sang of "motel money/murder madness." Precocious daughters. Sculpted mothers. Men on the hunt for wealth and reward. Scientology, est, Synanon. Through the canyons and flatlands, the remnants of the Manson family slithered along the same streets Connors trekked to all across Los Angeles, in order to play on private courts and hyper-competitive tennis spots such as UCLA, USC, and the LATC. As Connors told me years later about that era, "it was creepy, unreal."

By the summer of 1970, Connors was the best junior player in America, making a splash not only with his forceful ground strokes, but with theatrics never seen in tennis: the scowl of a boxer, the gestures of a bullfighter, the quips of a nightclub act. "I must have been born arrogant," said Connors, "because I came out of the womb walking that way."

"It's questionable whether or not Southern California can survive the antics, explosions, and amazing tennis talent contained in this youngster from St. Louis," said an article from the August '70 edition of *Tennis West*. "Southern California racqueteers beware: THIS IS A NEW BREED OF CAT."

Trabert, Kramer, Olmedo—mere crooners, understated with their tidy haircuts and wood racquets. Not Jimbo. Propelled by his squeaking feet, flying Prince Valiant hairdo, and scalpel-like steel racquet, Connors had become tennis' first rock star. In 1977, upon hearing of the death of Elvis Presley, he said, "What a shame, there are only a few of us kings left." In a city where such iconic athletes as Sandy Koufax, Deacon Jones, and Jerry West had long garnered headlines, Connors had thrust tennis onto the front page.

"Guess what?" I asked my older brother Ken one December afternoon. "Tomorrow is Julie Heldman's birthday." Heldman was one of America's ten best players.

"You know," he said, "if you spent a little more time playing tennis than reading about it, you might become a good player one day."

A good player.

Shortened simply to a word frequently heard in LA during those years: "a player."

> *"What kind of player are you?"*
> *"He's a player."*
> *"She's a player."*
> *"Are you any kind of player at all?"*
> *"Is he a ranked player?"*
> *"That's a serious player."*
> *"That guy, he's what you call a player."*

Was being a player only about tennis? Did it have to do with the blonde and the warm-up suit? Or was it deeper? A player didn't just ponder from the sidelines. A player participated. A player had something to offer. As Connors liked to ask when told about an opponent, "What's he got?"

From 1973 to 1977, I played tennis 330 days a year. My opponents covered the waterfront. Men over age fifty with goofy strokes. Basketball players who figured their athleticism would make tennis simple. Wives of doctors. Sleek-nosed shiksas from Pacific Palisades and Santa Monica. Boys with more money. Boys with less money. Boys with better strokes who mocked mine. Boys with worse strokes who trash-talked me. Boys who wanted to take away my singles spot on the high school tennis team. Schoolteachers, from the nebbish math teacher to the blonde female marine biologist to my alternative high school history teacher, a Socialist who told me that the pursuit of victory at all costs had been a major reason for Nixon's downfall. Wannabe Hollywood types who showed up at the courts by three o'clock because by then they knew they'd never hear back from that agent. Real estate developers who said to me, "I don't fear you." Drug dealers headed up Beverly Glen. Or was it Benedict Canyon? A sixties surfer icon, allegedly on the 1:00 a.m. Actors from fifties and sixties TV shows. Constantly, the so-called "tennis bum"—instructor, prophet, hobo.

Barrington Park was within walking distance, but it was only one venue. Until I earned my driver's license on the first day of the summer of 1976, I traveled as far as the Santa Monica bus schedule would take me. West to Santa Monica and Lincoln Park, where I first saw future world number one Tracy Austin, at age ten already an assassin in pigtails. East to UCLA, a frequent Connors practice venue. South to Stoner, east to Rancho. Occasionally, there'd be access to a private court, invariably accompanied by mention of the Hollywood icon who had once lived there. Joan Crawford. Dustin Hoffman. Joseph Cotten. Then there were junior tournaments. To steal the line from Jerry Dunphy, the CBS newscaster of that period, these took place from the desert to the sea. At 6:00 a.m. one summer morning, I stood at the corner of the Pacific Coast Highway and Will Rogers, awaiting a ride from Billy Moss and his father Barry to Santa Ana. Whittier, Fullerton, Long Beach, Santa Monica, Beverly Hills, Glendora, Northridge, Redlands, Carson, Arcadia, Hollywood. Once I'd lost, I'd ingratiate myself to a parent and get a ride back near a Blue Bus. The year I started driving, I played twenty-seven tournaments.

Further evidence of tennis' increased popularity came in 1975. For nearly fifty years, the Los Angeles Tennis Club had hosted the Pacific Southwest Championships, a major pro tournament Kramer later told me was harder to win than Wimbledon. But by 1974, it had outgrown the LATC and relocated west to Pauley Pavilion on the UCLA campus. For me, this was a gift. While the LATC was located in Hancock Park, an unreachable distance, UCLA was a familiar number two bus ride away.

Inspirational as it was to watch pros up close, nothing dazzled me more than what I saw prior to the Saturday night session. In their own private dining area, tucked away adjacent to Pauley Pavilion's outdoor food court, were many notables from the traveling tennis circus. There was Arthur Ashe, the former Bruin who that summer had beaten Connors in the Wimbledon final, with his cool necklace and crisp collared shirt. There was Ashe's agent, Donald Dell, a former assistant to Bobby Kennedy, huddled with Kramer. There was former USC standout Raul Ramirez, chatting with veteran Marty Riessen (author of a book I'd read two years earlier). Each wore an Adidas warm-up suit; Ramirez sleekly ambled in orange, Riessen clad in powder blue. Wealthy men and lovely women circulated.

"Can you be another Connors?" the man asked me. This was Jerry Paris, former director of *The Dick Van Dyke Show*. Paris' son, Tony, was friends with Ken. We were at the Paris' house on San Remo Drive in Pacific Palisades about to head to the Coliseum to watch the Rams play.

The answer: no way. Perhaps it was genetic. Perhaps it was because I hadn't entered a tournament until the late age of thirteen, three to five years later than most fast-track players. But, unquestionably, it was because, while I loved tennis—that is, to play a set or two a day and to think, read, and talk about it constantly—I lacked the desire to put in extra time to make significant improvements. I was more prone to read a book than hit one hundred practice serves, call a girl than go for a run, attend a party than get the best possible sleep the night before a tournament match. It was one thing to reach the finals of a "B" tournament at Stoner and Rancho. But in the high-octane world of SoCal junior tennis, I was content to win one match, elated to win two—and probably, given what my lifelong vocation became, happy merely to arrive at the tournament and participate as both competitor and observer.

"Are you any good?" The question came from a lawyer's wife who wondered if she should let me use her court off Kenter Canyon a few hours a week so I could give lessons on it for seven dollars an hour. My rapid-fire answer: "Yes." So what if just the previous week in Pasadena I'd lost my second round match in less than an hour. Another tournament was happening soon at Rancho. I'd just won a few challenge matches. Did this sneering richie dare think I was anything but a player?

No one legitimized that self-definition more vividly than Jimmy Connors. He'd proven emphatically that tennis was no longer a sissy sport (take that, PE teacher). On the morning of the 1976 US Open final, with Connors up against his fiercest rival, Bjorn Borg, I went to Barrington and saw my friend Tom, a thirty-eight-year-old runner, trying his hand at tennis.

"How could someone like you, Joel," asked Tom, "like an asshole like Connors?"

"And a damn successful asshole," butted in Sid Young, clad in his white Adidas jacket. That spring, Sid had moved from the flatlands near Fairfax Avenue to a home north of Sunset with a court (starfuck product placement: once occupied by actor Van Heflin). Tom lived in a small rental on Barrington near San Vicente. What Tom felt was conceit, Sid viewed as rocket fuel.

The truth was that I, too, had been initially ambivalent about Connors. In September 1974, Connors and his then-fiancée, Chris Evert, had looked at an apartment in my building. *Maybe*, I thought, *Connors will help me with my return of serve.* What an asshole—both him for his behavior, and me for thinking he'd ever lift a calloused finger for me.

But by the time I spoke with Tom and Sid, I'd learned that to be an asshole was viable, perhaps even necessary. The staff of Innovative Program School, the alternative high school I attended at University "Uni" High School, had all taken est. Wholesaling est argot, my teachers were fond of telling us, "You are all assholes." To make your life meaningful, you needed to cast off your belief in cool and shake the world by its throat—the asshole in each of us that was less concerned with fitting in and more eager to stand out. As Ruth

Gordon said in that zeitgeist-capturing 1971 cult movie *Harold and Maude*, "everyone has the right to make an ass out of himself." Or as Connors used to say, "people don't understand that it's a goddamn war out there."

If you wanted the Adidas warm-up suit, if you wanted the blonde, if you wanted the Mercedes 450 SL, if you wanted to beat that snotty kid who lived north of Sunset and went to Harvard and refused to play with you because he didn't think you were good enough, well, then, you needed to throw yourself in, even if a bayonet was required. And why not let tennis lead the way? "Tennis is a great test of democracy in action," said Segura. "Me and you, man, in the arena, baby. Just me and you, baby. Doesn't matter how much money you have, or who your dad is, or if you went to Harvard or Yale, or whatever. Just me and you."

December 1975. Court One at UCLA. This was the court Connors often hit on. But on this day, the player was me, embroiled in a challenge match for the last singles spot on our high school team versus a player I'll call Jason. Two years earlier, Jason and I had been quite close. But everything from adolescent neurosis to competition had torn us apart. Jason took a big lead. As Jason toyed with me, Sid Young—delighted to see two teens locked in combat—watched and laughed. But I persevered and eventually won. During that match, I wore a Fred Perry vest, the same model Connors frequently wore. Unlike the Adidas warm-up suit, though, this piece of clothing was affordable. Six months earlier, after a loss in the first round of the sixteen-and-under sectionals at the Los Angeles Tennis Club, I'd stolen it from the club's pro shop. Upset that I'd lost, miffed at a club that excluded Jews, perhaps even drawn to Connors' rebellious qualities, what was so bad about a little renegade behavior at the ends of the tennis establishment?

So there it was, me wearing Connors on my sleeves. "For better or worse," said a 1975 *Los Angeles Magazine* article, "he is ours." Connors, briefly managed by the father of a high school classmate. Connors, his racquets strung at Westwood Sporting Goods, where Trabert, Kramer, the UCLA squad, and my high school team took our frames. Connors, in a Nike poster, my close tennis buddy Steve Smooke in the picture as the ball boy. Connors at the Beverly Hills Tennis Club, hitting for a week with my high school teammates, Ed and Ronnie Berman. Connors, inspiration for the laser-like two-handed drives of my closest friend on our team, Mike Anderson.

April 1978. Mike and I drove east to the LATC. A year earlier we'd played a doubles match in a tournament there, and a prominent Southern California umpire—the same one who'd been in the chair for the '76 Connors-Borg US Open final—had called it "the worst match in the history of center court at the Los Angeles Tennis Club." But at least we'd won.

On this day, though, we just glanced at the club we loved and then headed west on Melrose, north on La Brea, west on Sunset to Tower Records. There was one space left in the parking lot, but a Porsche was angled into it from another spot. What asshole took up two parking places?

As if I had to ask.

As I squeezed in, Mike noticed a man in a Prince Valiant haircut slumped into the passenger's seat.

Asked Mike, "Who's that, Jimmy Connors?"

It was.

"Hey, Jimmy," I said.

"Hey boys, what's shaking? How's everything?"

"Jimmy," I asked, "are you going to be number one again or what?"

"Well, we'll have to see about that son, won't we?"

That year, 1978, was the peak of the tennis boom. Those who'd bought the cool racquets and could afford the slick warm-ups learned that it took a lot of skill to become even a plausible player and soon ditched tennis. Jane Fonda and Richard Simmons offered forms of exercise that took less time, and were far less combative. Golf ascended. Tennis continues to have its stars, be it a John McEnroe or Andre Agassi, or more recently a Serena Williams or Roger Federer. But those heady rock star days of the seventies, when the luscious warm-up suit was wed to tennis and more, are long over.

Nineteen-seventy eight was also the year I graduated high school and went to Berkeley, convinced that my days as an ambitious competitor were over. Since I wasn't good enough to play for a top school like UCLA, USC, Stanford, or Berkeley, why even bother pursuing more? To my regret, such was the tennis language I absorbed.

But there was something else I felt deep in my bones. As a child of the tennis boom, in the shadow of Connors, through time with Jason, that kid from Harvard, and so many others, I had engaged in hand-to-hand combat. Observer? Often. Participant? Always.

Just before I entered college, Connors won the US Open. On my dorm room wall, I taped the *Sports Illustrated* cover shot of him that proclaimed, "Connors Comes Through." Connors' manner inspired me all through college. *Top-of-the-pile.* Most students, a professor said, were reluctant to throw themselves and their opinions stridently into their papers. "But you," she said, "You scare me... you're pathologically subjective." Of course she had no idea that, like Connors in his matches, I often put on a pair of wristbands just prior to final exams.

Five years to the month of when Mike and I had seen Connors at Tower Records, I interviewed him at the Beverly Hills Tennis Club. By then, I'd started to write about tennis. I'd found my own way to the circus.

On the court in front of us, Connors' aide-de-camp, Lornie Kuhle, played my high school doubles partner, Ronnie Berman. Pointing to Berman, his one-time hitting partner from a half-decade back, Connors asked me, "You know that guy?"

"Know him? That guy once threw a racquet at me in the middle of a challenge match."

Connors turned his head to me and squinted. *What's he got?* And then he said, "I can see that."

For a brief moment, Jimmy Connors looked at me and only saw a player.

Joel Drucker's *career in communications covers many industries, including information technology, consumer marketing, business-to-business, professional services, and nonprofits. He spent a decade in the public relations agency business as an account director at leading international firms Burson-Marsteller and Edelman. He also currently works as a print and broadcast journalist, his work appearing in such outlets as* Forbes FYI, ESPN, Los Angeles Magazine, *and* Tennis Channel. *His first book,* Jimmy Connors Saved My Life, *was published in 2004. He has taught media training at Stanford University and earned awards from the Public Relations Society of America and the International Association of Business Communicators.*

RITAM BHARA PRAGYA

by Howard Gewirtz

LUCKY FOR ME THE CAT KNEW CPR

I WAS LIVING IN a dump, a gloomy gray, old, dilapidated A-Frame house built a hundred years ago, when Jamaica, Queens, was farmland, before the sketchy neighborhood grew up around it. That Saturday night in 1973, as my three roommates had gone out to a party, I was alone, with only a tomcat that we imaginatively named "Cat" for company. Cat wasn't a pet; he came and went as he pleased through the porous openings of this crumbling place, and tonight he just happened to pop by to hang out.

I was sitting in the red-walled living room, finishing up a pint of J&B while toking on my brass hash pipe. The Grateful Dead was blasting from the stereo on the cinderblock shelf as I lay down amidst the pretzel crumbs on the twenty-nine dollar green shag rug.

I closed my eyes and suddenly had the sensation that I was falling—faster and faster like a thrill ride that I never wanted to end, but then Cat rudely jumped on me, claws dug in my chest, meowing furiously in my face. Suffice it to say, this was very odd behavior for the aloof Cat. I'll translate what Cat meowed:

"Hey! Get the fuck up you asshole! You mixed alcohol, hash, and ten milligrams of Valium in your 120-pound body and your pulse is down to thirty beats a minute. You're dying, you idiot! Snap out of it now!"

I started coming around and Cat, satisfied I wasn't about to die, pulled his claws out of my chest and sauntered away, shaking his head and mumbling, "Fucking moron." I had heard of animals saving people's lives before but never through medical intervention. Cat never stopped by again after that, but later on I did pass him on Hillside Avenue and he snubbed me, so I never got a chance to thank him.

Here I was, a twenty-one-year-old alcoholic, pothead, pill-popping NYU film student with greasy hair and a perennial three-day growth of beard, smoking two packs of Salem 100's a day. Something had to give. My junior high school friend Barry had initiated me into Transcendental Meditation two years before, but I'd quit. Now Barry told me Maharishi Mahesh Yogi was holding a two month long symposium at Humboldt College and he was going. Desperately needing to turn my life around, I asked if I could come too.

I'd dreamed of California ever since I was a kid growing up in working-class Rego Park, Queens, and now I was on a plane to Humboldt County for a month of meditating. I was in the smoking section, which people obviously took to mean you were required to smoke, which everyone did for the duration of the flight. You couldn't see the brilliant blue sky outside for the malignant blue haze inside.

I got to beautiful, bucolic Humboldt College, and when I saw the the Pacific Ocean and the majestic redwood trees for the first time, I lit up a cigarette. A symposium leader politely pointed me to a corner of a parking lot, the one place on campus you were allowed to smoke. I joined three dismal-looking people who were lighting up, and as meditators passed by they looked at us with contempt, disgust, or just looked away out of embarrassment. I couldn't take the ostracism. So I tossed my Salems in a trash basket and never missed them. No patches, no withdrawal. Such was the healing power of being in this rarified atmosphere of dense forest with five hundred people meditating. At least that's how it was for me.

Maharishi had only been there for the first month and then left, as did Barry, so I didn't know a soul. Our days were spent watching videotaped lectures of Maharishi, discussion groups about the tapes, watching more Maharishi, and "rounding," which was a round of TM, asana yoga poses, then more TM. After dinner we'd do a powerful group meditation in the large meeting hall. This never varied, even on weekends, and we never left campus.

The symposium turned my life around 180 degrees. Even Cat wouldn't have recognized me as, back at NYU, I went from a scuzzy junior to a clean and sober senior and graduated with a BFA in Film and Television. I spent that summer sending my admittedly trumped-up resume around to every film and TV production company in the Manhattan Yellow Pages. Not surprisingly, there were no bites. Then someone showed me the industry handbook, the Hollywood Creative Directory, and I made an astute observation—Hollywood was where most of the jobs were, so maybe I should move there.

IS HOLLYWOOD AN ACTUAL PLACE?

I HAD NO GAME plan and no idea if Hollywood was an actual place or just a term they used to denote show business. I rented a little Camaro and zipped up the 405 to gain my bearings when, just past Mulholland Drive, the entire San Fernando Valley opened up before my eyes with actual mountains (city kid here) on the distant horizon. Then I noticed the yellow, pea-soupy air that hung over the Valley— the smog I'd always heard Johnny Carson joke about.

Within a week I'd moved to a two-story apartment complex at 2001 N. Beachwood Drive, right under the Hollywood sign. The walls of the building were so thin you could hear a fart two units over, which meant I had no problem hearing the nonstop music blasting, guitar playing, and sex being had by my neighbor Al and his sixteen-year-old child bride, Jackie. Kevin, my black downstairs neighbor, was a big, gregarious roadie who, in any conversation, found a way to name drop his "best friend" Dallas Taylor, the junkie drummer for Crosby, Stills & Nash. Our mustachioed, cigar-chomping landlord was constantly yelling for the rent from these deadbeats like some old silent movie villain. But this seedy apartment building wasn't my biggest problem. Unemployment was.

A typical day of job hunting went something like this: I'd cold call some production house where, behind every reception desk, there was a stunningly beautiful girl who intimidated the shit out of me. I'd apologetically ask if they were hiring, and the Charlie's Angel would say "no but we'll keep your resume on file. Have a nice day." In LA everyone seemed to say "have a nice day" but never really meant it. Eventually this routine became so humiliating that I'd just fling my resume to the hot babe behind the reception desk and flee. After three soul-crushing months, I had enough rejection letters to paper the paper-thin walls of my apartment.

One day, a work call finally came through from Susan at Wakeford/Orloff, a company that had produced the Burt Lancaster film *Executive Action*. Susan cheerily said, "Howard, are you ready to work next Friday?" My heart was beating but I knew I had to keep it cool. I said, "Sure, fill me in." Susan continued, "We're filming at Sunset Gower Studios and…ooh, I have the wrong party. I'm sorry." I said, "Wait! My resume is on file at Wakeford/Orloff and I'm available for work." "No," she said. "I'm really very sorry. I made a mistake." Susan did, indeed, sound sorry but this convinced me that it was time to call it quits.

THE MEDITATION TV STATION

MY FATHER WASN'T ONE bit surprised that I'd failed. He even helpfully picked out my new career: optometry. As numbingly dull as that sounded, I didn't have any better ideas. Just as I was about to book a flight back to New York, my friend Barry phoned and mentioned that Maharishi Mahesh Yogi was starting a TV station in Los Angeles, so maybe I should look into that.

A TM TV station? I thought. They had to be kidding.

They weren't. I called Stan Becker, the President of Maharishi's Global TV and he invited me to a meeting that night at their studio on Cotner Avenue in West LA. When I walked in I saw that the studio wasn't a studio, it was a dress factory with rows of fluorescent lights hung at chest level so the workers could better see what they were sewing. About thirty staff members of Global TV had their chairs arranged in a circle and Stan announced the agenda for tonight's meeting—me. Apparently when I said I had a Bachelor of Fine Arts in Film and Television from New York University, I might just as well have said I was the president of NBC. No one else in the meeting had any background in television. In fact, half of them didn't own one.

To say Stan Becker was soft-spoken would be an understatement: he was barely audible and wafer thin, with the complexion of a powdered doughnut. Stan introduced me to the others, and when they heard my impressive credentials—the same ones, mind you, that couldn't get me a job as a gofer anywhere else— the room buzzed with excitement. Stan said that Maharishi wanted to see some TV pilots that might air on KSCI (the station call letters stood for K Science of Creative Intelligence) and the group figured they could shoot them on sixteen-millimeter film. This was such a patently bad idea that for the next hour it wasn't hard for me to sound brilliant. I told them that it would be better to shoot on videotape; then, drawing on my experience getting rejected from every production house in town, I rattled off the names of several locations where we could rent a mobile production van or buy studio time.

Finally, Stan asked me if this facility—where, currently, illegal immigrants sewed *schmatas*—would make a good TV production facility. Up to that point, my only real experience in a TV studio was a grade school stint in the peanut gallery on the *Bozo the Clown* show and doing television production at New York University, which at the time was still using black and white cameras from the defunct Dumont Network. I sized up the dress factory, saw that it was at least as big as NYU's student production space, and uttered the fateful words, "Yes, this would make a great TV studio." In truth, it was too small for a professional facility, but damned if in two years KSCI wouldn't be broadcasting its first shows from 1950 Cotner Avenue on UHF, Channel 18, San Bernardino.

KSCI had found its new Head of Production: me.

But San Bernardino? Wasn't this station supposed to be Los Angeles-based? It was going to be…sort of. Our chief engineer had a devious plan. He was a boisterous Texan with the awesome name of Cecil Fluker, and a broadcast engineer—along with being a general contractor, real estate agent, junior high school teacher, and pilot. When Maharishi and the leaders of the Transcendental Meditation

Movement decided they wanted a TV station in LA, they soon learned that getting a Los Angeles broadcasting license was too expensive and too competitive. However, San Bernardino, just sixty miles east of LA, was wide open. But who the hell wanted a station that just broadcast to "San Berdu"? Here's where Cecil's brilliantly devious plan came in. He designed a broadcast tower to be erected on Mount Baldy with a "cardioid broadcast pattern," meaning our antenna would actually beam its strongest signal out to Los Angeles.

My salary at KSCI was a fat $500 a month, which made me the only high-powered TV executive who still needed an allowance from his parents. However small this stipend was, it didn't really matter because for me this had become bigger than just a job. My coworkers were now my best friends, and I fully embraced the TM culture. I wore a suit and tie practically everywhere, because that was the uniform designed to present TM as a tool for businessmen and women. Maharishi learned in the late fifties when he formed the Spiritual Regeneration Foundation that very few Westerners sought Higher States of Consciousness, but almost all of them sought lower blood pressure, sounder sleep, and fewer headaches. That's how TM was presented, and the Movement grew large. There was Maharishi International University (MIU) in Fairfield Iowa, and Maharishi European Research University (MERU) in Seelisberg, Switzerland.

Also, KSCI wasn't the only TV production arm of the TM Movement; they had a state-of-the-art studio at Livingston Manor in the Catskills in New York, a studio at MERU, and a *TV Guide* article of the period titled, "Cue The Maharishi! TM Discovers TV!" stated that "about 1,000 copies of one-hour color videocassettes flow from the Livingston Manor facilities each month to 460 TM centers around the United States and in eighty-eight other countries. A third production center has recently begun operation in San Bernardino, California." *TV Guide* wildly overstated that we'd begun operation while we had yet to remove the dress factory lights.

Legally we had to have offices in San Bernardino, so Stan sent a scouting party there consisting of yours truly, Cecil Fluker, Michael Necessary (another tailor-made name), and Ed Hinch, a quiet guy whose personality type could best be described as "zero." The four of us piled into Cecil's Bonanza B four-seater with its single prop engine and took off. It was only when we were airborne that Cecil told us the Bonanza B was a junker that he'd bought for $3,000 and that he'd overhauled himself, which may have accounted for the alarming engine rattling noises. However, Cecil was so buoyant and confident that I wasn't worried…until he placed my hands on the control yoke, pointed out the center stick, the throttle controls, and turned around to joke with Necessary and Hinch while I flew the plane. I thought, *Cecil wouldn't hand me the yoke if there was any danger*, though it didn't entirely escape me that we seemed to be flying straight into a mountain. Somehow, and maybe with the help of my meditative principles, I had just convinced myself that this must be some sort of optical illusion when Cecil finally turned back around, went white, and yelled, "FUCKKKKKK!!!!" He immediately grabbed the yoke and pulled back on it as hard as he could, and we cleared the mountain by just about forty feet. When he got his color back he laughed his ass off. "Whew! It don't get no closer than that!"

BUCKMINSTER FULLER PLAYS BALL, BUT MARGARET MEAD IS NOT AMUSED

As the year progressed, the studio was slowly coming together, and they hired Steve Baleen, another TV director, to work with me. Steve was an ex-marine and a certified adult with worldly experience, something the rest of us lacked.

One day, Stan called us into his office and told us that the UN was holding a conference in Vancouver called Habitat, and that Maharishi was going to be one of the key speakers. Our mission was to gather Necessary and Hinch and fly up that afternoon. At last, actual production! Baleen the ex-marine took care of our travel arrangements and before long he and I were enjoying a gravlax appetizer on Air Canada Business Class to Vancouver. When I asked him where Necessary and Hinch were, with a mouthful of lox he said, "coach." We arrived in Vancouver and Steve booked us into the luxurious Four Seasons Hotel. When I asked him where Necessary and Hinch were, he said, "Econo Lodge." Settling into the bubbling Jacuzzi tub in my mini suite, I decided not to quibble.

We'd need press passes to tape Habitat, but our only credentials were our (cheap) Global Television business cards. For the super friendly Canadians, this was apparently good enough; not only did they give us our passes, but they hipped us to a VIP cocktail reception happening that evening. We'd need wheels to move our equipment, so we asked the local Vancouver TM Center if they could lend us some kind of vehicle. The Canadian TMers were even mellower than LA TMers, which rendered them practically catatonic. They looked genuinely pained and confused at the quandary we were in due to our lack of wheels. I saw Baleen's reptilian eye looking over at a beat up van parked outside. He asked who it belonged to, and a timid soul said it was his work van.

"But I couldn't..."

Baleen interrupted, "Standard shift?"

"Yes but—"

"Gassed up?"

"I'm afraid I can't—"

The ex-marine held out his hand and barked, "Keys."

The KSCI crew careened through the streets of Vancouver as Necessary, whose stick talents were rusty at best, drove erratically. We showed up at the VIP reception and flashed our press passes and the friendly Canadian security smilingly waved our rusty, noisy, very suspicious-looking van through (I get misted-up remembering how unthreatening a conspicuous van was considered back then). The VIP reception was held at an elegant outdoor garden. I was no more than three steps inside when I spotted Canadian Prime Minister Pierre Trudeau. With my trusty Sony camera mounted on a brace at my hip, I stalked him, moving closer and closer until I was just about to knock him over.

His lone bodyguard said, "Hey, get back, eh?"

(Today I'd have been shot. I'm misting-up again.)

Under the watchful eye of apparently no one, I was free to badger people. Out of the corner of my eye, I saw Buckminster Fuller, the philosopher, architect, and inventor. I boldly went up to Bucky and started to speak, but he cupped his ear, which reminded me that he was all-but-deaf.

"Mr. Fuller! I'm with the Maharishi in Switzerland!"

I knew that Bucky had participated in symposiums with Maharishi and I shouted to him we were doing a show on the conference. Bucky, who didn't hear a word, just pointed to his nephew Roger, a hip, good-looking guy who handed me his card and said Bucky could be available for an interview tomorrow. Freshly emboldened, I spotted world-famous author and cultural anthropologist Margaret Mead, and before I knew it, she, too, had agreed to an interview. All I needed was to figure out where the hell any of this was actually going to happen.

Baleen booked a small room at a staid, quiet hotel where we set up our equipment. We wrangled an MIU professor, Edward Smucker, to do the interviewing. Buckminster Fuller showed up right on time and, cutting to the chase, asked how long the program was. "Thirty minutes!" I yelled into his semi-functional ear. Bucky could give you any length version of his lecture that you needed, so he spoke for thirty minutes precisely to the second. "We take one tetrahedron and associate it with another tetrahedron. Each of the two tetrahedra has four faces, four vertexes, and six edges..." All Smucker could do was smile dumbly on. Whatever this was, we at least had it in the can.

Then Margaret Mead showed up, remarkably unescorted. Looking back, if I had to point to the exact moment her mood fouled, it might have been when she took one look at the little room, the little cameras, and the little crew with the unknown interviewer. Smucker's agenda was only partially to interview Professor Mead, and primarily to coerce the conversation toward TM.

He began, "Dr. Mead, would you agree that consciousness is the basis for action in the societies you've studied?"

"What? No, I certainly would not agree with that. I don't know what you're talking about. And what does this have to do with the consequences of rapid urbanization and Habitat?"

She was right. We didn't give a shit about urbanization or Habitat; we were there to enlighten the world through TM. The interview mercifully ended after fifteen painful minutes. When she left, we learned that there had been a slight foul up at Movement headquarters. Maharishi wasn't to be a key speaker at Habitat after all, but he'd be welcome to speak at the "public forum." In other words, he wasn't a headliner but they'd let him get up at open mic night. Maharishi declined, and so for us—as well as iconic anthropologist Margaret Mead—the shoot was a bust.

THE KEY LIGHT IS TOO HOT

IN TIME, CECIL FLUKER finished building the broadcast tower on Mount Baldy and the studio was finished. Maharishi was coming from Switzerland to do an appearance on *The Merv Griffin Show*. Merv was a big TM advocate, and Maharishi's first appearance had boosted TM Initiations 1,000 percent. He appeared with celeb TMers Mary Tyler Moore and Clint Eastwood, and when Dirty Harry approached Maharishi he reached into his jacket pocket and drew...a flower. While Maharishi was in Los Angeles he'd also inaugurate KSCI, which was now a functioning, though still too small, television studio.

Maharishi's visit to our studio was as momentous to us as a visit from the Pope. When he arrived, hundreds of men in business suits and women wearing long, conservative dresses or Indian saris crammed the narrow hallway and folded their hands to their foreheads in *namaskar* as Maharishi slowly made his way toward the studio. He smiled benevolently and the only sound that could be heard was Maharishi quietly saying "Jai Guru Dev" and the devotees quietly saying back, "Jai Guru Dev, Maharishi."

He was led into our studio where saffron-colored silk was draped over a sofa and an aide quickly laid down the traditional deerskin just before Maharishi sat down cross-legged, surrounded by vases with lush flower arrangements. Positioned behind him was a painting of Guru Dev, his master. The first words Maharishi spoke at KSCI were "the lighting is terrible." He continued in his accented English, "The key light is too hot, the kick lighting is no good, and the backlight is creating flares." So Maharishi took over as director of photography from his saffron sofa and relit the set.

When it was finally to Maharishi's liking, Stan Becker led in two people: a large, ruddy-faced man who was Head of the

Chamber of Commerce and an imposing black woman who was a City Councilwoman. By their baffled expressions, it was clear they were clueless as to why an Indian guru was inaugurating their San Bernardino Public TV station. Michael Necessary silently counted down, "three, two…" and the program began. The ruddy-faced Chamber of Commerce man raised his finger to speak but Maharishi, in a cheerful, celebratory tone, quickly cut him off.

With a high but authoritative and commanding voice Maharishi began, "It is a great joy today to inaugurate this television station, KSCI. K Science of Creative Intelligence. What better place to have this first intelligent TV station than San Bernardino. 'San' means saint in Spanish. Saint Bernardino! Saint Bernardino is smiling down because now there is Global Television that will enlighten the whole city…"

When the taping was over, Stan Becker escorted me over to Maharishi and cut in the long line of devotees waiting to give *namaskar*. Stan introduced me saying, "Maharishi, this is the man who built the TV station." Maharishi smiled at me and exclaimed, "Ah! Good! Good! Good! Good! Good!" Then he handed me a flower. I had just received *darshan* from the master.

The next morning, I got called into Stan's office, where I was introduced to a tall, striking blonde dressed in a crisp, tight-fitting business suit who was sitting behind his desk. As I stood there, distracted by her hotness, Stan broke me out of my reverie.

"Howard, Cecilia is going to be replacing me."

Maharishi didn't like how sallow and exhausted Stan, who'd long been one of Maharishi's favorites, looked, so Maharishi was taking Stan back to Switzerland with him.

"Howard," continued Cecilia, "we'd like you to go on Teacher Training at MIU."

I immediately demurred saying that I had too much work to do, too much programing to figure out.

"I don't think you understand. You're going on teacher training." It was decided that from now on everyone working at KSCI had to be a TM teacher.

I spent a summer at Maharishi International University in Fairfield, Iowa, which was on the site of the old Parsons University (which itself was more commonly known as Flunk-Out-U. No matter how dumb you were, you could always go to Parsons, but when they lost their accreditation, the Movement swooped in and picked it up for a song). Then, surprisingly, my old friend Barry showed up after a six-month course in Switzerland. I met him that night at ten after lights-out and he looked great—tall, straight, practically glowing. After a manly hug, I asked, "How are you?" which really meant, "What's it like living in Enlightenment?"

Barry moaned, "Oh god, I'm miserable!" It seems that his girlfriend of two years had broken up with him, and Barry was a bit manic as he wondered aloud what the hell had happened to the relationship. Did she meet someone else? Was she bored with him? Would he ever meet the right woman? The only state Barry seemed to be in was panic.

Barry had given me Transcendental Meditation, which had saved my life, and KSCI, which had saved my professional life, and now he gave me something else—a slap of reality with a sense of perspective. I wasn't going to finish teacher training and I wasn't going back to KSCI.

There is one final thing. On the night of his lecture, Walker Collins taught us the Sanskrit phrase, *Ritam Bhara Pragya*, which, loosely translated, means that as you continue to meditate and grow in consciousness, the right thing to do in life—your *dharma*—will come to you spontaneously. My roommate, David, was thinking of writing a "Barney Miller" script on spec and asked if I wanted to be partners with him. I had never considered writing before, but as we worked I found that the dialogue flowed naturally and I seemed to know instinctively how to structure a scene. KSCI signed on the air June 30, 1977, broadcasting "good news" stories, prerecorded lectures, and variety shows with TM celebrities. On that very same day, David and I walked through the gates of Paramount Pictures for the first time to begin our careers as comedy writers.

A Final Note: KSCI broadcast TM-themed programming for a few years, then became a commercial station. In October 1986, the station was purchased by a consortium of international investors for $40.5 million, a 4,000-percent gain in profit from the roughly $1 million TM spent getting it up and running. Its call letters remain to this day KSCI, which now stand for K Southern California International, and it broadcasts programs in fourteen languages.

After walking through the gates of Paramount Studios for the first time in 1977, Howard stayed for years producing the Emmy Award-winning shows Taxi *and* Bosom Buddies, *and was the showrunner of* Wings *for four seasons. He also was on the original staffs of* The Larry Sanders Show *and* Everybody Hates Chris, *where he executive produced the pilot. He created the semi-autobiographical series* Oliver Beene *that ran on FOX in the early 2000s, and along the way also wrote episodes of everything from* Three's Company *to* The Simpsons. *Howard has continued to work successfully in sitcoms up to the present and is now branching off into dramatic series. He lives in Los Angeles in the Brentwood area with his artist wife Karen and seventeen-year-old, national award–winning artist son, Connor.*

"ME? I'VE GOT A PILOT."

by Ken Levine

EVERYONE IN LOS ANGELES has a pilot.
A pilot is a prototype episode of a television series. Networks determine their prime time schedules based on how these pilots turn out. ABC won't commit to thirteen episodes on the air based on the pitch: "Imagine a family moves to the suburbs and then discovers all their neighbors are aliens from outer space." They might want to *see* what that looks like first. Execution is key. You could have the following series premise: "A group of travelers is marooned on a tropical island." Well, that could be either *Lost* or *Gilligan's Island*.

So networks hire writers and producers to draft pilot scripts. NBC might commission sixty scripts (in comedy and drama) each year. From those sixty they'll make twenty. Six or seven might get on the air. Between the four broadcast networks, that's roughly 240 pilots. And now there are so many more cable networks and streaming services buying original programming that you can probably add another hundred pilots to that pile.

So why does everyone in LA say they have a pilot? Status, for one. It's not enough to be a waiter, or car salesman, or neurosurgeon in this town. You have to be in "the biz."

Second and most important: pilots are stealth. Until they're greenlit for production, no one other than the buyer knows they exist. There's no way to prove that you're lying when you say you have a pilot. It's not like you have to convince anyone at a party that you're the Chairman of the Joint Chiefs of Staff. If you boast that you're on a show or wrote an episode of *The Walking Dead*, someone can go to IMDb and see you're full of shit. But you can easily say, "I'm writing a pilot," "I'm waiting on a pilot," "Meryl Streep and Jeremy Irons are considering my talking cat pilot." Who's going to know?

However, there are a lucky few who *do* get pilots. I am one of them. There are generally two ways to determine if someone has an actual pilot. A track record (that you can look up), or at a party he's the one who *doesn't* tell you he has a pilot.

Along with my partner, David Isaacs, I've had many pilots over a forty-year career. Several were made, three became series; one lasted two years. Some were good experiences, others were wisdom teeth extractions, but maybe the weirdest was the pilot we did for CBS in 1978 called *The Music Booker*.

At the time David and I were the head writers of *M*A*S*H*. That kept us kind of busy, but still—a PILOT!

Our agent arranged for us to meet Allan Carr, a producer who had a pilot script commitment from CBS but needed writers.

Allan Carr was a rather flamboyant character who was riding the crest of his popularity at the time. Originally a talent manager (Rosalind Russell and Paul Anka), he transitioned into producing such movies as *C.C. & Company* and several of Ann-Margret's TV specials. He made millions on a cannibal exploitation flick called *Survive!* But his big home run was the film version of *Grease*. This netted him all kinds of awards (that weren't Oscars) and a coveted cameo acting performance on an episode of Angie Dickinson's *Police Woman*! (He is also known for producing maybe the worst Oscarcast in history: 1989. That was the Academy Awards show with those horrendous lavish production numbers—most notably the one with tone deaf Rob Lowe and Snow White. Go to YouTube. You've got to see it.) Later he would produce the musical *La Cage aux Folles*, for which he would win a Tony. But if he ever wanted an Emmy, he had to go through Levine and Isaacs first.

The meeting was set for 6:00 p.m. at Carr's home. He lived in a mansion called "Hilhaven Lodge." It was not hard to find along winding Benedict Canyon; we just looked for the estate with the giant Oscar statue in front (LA's version of a garden gnome). Previous owners included Ingrid Bergman, Kim Novak, and James Caan (the house is now owned by movie and TV mogul Brett Ratner).

One Allan Carr add-on of note to "Hilhaven Lodge" was the orange-and-mirrored King Tut Disco he had built in the basement. This was the seventies, and both disco and Egyptian pharaohs were very much in. David and I were never invited to any of Allan's disco parties—we weren't on the "A-List" (we were more likely on the "C-List"), members of which included Old and New Hollywood celebrities and neighborhood pool boys, but we were permitted to wait in the living room, which I think they later used as the set for *La Cage aux Folles*. The leopard spot carpeting was a subtle touch.

Allan swept in twenty minutes fashionably late. He was just coming from the set of *Grease 2*, a clear indication that he was transitioning from King Midas to King Tut. Carr was a short, bespectacled, cherubic-looking man of forty. Picture Paul Williams or Louie Anderson or Ellen in a fat suit. He was wearing a black T-shirt and jeans—the producers' uniform.

He sat down and immediately launched into his pilot idea. At the time, there was a late Friday night show on NBC called *The Midnight Special*. Musical acts of the day like Alice Cooper, David Bowie, and Helen Reddy would perform. Allan wanted to do a "behind-the-scenes" sitcom set at a rock music/variety show and center it on the girl who booked the artists. Kind of like *The Mary Tyler Moore Show* meets *Soul Train* for white kids.

The premise seemed intriguing and I had been a Top 40 disc jockey before wising up and getting into TV writing, so I had some exposure to the music scene. (Not enough that anyone offered me payola. I was on that "C-List" too.) We figured we could fill the show with colorful rock stars, bizarre managers, roadies, and groupies, and have our star be the only character in the show not on heroin. So we took the assignment.

For research, Allan suggested we attend the Don Kirschner Rock Awards. This was a bullshit, network made-up award show, a predecessor to the American Music Awards or MTV Awards, or the iHeartRadio Music Awards. We were to mingle with the stars, get a sense of the world, compare drug prices, etc. The tickets were free, so what the hell? It was broadcast live from the historic Hollywood Palladium at 5:00 p.m. (8:00 p.m. in the East). We were given house seats and told to dress black tie. So we had to hit the rental store. When the salesman learned the occasion he said, "You can't just get black tuxedos. Not for the Don Kirschner Rock Awards. Are you nuts? You've got to wear something much hipper than that." Considering we were less hip than accordion players, that made sense. We wanted to fit in. Didn't want Helen Reddy thinking we were not happening. So we said, "What do you got?" The day of the show we picked up our dates at about three o'clock. They got one look at our outfits and both almost busted a gut. Like two complete idiots, we were wearing matching brown tuxedos with peach-colored ruffled shirts. All that was missing was kilts.

Obviously, it was too late to procure other tuxedos (or ski masks) so off we went to the Palladium. And, big surprise, we were the only two nimrods in the entire cavernous auditorium wearing brown tuxedos with peach ruffled shirts. Our dates were still laughing. Actually, the sound of snickering seemed to follow us wherever we went. Gone were my fantasies of Olivia Newton-John slipping me her number.

It's now four forty-five. We're seated. The stage PA calls out, "Chaka Khan? Is Chaka Khan here?" I don't know what possessed me, but I raised my hand and said, "Here!" The woman sitting right in front of me whirled around and said, "Hey, Fuckhead! I'm Chaka Khan!" So much for my mingling with the stars.

Quick note: Allan Carr himself did not go to the Don Kirschner Rock Awards. He was probably in his disco getting "bump" lessons.

After suffering through the show ("Oh wow, man. I can't tell you what an honor it is to receive this, uh…what is this again?"), we got out at about seven thirty. Unbelievably, we weren't invited to any of the after parties. When Alice Cooper laughs at your outfit, you know you look like an imbecile. So now we had to get dinner. Where do you go on a Tuesday night in Hollywood dressed like the groomsmen of Liberace's wedding?

Thank God for Kelbo's!

Longtime Angeleno residents are familiar with this local treasure. Kelbo's was a super-tacky Polynesian-themed restaurant with several LA locations. Picture Trader Vic's for Homer Simpson. They're gone now, but back then there was one right across the street from CBS Television City.

(Side note: CBS Television City is in the heart of the Fairfax district, a decidedly Jewish section of town. The joke is to get to CBS, just drive down Fairfax Ave. And the first window that doesn't have a chicken in it is CBS.)

We walk into Kelbo's, two Jerry Vale impersonators and their dates, and make our way through the palm fronds, tikis, and roasted pig fire pits to the hostess stand. She glances at our outfits and doesn't even bat an eye. Shows us to a booth and even offers us complimentary drinks in flaming skulls. Finally! Some Kelbo's customers who knew how to dress!

Then I get home and watch the tape-delayed replay of the show. Chaka Khan wins an award. Jumps up. And there we are, in a lovely two shot, on national television. And it was an extra good idea to sit right next to each other.

A few years ago I came across this item below on a fashion website (don't ask what I was doing on a fashion website):

> "If you are trying to decide the perfect outfit for your special man to wear on your wedding day, well don't get stuck on the typical black tuxedo. For 2007, the hottest color is chocolate brown. Elegant brown is the new black! Many of the top designers have a handsome chocolate brown tuxedo for the new year. Check with your wedding planner to find out about specific designers offering brown tuxedos for 2007."

How 'bout that? We were ahead of our time! You can wear anything in Los Angeles and at some point it will be the fashion rage. Which brings me to the second part of my tale.

From there we put together our outline for *The Music Booker*. This took some time because we were used to plotting stories with amputations and hemorrhaging. Getting a rock star red M&M's for his dressing room was an adjustment. We thought we'd treat ourselves and have one rock star come down with malaria but ultimately decided against it. Once we cobbled together a story we liked, we arranged another meeting with Allan Carr to pitch it to him. We were summoned once again to "Hilhaven Lodge" for a 6:00 p.m. confab the following day.

We showed up and were told by the formal butler with white gloves that Mr. Carr is not ready. He had just left the set of *Grease 2* and would be arriving shortly. The butler ushered us onto the lovely outdoor patio where a bottle of wine was waiting for us, alongside an ice mountain of fresh seafood from Chasen's. Considering all the lobster, crab, and shrimp that was wedged into this three-foot snowball, it must've cost $500 in 1978 dollars. And the wine wasn't "Two Buck Chuck" either. At least we had gotten the "A-List" snacks!

An hour later we were still waiting, although the bottle was now empty and you could ski down the ice mountain unencumbered by lobster chunks. And we started getting a little giddy. We were wondering how we could steal one of Allan Carr's ceramic flamingos. Would Allan notice the two long flamingo legs sticking out of my briefcase? We were really starting to get punchy.

Finally, we heard, "Hellooooo, helloooooo" and quickly put on our game faces. A moment later, Allan swept in, wearing nothing but a flowing white caftan...and a layer of thick white cold cream all over his face.

Holy shit! We almost lost it.

And then, not only must we somehow maintain decorum, we had to pitch a complete pilot story. Behind Allan sat the flamingos, making it even worse.

We somehow managed to get through it. Imagine this surreal scene—a normal pitch meeting, the producer and writers polishing a story, trading ideas, everyone acting as though there's nothing unusual even though the producer is in a dress with Crisco dripping from his face. (Okay, that may be the one look that doesn't catch on—even in Los Angeles.)

We wrapped up the meeting, said goodbye, shook hands, he closed the front door, and we rolled around on his front lawn for forty-five minutes laughing.

The pilot didn't go. We weren't heartbroken. Shortly after learning our fate, Allan had his stomach stapled. Lord knows what the story meetings would have been like following that. (One of the reasons CBS rejected *The Music Booker* was that Allan refused to go to CBS for meetings. He claimed network executives should come to him. Personally, I think he didn't want to go to CBS because it was across the street from Kelbo's.)

Everyone in Los Angeles has a pilot. No one believes them.

We did have a pilot. I still can't believe it.

Ken Levine *is an Emmy-winning writer, director, producer, and Major League Baseball announcer. In a career that has spanned over thirty years, Ken has worked on* M*A*S*H, Cheers, Frasier, The Simpsons, Wings, Everybody Loves Raymond, Becker, Dharma & Greg, *and has cocreated his own series, including* Almost Perfect *starring Nancy Travis. He and his partner wrote the feature film* Volunteers. *Ken has also been the radio/TV play-by-play voice of the Baltimore Orioles, Seattle Mariners, and San Diego Padres, and has hosted* Dodger Talk *on the Dodger Radio Network. His blog, "By Ken Levine..." was named one of the Best 25 Blogs of 2011 by* TIME *magazine.*

SHITTY LEAD GUITARIST TAKES CALIFORNIA BY STORM

by Geza X

NINETEEN SEVENTY-FOUR BEGAN WITH a whimper. I stayed briefly with my dad, but his new girl was the same age as I was and I felt awkward. They couldn't deal with me sleeping on the couch all day. I fell into a black depression, not knowing how to tackle the Herculean task of making a name for myself in LA, which I considered the hell-pit of the satanic music industry. One day, sitting at a lunch counter on Hollywood Boulevard and chatting with the person next to me, I asked for advice on how to get started. He told me to get a job doing the "second best thing," so I could get close to what I wanted and learn by observation. He wanted to be a movie director so he got a job as cameraman. That inspired me to start engineering and producing records. I wanted to play the clubs and be a rock star, but Hollywood was just too confusing and intimidating for a yokel like me with zero connections. I bought a four-track tape recorder and started learning how to use it.

Meanwhile, I started checking out the endless "singer-songwriter showcases" that were prevalent at the time. It was really the only game in town, circa 1975. Glam was dying and amplified music was nearly nonexistent in the shadow of disco. I hated disco, hated mellow rock, and semi-hated glam, so I was shit out of luck in the cultural vacuum of mid-seventies Los Angeles. Signing up for all the "showcases," which really meant playing for free, I screamed my Dada angst into one microphone after another, finally landing on *The Gong Show,* an ostensible "talent show" that searched for the most ridiculous acts and then expelled them with a giant gong if they were bad enough. I wore what I called The World's Worst Haircut to the taping, hacked and shaved and painted every which way, with eyebrows to match. About halfway into my song about a character named Con Ed, who'd steal your electricity and sell it on the black market, I got gonged by Jaye P. Morgan. I refused to give up the stage, shaking my guitar at them and yelling, "You can't Gong ME—would you Gong Moses? Would you Gong Jesus? WOULD YOU GONG IDI AMIN?" They called security and wrestled me out of the studio.

Somewhere along the circuit I ran into a thin little Dylanesque songwriter named Cotton. He was an incredible talent and quite popular locally. We hit it off and he began introducing me into various cliques. For all the sunshine, Hollywood is the kind of clique in which you need an Eskimo to bring you in from the chill. That ended a dark period of loneliness and brought the crazies back into my orbit. There was a band called Manuel and the Gardeners, who played colleges and parties locally. Their keyboard player was a shy, witty young girl named Charlotte Caffey, who would later go on to become one of the major creative forces behind The Go-Go's. She introduced me to the local Hollywood Hills party circuit. Her soon-to-be ex-boyfriend, Tim, played in a local band called The Pop, so they knew everyone. Among her friends was a guitar player named Joe Ramirez. He was of Colombian descent, handsome and dark skinned, with frizzy Afro-style hair. He played a gorgeous custom-made rosewood Telecaster. Both he and the guitar had a unique, brilliant sound, since he played in open E, a tuning usually reserved for slide guitar. The two of them eventually teamed up with eventual X drummer Don Bonebrake to form The Eyes, an early band to hit the punk scene and one of the first to record on Dangerhouse Records. We all jammed with Cotton and Tito Larriva, who eventually formed The Plugz. They were all unusually funny people who could have easily become comedians rather than musicians. We spent a lot of time drinking, writing songs, and howling at one another's mad stories.

I rented a four-bedroom house in the middle of Hollywood and we all moved in. Some of us lived there and others used it as a clubhouse. I christened it "X-Projects" and demanded that we all answer the phone that way. People came and went. It was a party house, with gin and tonic being the drug of choice. I turned one of the bedrooms into an impromptu recording room, having just bought that nice four-track Dokorder. We all took turns recording our pre-punk experiments there, using each other as backing musicians. It was a very good band, one we called Tornado Babies and, briefly, Band X. We would all go see shows by Roxy Music and Sparks, as well as by local bands The Quick and The Pop.

I owned a small PA system with some mics, so I put an ad in the local papers for work. We called the company "Surgical Sound." Joe Ramirez, Charlotte, and I would show up in lab coats, haul the PA out of the van, and deliver "perfect sound every time." That was our motto, which we printed on the business cards. We met a lot more bands and became familiar with the smaller clubs and coffee shops that way. Some of the gigs were in rough parts of town like Compton. But we weren't exactly run-of-the-mill neighborhood types in our lab coats either, so no one bothered us much. In fact, we built a good clientele who called again and again. Sometimes, they told us the lab coats threw them at first but they liked our mixes so much they called us back. As I've learned so many times: a little calculated weirdness is actually an asset.

After a year or so, we got evicted from X-Projects. Property values were improving and they wanted to raise the rent. This incensed Joe Nanini so much that he went all punk and *demolished* the house while I went to get a U-Haul trailer. It was bad. When I returned, there was rice in the carpets, pancake batter in all the drains, spray paint all over the walls. And he had kicked *holes*. I was appalled. You could see right through from one room to another! I panicked and drove to Charlotte's apartment, hiding out in terror until I could figure out what to do. Finally, I called the landlord and explained what had happened, knowing I was liable because it was my name on the contract. I apologized profusely and said it had all happened while I was gone. I told him would never have done anything like that myself. And he said, "...You know what? I believe you. You've always been honest with me. I'm gonna let the insurance company handle it." I put the phone down in disbelief.

Looking for a new place got me making the rounds of local studios. I knew how to repair electronic equipment and was hoping to parlay that into a living situation. One day I stumbled into a little dive called Artist's Recording Studio. The owner Pat was a scam artist who had multiple hustles going simultaneously. But he hired me to build a rehearsal room in a vacant part of the studio. He also let me sleep on the floor of the studio workshop, where I started fixing their old microphones and generally upgrading things. For some reason, he always got mad when I did that. Later, I discovered he was running two sets of books. One showed profits and the other showed deep losses. He would put an ad in the paper and sell "partnerships" in the studio for $10,000 to $20,000, then drain the "partner's" money and show a loss. He would buy back their share for pennies on the dollar and then go do it again. He also had nursing hospitals up north and took fiendish delight in telling us how he would torment the elderly patrons by starving them and keeping their Social Security money. A real gentleman. I guess the broken equipment in the studio was part of his multilayered rip off.

But the most interesting scam was "investment securities." Apparently there was a tax loophole given to record companies that allowed them to lose record amounts of money in the mid-seventies and actually *make* money that way. Pat used that loophole to sell write-offs to doctors, lawyers, anyone who wanted to take home a yacht for Christmas. The general idea was to recycle an old master tape off the shelf—studios always have a stack of loser demos that never got finished or paid for. They would hire a musician to add a few synthesizer lines and make it sound more modern. Then they would mix it and send it to an A&R person at a record label, who would sign a document saying it had "commercial potential." All of this cost next-to-nothing. Then the studio would generate a *huge* fake bill for the studio time and production. Anything from $20,000 to $200,000. The "client," a rich doctor or something, would pay the studio $5,000 or so of (nearly) free money for putting the scam together. Then he would put the tape on a shelf forever and amortize the whole amount over seven years. It was a huge tax write-off and would depreciate slowly, so he could deduct quite a large sum every year and spend that on whatever he wanted. That loophole finally got closed, but for a few years labels could write off the full (scam) amount of any losses, making it counterproductive to actually produce a record and market it. It was more profitable to *lose* money and write a hundred percent of it off.

The thing people always say is that if you want to work as an engineer in a studio, which is a competitive field, get a job doing *anything* there; because one day their regular engineer won't show up and the studio will put you in the driver's seat rather than lose the session. That's exactly what happened to me—the main engineer lived over a hundred miles away and sometimes he didn't want to drive in for the smaller sessions. I started learning to record mariachi, funk, and disco, doing the "second best thing" to what I loved, which was playing loud, crude rock. And it was exhilarating to be using real recording gear at last. I became a passable engineer after a few months.

Meanwhile, a rehearsal space called The Masque was opening directly across the alley from the studio, run by an Englishman named Brendan Mullen. A few proto-punk bands like The Berlin Brats were rehearsing there. Charlotte and I had gone our separate ways. She and Joe Ramirez were starting The Eyes. This began a peculiar "in-between" period in LA history. There wasn't much action, but a lot of things were bubbling under. A few rock shows were springing up in rented halls. Photocopy places were also springing up all over town, which turned out to be an important development in the burgeoning punk scene. People started putting up flyers as DIY advertising on telephone poles and walls. The flyers were like collages, and a whole style was being created from that. We started to notice the ads, and everyone from the proto-punk scene attended most of those local shows. For those of us who liked amplified music, it was like throwing a starving dog a bone. We saw The Dogs, The Motels,

The Pop, The Quick, and many other pre-punk bands. As I discovered later, several of those bands were rehearsing at The Masque.

Somewhere along the way Joe Nanini, now in a new apartment with Stan Funston (later Stan Ridgway), sat me down on a chair to listen to a new record. The twelve-inch single was called "God Save the Queen," by the Sex Pistols. Well, needless to say, it didn't require any explanation. I felt like pulling all the skin off my face and screaming "IT HAS FINALLY HAPPENED!"

Things moved quickly after that. Joe was about to join an all-girl band called The Bags. But there weren't enough girls playing instruments yet. They needed another guitar player and he talked them into auditioning me. Alice and Pat, the matriarchs of the Bags, had recently abandoned the glitter scene and had a new fashion idea: they wanted the band to wear paper bags on their heads. They said it would get us instant notoriety. I loved the idea, of course. We would go to early punk shows and circulate around with our bags on. Mine had tampons with fake blood pinned to it. Everyone wanted to know who we were. We would disguise our voices and say we were The Bags. Then, we would do a quick costume change and reappear as "ourselves." People who knew us would run up and tell us about this new mystery band called The Bags. It was exciting to be an invisible celebrity! Alice and Pat were popular girls and, tagging along with them, I quickly became popular, too, both as Geza X and the mystery guitarist of The Bags.

The Bags played one of the first shows at The Masque. Brendan had just built a "stage," a six-inch-high platform of wood barely above crowd level. I think he had no idea that the newly safety-pinned punk scene was going to invade his rehearsal hall and turn it into ground zero, but that's exactly what happened. The Bags played The Masque, Troubadour, and other venues. *Every* single time, the audience would riot. We were quickly banned everywhere and the Troubadour never booked a punk show again. The girls were right, the bags had an amazing effect. But my antics were too much, even for the riot-provoking Bags. They hated my tampons and my tendency to pull my pants down at the slightest provocation. They wanted to be stylishly weird, not gross. Joe Nanini was just as bad; our contingent brought a little too much John Waters trailer trash and not enough Rocky Horror Show decadence. So they fired us. I went on to join The Deadbeats and start my record production career. Joe joined Black Randy and the Metrosquad and Wall of Voodoo.

One day Joe sat me down again and we listened to the whole first Ramones album together. He had just bought it. He mentioned that they would be playing the Whisky soon with some local band called The Weirdos. We could feel the wave coming and wanted to be on it. So we went to the Whisky to investigate The Weirdos and the Ramones, but it was empty. The only other people were a young blonde kid and three matching blonde girls. The girls followed him everywhere, weeping and bringing him anything he demanded, whispering secrets as if he had terminal cancer. I took an instant revulsion to him and his obvious manipulations. He stood in front, right by the stage, deeply memorizing every move the bands made. I later found out that this snotty kid was Bobby Pyn, soon to become Darby Crash, suicidal singer and cult leader of the Germs. And the girls were Belinda Carlisle, Melissa Hutton, and Lorna Doom. As for the show itself, it was one of the best rock shows I've ever seen. I felt like I had finally found home.

Around the same time I talked Brendan into renting me a room and took up residence in The Masque. I literally walked across the street from the workshop of Artist Recording Studio with all the stuff I had bought with my engineering money. I had a PA, microphones, and a tape recorder, not to mention guitars and amps. That fueled much of the early scene, because everyone was impoverished and even the musicians didn't have gear. Pat Smear borrowed my guitars for many of his gigs, including the Firebird he played in "The Decline of Western Civilization." There were only a few of us actually living in that stinky basement: Brendan, Spazz Attack, Bruce Barf, and me. Bruce and I set up the PA's for rehearsals and gigs. And all of us cleaned up the vomit and piss after shows. The place quickly turned into a tapestry of interwoven graffiti, as punks flooded in with spray paint till it was many layers deep.

The Screamers were one of the biggest bands; they and The Weirdos ruled the new scene. I became The Screamers' personal roadie and sound man. Their look was minimal to the extreme and their sound thin and harsh. I fixed that with some electronic trickery: I divided the keyboard, literally cut the internal wiring, and sent the low notes to a bass amp and the high notes to a guitar amp. I took the bottom heads off from underneath the drums and put the drum mics way up inside there instead of on top, which was more typical. Also, I added a Roland Space Echo unit to the board mix, to create sweeping collages. That became the huge, orchestral, trademark Screamers sound. It would baffle the eye—you'd see tiny tinkertoy instruments onstage but hear enormous waves of sounds rolling out of the PA. The Screamers were arguably the best band on the scene and played up their cult status with an air of mystery and snobbery that somehow added to the appeal. As their semi-invisible fifth member, I got to tour with them to New York and mix them at CBGB and Hurrah. Despite their public snobbery, they were gents and treated me like gold. They paid well, and working so closely with them gave me quite a bit of social capital in the scene.

All of this sonic manipulation and access to bands made it possible for me to spread the word that I was a "record producer," something I had never actually done. I had a bit of studio experience and had done demos on my four-track but that was about it. One night at The Masque, Darby Crash of the Germs tapped me on the shoulder and said, "…You're a producer, produce the Germs!" That was his inimitably bossy way of saying everything. As it turned out, *Slash* magazine, the mouthpiece of the early LA scene, was about to release its first record. I went out of my mind with excitement, it was a golden opportunity and I knew it. Everything in those days happened so quickly and drunkenly. You could hardly keep track of developments; every day was a party or a new event.

So they threw us into a five-dollars-per-hour eight-track studio for a total of five hours and told us to make a record. If you're unfamiliar with recording, that is barely enough time to set up the gear. The *Lexicon Devil*/"No God" single was tracked inside the former vault of a Security Pacific Bank, in a basement under Hollywood Boulevard near The Masque. Don Bolles had just joined the band and didn't know the songs yet so Nickey Beat played drums. Pat and I had both neglected to bring an amp so I took the guitars directly into the board through some effects pedals I had. We were more like kids having fun than big bad punk rockers. And, squeezed for time, we did manage to make a pretty decent recording and mix it. *Slash* released it shortly afterward, the first Slash Records release as well. It was one of the first punk records to come out of LA and it swiftly achieved cult notoriety.

A short time after that, Jello Biafra of Dead Kennedys gave me a call. I first met Jello and East Bay Ray during a Screamers video shoot at Target Video in Oakland, California. The Screamers saw the future of video well before it happened. Joe Rees, the very talented owner of Target, was one of the few people actually doing video. It was a new thing. He made eye-popping collages of war footage mixed with excerpts from TV and other sources. Thankfully, he also recorded many live bands at clubs in the San Francisco area. He had a nice studio I camped at frequently during my forays up north. So we made the trek up there to do a Screamers shoot with him. I did the sound, as usual. There were some scenesters hanging out, as the Screamers were a popular band. Two of them invited us all to Zim's, a Denny's-style restaurant in San Fran. When we got there, one of them introduced himself as Jello Biafra and began ranting about their new band, Dead Kennedys. I instantly liked the name, wondering if these young college kids would be able to live up to it.

On my next expedition to Mabuhay Gardens, SF's seminal punk club, I got a wonderful surprise. I remember walking into the club shortly after the night began. I heard fat thunder rolling off the stage so I crept closer to see who it was. The club was packed, a good sign. I stood right next to the giant PA speakers by the side of the stage because it was impossible to get any closer. It was the Dead Kennedys. They had just finished playing their first single, "California Über Alles." Then I heard Ray's trademark Echoplex guitar start playing a haunting riff and build it up to a climax till the drums came in, wickedly pounding out a hypnotic beat. Then the bass guitar started throbbing, and finally Jello's mighty vocals, singing *…so you've been to school for a year or two, and you think you've seen it all…* The song was "Holiday In Cambodia," and I immediately knew it was a hit. I decided I would do anything to record that song.

So when Jello called and said they were going to record their second single and they wanted me to produce it, my only question was, "What song is it?" When he said "Holiday In Cambodia," it was an epic moment because I knew I could make that song sound enormous. I went back up to San Francisco, into a vintage studio they'd rented called Tewksbury. There was something wrong with the brakes on the tape recorder, so I literally had to stop each rewind with my bare hands and got burn marks on my palms to prove it. It was all par for the course, though. In punk rock you earn your stripes by dying for your art, so I was proud of the pain and showed my scabs off for weeks afterward.

Tewksbury had another interesting thing—vintage microphones. The owner had a mic fetish and kept them arranged in a dresser on crushed red velvet like dildos. It was kind of weird. I was almost embarrassed picking them up. I had some experience with those postwar mics from my days repairing them at Artist Recording. He had everything, even the big phallic ones with the round tip like Hitler had used at rallies. So I tried a Neumann U47, a very beefy-sounding mic, on Biafra's big growly voice. It turned out to be one of the best pairings ever, one we used on all subsequent DK's records. "Holiday In Cambodia" got picked up by Cherry Red in England and the twelve-inch single got mastered by Porky Prime Cuts, an amazing engineer who brought every bit of brutal force out of the recordings. That single took the world by storm and put us all on the map. Howie Klein, then a reviewer for SF's *BAM Magazine*, said, "Geza X is the first, and so far *only*, producer to fully capture the power and compelling urgency of the West Coast Punk Rock movement."

The next band to contact me was Black Flag. They already had a thriving scene going in LA's South Bay but wanted to expand it into Hollywood and the rest of the country. They thought that if they did a record with me, they might get a little more attention. We recorded the whole *Damaged 1* album together, with Dez Cadena singing. Black Flag always had business resources, so studio time wasn't an issue. The album turned out great. But Henry Rollins joined the band shortly afterward so they rerecorded everything, much to my disappointment. Many singles were subsequently issued from that first batch of recordings, most notably "Six Pack," "I've Heard It Before," and "American Waste."

All in all, I've produced over a hundred punk records. And the heyday of the scene might have come and gone, and real estate in our former Hollywood haunts might have gone from the basement at The Masque through the proverbial roof, but I have a killer new space downtown and I feel even more punk now, in my mid-sixties, than ever.

Geza X Gedeon *is a veteran record producer with forty years of experience documenting folk artists and pop culture. He was one of the first (and only) professionals to capture the punk rock explosion in 1977, creating seminal recordings of bands such as Dead Kennedys, Black Flag, The Screamers, The Weirdos, Germs, Redd Kross, and over one hundred other noteworthy underground bands. He had a double-platinum commercial hit with Meredith Brooks' feminist anthem "Bitch," which was RIAA-certified #1 on Billboard's Pop charts for four weeks. He has written about pop culture and recording for* SPIN *and* LA Weekly, *and has been featured in innumerable interviews and several history textbooks. He is currently working on an archival four-part documentary film series on the origins of California punk rock.*

MERGING WORLDS: LOS ANGELES, 1979

by Mitch Schneider

W HEN I FIRST MOVED to Los Angeles in January 1979, I had no idea of the good times I was about to experience. The city was—the most amazing thing about it, especially looking back now—relatively uncharted

I didn't come to LA by choice, per se. In 1978 I was living in the Bronx and working as a freelance writer for various publications, including *Rolling Stone, Crawdaddy!, Circus, Good Times,* and a few others. Even back then being a rock critic didn't promise a rosy financial future. I wanted to get a job as a publicist, but there were no positions available in New York City at the time since the music biz was so much smaller then. I went ahead and sent my resume out west, landing a job as a junior publicist at Solters/Roskin/Friedman after an interview in their New York office. Company head Lee Solters, who would end up becoming one of my first mentors, was a publicity legend. He represented Frank Sinatra and Barbra Streisand, among others.

I was looking forward to it, but definitely apprehensive about moving. My vision of LA consisted of bland images from even blander TV shows, like *CHiPS* and *Starsky & Hutch*. I was too young to have experienced firsthand the magic of West Coast tastemakers like

The Beach Boys, The Byrds, Buffalo Springfield, and The Doors when they happened. Plus, being a New Yorker from the Bronx, *Annie Hall* made California, and LA in particular, look like an utter wasteland; it would be decades before Woody's famous line about right turns on red lights and awards ceremonies were no longer applicable. Simply put, it wasn't the cool place to be. It was frowned upon by the Big Apple. Then again, I did need a job.

I took the gig, packed my things, and moved here, sight unseen, when I was twenty-three. I pulled up to the City of Angels in my decidedly un-angelic, pimp-green Buick Skylark, complete with a white vinyl top and nostrils on the hood.

I was immediately struck by the spectacular geography: the mountains, palm trees, and beaches were daytime eye candy, the likes of which this hardened Bronx native had never seen. At night, I fell right in to the would-be stars and star makers of the rock world. The *LA Weekly*, which began publication the same month I moved here, was more than happy to point me in the right direction (it still does). *Rodney on the Roq*, the eponymous show hosted by the unofficial mayor of the Sunset Strip, Rodney Bingenheimer, was on the outer reaches of FM radio, at 106.7 KROQ. A first-rate tastemaker, Rodney spun singles from Los Angeles bands like The Weirdos and X. Outside the radio, on the actual Strip and beyond, there were shows nearly every single night. You were in the mix at the very minute the scene was going down. It was heart-pumping, exciting, and wild. It wasn't just cool, it was Big Apple–worthy cool.

I lived in West Hollywood on Norton Avenue, not far from the intersection of Fairfax Avenue and Santa Monica Boulevard, and I was working on Sunset Boulevard, at the edge of Beverly Hills, in the Solters/Roskin/Friedman office. My job was fun, but definitely mainstream; as a junior publicist, I worked on Melissa Manchester, Dolly Parton, Leo Sayer, and teen star Leif Garrett. I also worked with Bernie Taupin, so I'd get invited to all of the Hollywood Hills events and parties. Back then disco was hot—the glossy soundtrack of Sunset Boulevard in West Hollywood where Donna Summer's "Bad Girls" and Chic's "Good Times" were always on the car radio. That party felt like empty hedonism whereas punk felt both visceral and cerebral to me.

Before I moved here, I didn't know you could go from the beach to the hills to downtown, all in one day. There were no bridges. Home was the exact opposite; in New York City, there were toll bridges between the boroughs, which created geographical—and psychological—boundaries. Los Angeles was free and sprawling, and it felt less divided. Everybody was on the streets—or, if not out on the streets, en route in their cars. It was a city on the move; you were free to roam throughout the city and experience the wide range of music, both mainstream and underground, it had to offer.

One of the most influential clubs in Los Angeles was The Masque. Started by an English impresario named Brendan Mullen, the equally beloved and maligned punk club (for all the attention it got, it was physically little more than a basement with a filthy bathroom) closed in 1979, so I only got to go to one event there, and at a spin-off location, no less. I did, however, spend a great deal of time at the Starwood. At the intersection of Crescent Heights and Santa Monica Boulevards, it was as good as clubs got: a super-sized space with two large rooms. Bands played live in the big room while Rodney Bingenheimer spun punk and New Wave records on the two New Wave nights every week, Tuesdays and Wednesdays, in the smaller room. It would ultimately go the way of the wrecking ball, officially due to resident complaints about punked-out clubgoers spilling out onto the neighboring streets after the shows. It also didn't help that it was owned by Eddie Nash, who was suspected of dealing drugs out of the club and would later become infamous for ordering the murders of a group of miscreants who, with the help of porn star John Holmes, stole a massive amount of narcotics, cash, and jewelry from him in a brazen home invasion (the case, which was marked by one of the most gruesome crime scenes seasoned cops had ever seen, would come to be known as the Wonderland Murders and would be depicted in the Val Kilmer film *Wonderland*).

The nature of the clubs I went to—and bands I saw—depended on what neighborhood I was in. On the Sunset Strip, I'd go to The Roxy, the Whisky A Go Go, and Gazzarri's, which played a wide spectrum of well-known and less well-known bands, but were more or less typical nightclubs. Downtown, which was the seat of municipal power during the day and little more than a ghost town by night, had its own venues, and they weren't typical in the least. There were two Chinese restaurants right across from each other in the neighborhood's pagoda-themed plaza: Madame Wong's and the Hong Kong Café. Madame Wong's skewed toward New Wave and power pop, while the Hong Kong Café took a more radical approach by booking bands like X, The Bags, and the daring performance artist Johanna Went.

Unlike the self-aware vibe that permeated the Strip at times, the clubs downtown were amazing because they lacked pretense. A Chinatown restaurant-turned-rock-club would involve a walk past ancient and tourist diners, upstairs to the restaurant on the second floor where the bands played. It was different and random and very much conveyed the sense that anything was possible. And it did; you learned to expect the unexpected, and dispense with everything you'd ever been taught. What I was figuring out would ultimately shape my perspective on public relations and lead to me creating my own voice in a world of white noise. I was slowly realizing that the arbiters of taste—folks who dictate what is hip—didn't control it in Los Angeles. Musicians created their own scene.

See, growing up in New York City, especially back then (but I suspect that little has changed), it was ingrained in you that you were living in the center of the universe. There was this built-in elitism that wasn't even conscious anymore; it just was, and it shaped your entire outlook on the cultural hemisphere you inhabited. It wasn't entirely undeserved; New York, after all, was the city that spawned the Fillmore East and The Village Underground and Mercer Arts Center, which was the early epicenter for the glam rock scene. You had Max's Kansas City, Club 82, CBGB, and Studio 54. It was unbelievably influential, and I got to experience all of it. However, being in the eye of the storm wasn't always the most fun place to be. If you went from New York to Los Angeles you got kicked down a notch. You had to fight harder when you were on the outside. It colored the music in an interesting way.

Los Angeles beckoned the outsiders. They'd be driving around looking for parking spots. They didn't just roll up to concerts in cabs. Everybody was on the streets. You'd see the same people at night that you did during the day working at record stores and thrift shops. You'd become friends because you dug the same bands. When you went to shows, you felt like you were seeing family. The bands might've been competitive, but they were friends and would help each other out, too.

The scene was small, and it was friendly. It didn't feel like people were under the microscope. There was still some uncharted territory, which allowed the music to be different and find its own way. It was exemplified by the wide range of styles and influences you'd see in the bands from that era. The Screamers were basically an electro surf band, mixing synthesizers, surf beats, and damaged lyrics. Then you had Gary Valentine (an NYC transplant, ex-Blondie) and his band The Know, and the great Plimsouls doing their own version of garage rock and pop.

And then there was X. My introduction to them had actually come in November 1978 at Hurrah in New York. I had initially thought, "There's no way a Los Angeles band could be punk! They drive cars! They're not living in cold-water flats, playing colder-climate clubs. How is that even possible?" Then I saw them play. I was just blown away by their off-kilter male-female vocal dynamic (it was often said that Exene Cervenka sang "lead harmony"), the unlikely (for a punk band) rockabilly guitar style, and unflinching lyricism.

I'll never forget when I saw X at the Hong Kong Café. It was one of those nights where I'm sure I lost part of my hearing. I'll never regret it, either. Since we were in a restaurant, everyone was standing on tables and falling over. Before X played, this electrifying performance artist Johanna Went came on stage with garbage—she collected it from the streets—and dildos attached to her. She was a woman possessed— with a synth player and electronic drum pulse backing her—and it was mind-blowing. X came on right after, and it was one of the most exhausting experiences I've ever felt at a rock show, because there was no real barrier between the band and the crowd. The way everyone merged together took my breath away.

A band like X couldn't have been born anywhere else but Los Angeles. New York had plenty of punk and poetry, but the rockabilly kick that came courtesy of X's pompadoured guitarist, Billy Zoom, was the special sauce, the—pardon the pun—X factor that landed the band in elite musical climes. John Doe and Exene had come out of the bohemian poetry scene in Venice Beach. They documented the world around them on the seminal debut album *Los Angeles*, which instantly became my favorite album of all time. It perfectly captured a city, a time, and a place. It was an eloquent thematic concept album without trying to be one.

X's music was definitely not the "Hollywood" message the Chamber of Commerce was blasting out. It was gritty. It was situated below the surface. It was hard reality. For me, it was more interesting to have this vignette beneath the surface. You would drive east down Sunset Boulevard and see a different Los Angeles. It felt like there was something wrong there. You could almost physically see the divide between the haves and the have nots. When they sang "perhaps we're boiling over inside" from "The World's A Mess; It's In My Kiss," they were as visionary as any band had ever been. The second Los Angeles riots may have happened thirteen years later, but the album X recorded in 1979 tells you all of this clearly and concisely.

X's music was galvanizing, in ways I realized viscerally immediately, but that I wouldn't fully process cognitively until decades later. As I drove around the city, through all those parties in the Hollywood Hills, I couldn't help but realize that this was where privilege was, and that X was speaking about the divide between the haves and the have nots. It was there in songs like "Sex and Dying in High Society," "Johnny Hit and Run Paulene," and "Los Angeles." They even covered The Doors' "Soul Kitchen," a version that connected their album *Los Angeles* to The Doors, who were arguably the premier band of Los Angeles. Doors keyboardist Ray Manzarek gave their cover his seal of approval by producing "Los Angeles." Two generations, two entirely different Los Angeles movements, converged at that moment, and it made me all too aware of the two worlds I was straddling and would spend the rest of my career working to reconcile seamlessly in my own, unique way.

Lee Solters once said at a staff meeting, "If someone jumps off a bridge, figure out how to get your client involved." It was a valuable lesson in learning how to connect your client to what's happening in the news and pop culture, which could result in maximum PR. Years later, in 1986, when I heard Muzak was going up for sale, I called Ted Nugent and said, "Ted, we should make an offer to buy it." He said, "Why?" I said, "So we can destroy it if we own it." He laughed and said, "Go ahead." We came up with a publicity stunt—making an offer to buy it, knowing the offer would be declined, and then issuing a press release about it. To this day, people still ask me about it. It was a punk rock move, one that would never have been actualized were it not for what I learned that final year of the decade.

Ultimately, 1979 became an incubation year for me as a publicist. It was one year before Reagan was elected, one last year for me to be a kid, wildly lost and found at the same time. I attached myself to, and found my voice in, the antiauthoritarian music movement, and it later guided me to artists who were experts at disrupting the status quo. David Bowie, Ozzy Osbourne, Ted Nugent, Alanis Morissette, Korn, and other inspired troublemakers would all become clients of mine—drawn to me, I'm quite sure now, by my ability to move physically within the clearly defined topographical boundaries of the Hollywood Hills while allowing my soul to roam the boundary-free underbelly of the parts of Los Angeles the sun's beams never reached.

Nineteen seventy-nine rocked my world. I was a kid in a Buick Skylark bouncing around a city whose soul I was discovering without realizing it at the time. It was a city that was still viewed as a cultural abyss, that was marginalized by the cool kids on the East Coast, and that embraced outsiders in a way unlike any other. It was great to step outside the calculated cool of New York and dive completely into the chaos that defined Los Angeles rock and roll. It was damn fun. I'll never forget it.

Mitch Schneider *was a freelance journalist in the mid- to late-seventies in his native New York for* Rolling Stone, Crawdaddy!, Circus, Hit Parader, *and* Good Times, *the latter of which he also edited. He moved to Los Angeles in 1979 to become a music publicist for the entertainment PR firm Solters/Roskin/Friedman. In 1982 he left the company to return to freelance writing; his work appeared in* LA Weekly *and* BAM, *plus* The Rolling Stone Encyclopedia of Rock & Roll. *He subsequently joined Michael Levine Public Relations in 1983, becoming a partner in 1988 when the company became known as Levine/Schneider PR. In 1995, Schneider formed The Mitch Schneider Organization (MSO), an acclaimed PR and social media company. Based in Sherman Oaks, with an office in Nashville, the firm handles music, culture, and lifestyle projects with an artist roster encompassing the genres of rock, electronic, country, and pop. MSO was described by* LA Weekly *in 2010 as "...more than a PR company, it's a bonafide taste maker." Schneider is also a country music songwriter, living in the San Fernando Valley only a few miles from where The Flying Burrito Brothers wrote their classic 1969 country rock album* The Gilded Palace of Sin.

I WAS AN ILLEGAL...

by Jillian Franklyn

THIS STORY BEGINS WHEN I was fourteen. I recently changed my name. After you read this, you may wonder why it took me so long.

I was born here. Hollywood to be exact. Cedars of Lebanon. Now it's the Scientology building. My parents came from Jersey and I was conceived in the Beverly Wilshire Hotel. That makes me an official princess. Forever.

I wasn't a slut growing up. But I had the makings. I didn't understand it then as I do now. The reason you think you want to have a lot of sex is actually you just want a lot of different boys/men to want you and tell you you are pretty and desirable. It wasn't until my thirties that I got over my daddy issues. I won't digress, lest I never make it back.

So, it's the seventies and I'm a young teenager. I have braces and not the good, clear, aesthetically pleasing kind either, as they hadn't been invented yet. I had a mouth full of silver, and rubber bands that I was supposed to wear but never did. I chucked the night brace and retainer as well. Mouth closed, I was pretty, and my grandparents called me little Liz, thinking I looked like Elizabeth Taylor if she were Jewish and had hazel eyes. We might have had the same size boobs. To me that was the commonality. Regardless, in my brain I was certain my destiny was to be as famous as she was.

My looks would be my "in" to a new world. Not the world of high school, as I didn't care about anything so pedestrian as that. I wanted "after high school;" I wanted the easy money sequel without having to sweat through the hard-fought gains of the original. I wanted a key chain with keys to my car and apartment where I wouldn't have to share a bedroom with any siblings and I could eat cake for breakfast and not have a hemline restriction.

I can, and will, tell you about Bumbles and the Candy Store. The parties in Hollywood, and more. But first you have to sit through the why's. Why did I want to skip right over being a teenager? Why was I disconnected to the person I was supposed to be at fourteen? I was invisible. Not to my peers who saw me as a bitch because I wouldn't give them the time of day. I couldn't. I couldn't relate to anyone my own age. I had one best friend who will never talk to me again if I mention her. Let's call her Pamela because I don't know a Pamela.

I wanted birth control pills. A credit card. I wanted to look like I had responsibilities and affairs. I wanted to be away from my parents and on my own where I belonged. Where I thought I knew what I would do. I would be a grown-up. But I had a few years that I had to stick it out. I wanted what every kid secretly wants, except back then I thought I actually could, and should, have it.

I lived at home with my mother because my parents were, of course, divorced. It was the seventies. It was mandatory. My mother dated a lot and ate out of a gallon tub of ice cream in between. I wanted nothing to do with her. She wasn't going to let me buy clothes, stay out late, or go all the way with anyone. She had opinions about me, and because we couldn't communicate she would leave letters for me on my bed on legal pad paper. I could tell she wrote them in a hurry.

My father also dated a lot. Smoked pot. He got a new Cadillac every year for five years until the day he picked us up in a little Mercedes which was, by then, the ubiquitous car of middle-aged men. Mind you, middle-aged was thirty-five at the time. Thank God it was legally changed.

Dad was a handsome, handsome man, and every weekend he would come in and pick up my brother, sister, and me and we would go out to Malibu because did I mention it was the seventies? We would go for long walks on the beach and dad would share stories about the girlfriend of that particular month. All clichés notwithstanding, he did have some interesting Hollywood stories that stayed in my mind. He had gone motorcycle riding with a group of guys; the only one I remember was Steve McQueen, and not the designer either. My dad had hung out with Richard Chamberlain and Alejandro Rey. He and my mother knew Debbie Reynolds and Rock Hudson. Even though celebrities had more mystery and mystique back then, the chasm between regular and famous people seemed less canyon-esque.

As glamorous as they may have seemed to people other than myself, in my mind I had two parental figures oblivious of who I was. I began to stay in my room and write. I would write poems about death and sex and come out of my room and read the poems, awaiting the reaction. I imagined—not wrongly, either—that their first instinct would be to lock me up in a what was less-than-affectionately known back then as a "mental place." Again, did I mention it was the seventies? Today it would be rehab.

I remember coming out of my room one day and reading them a poem that began like this: "Sitting by my window, counting the distance to the ground…" Total crickets. A few minutes after my invisible cry for help, we all went to Baskin-Robbins. And so, naturally, I began to act out (is what a therapist would say—to me, this was when life finally started to get better, more tolerable). I'd come home from school around three, and from that hour until dark I would try on my outfits, my favorite being my tie-dyed hot pants and lace-up wedges (oh, to have those flawless legs again just for one night!). Then Pamela and I would call each other on the phone and talk about our outfits, which we found ceaselessly profound.

We lived for shopping, older men, celebrity sightings, dancing, drinking, and sex. The street that you had to be seen on at that time was Beverly Drive, and Nate'n Al's was where you had to be on Sunday mornings. If you didn't know someone who worked there, you didn't get the better booths. We got the better booths because we were illegal. Brooke Shields was about to make *Pretty Baby* and Woody Allen was dating a seventeen-year-old in *Manhattan* and it seemed as though the entire country had a lax view about relations between older men and far-too-young younger girls. As far as we were concerned, we passed muster and could get almost whatever we wanted, whenever we wanted it…and with almost whomever we wanted.

One Sunday brunch, we sat next to Milton Berle. He asked us if we wanted to smoke some pot. We demurred; we might have been obsessed with older men, but we did have an age limit. We saw no irony in going from brunching with older men to dessert at Wil Wright's Ice Cream Parlor, which truly was a shoppe: pink and white stripes, stools, a giveaway little almond cookie, and stuffed animals everywhere. It was a little girl's dream, and I loved it even though I barely had any little girl left in me.

All of our aging-up required tremendous amounts of shopping. Fred Segal's was the place, even more so than today, and I worked there. I saved my earnings to put them right back into the store. I couldn't "legally" work there because of my age, but I knew a guy that knew a guy…ad nauseam. It was amazing that anything actually got done besides drugs and fellow coworkers in the bathroom stalls…

I experienced getting hooked up to a lie detector test. Knowing that I was an almost pathologically bad liar, I just copped to stealing a T-shirt. In my less-than-innocent mind, that was tantamount to being innocent. I also worked at Theodore's on Rodeo. You had to wear the prerequisite white sheer cotton pants and top, which I didn't mind at all, nor did the older men that showed up every day. Vidal Sassoon was next door. And just south of it all on Beverly Drive was Mr. Mike, more of a jean store that employed me until I got fired for one reason or another.

On a slightly lower scale, but still popular, was Century City. It was more rock and roll than Beverly Hills, but life was about balance. I worked there after flaming out in Beverly Hills, since in my mind, this was what adults did when they were forced to pick up the pieces. Judy's was the store to work at and BIBA makeup was the rage. I wanted to live in London where it was made, so in my mind my thoughts took on English accents. When Cher came in with her entourage I hid behind a rack and watched her the whole time, which culminated in my getting fired.

Ultimately, I realized that I hated employment. I hated "the man." I started spending days lurking around Gucci, angling for Jaclyn Smith sightings, which was almost all it took to constitute being classified as a good day; the truth was, I couldn't actually afford Gucci except for the keychain! Yay, my keychain! Even though I had no keys to anywhere.

Bored and seeking inspiration one day, we followed the other Jacqueline (Bisset) all the way to her house in the canyon. We decided to make it our stake out. We'd smoke a joint, stop at Baskin-Robbins, then drive to her house and wait to get a glimpse of beauty and celebrity, hoping we would one day live the dream. I'm not sure how I got away with this secret life other than that my parents' complete self-absorption—not entirely uncommon, but a bit excessive even for the day, from what I'm now finding out—allowed me all the freedom I could ever dream of.

I continued to dream of being a movie star. Of people following me around and revering me, just for being me. I would sit in my room and write poem after poem about love, sex, and suicide—sometimes all at once, and sometimes not in that order. Looking back, I realize that I was more dramatic than suicidal and thought it would bode well for my movie star (note: not acting—movie star) career. I had no idea that all my angst was not meant for the big or little screen but for the written word; that didn't appear in my brain until way later.

My mother was always out, so she never knew when I left the house in hot pants and a sheer crop top. I still had silver braces, but when you're pretty and a healthy 34D no one is really looking at your mouth. Pamela and I became regulars at the clubs. We drank. We smoked Shermans (I didn't even know how to inhale, but no one ever called me out on it). We smoked pot. We played backgammon. I hadn't even yet had a molar pulled, yet in my mind my mouth was nothing but wisdom teeth.

One night we went back to an apartment with two cute Persian friends we had met at Bumbles, who wore patchouli and shared a yellow Corvette, clearly enjoying freedoms their compatriots back in the newly-minted Islamic Republic could only dream of.

While Pamela and her date were having a fine time, my guy was frustrated because he couldn't figure out why his penis wouldn't get hard. He'd get almost all of it inside and then get this look on his face like he was about to cry (clearly, both of us were frightened in our own way), then…nothing. I didn't realize until I got home that I had forgotten to take out my Tampax because…well, I was fourteen. I didn't realize until later it was a story I could tell forever.

We partied. I didn't really know who Roman Polanski was when I met him one evening, but I thought he was sweet. Truth was, across the room playing pool were Warren Beatty and Jack Nicholson, and I would much rather have been sitting with them.

On some level, I knew I was fourteen and I shouldn't be living this secret life. You would think, night after night, this would become a bore, but it didn't. It lasted two years. Happy sweet sixteen to me. I got an IUD.

There were no friends in my life besides Pamela; for some strange reason, she was the only person I knew who wanted to walk around, hungover all day, speaking in fake English accents and chewing Midols and Certs, so my party consisted of my parents and their friends. I got a car. It was a Datsun 240Z, but I pretended it was a Ferrari Daytona.

How did I get the car? I had made a deal with my father, since I was getting straight Ds, that if I got straight As he'd get me a car. We shook on it. I took tennis (it was, after all, Beverly Hills High) and cooking, but I also took psychology and creative writing—classes seemingly centered around having a completely messed-up mental state. I got an A in both classes, but a B in cooking (my dream wasn't to cook for a man, but rather, one day, to have many manservants, so my efforts were less-than-enthusiastic), and I got the car anyway.

To me, it finally felt as though I was growing up. As far as I was concerned, I would be happy as soon as I was almost out of the house technically, but able to drive away from it any time I wanted legally.

Little did I know, my mother had the same dream: to get me out of the house. Little did I know, we had something else in common, too… We didn't have a lot of blood relations, so my parents tended to adopt people and give them the title of "family." We had an "Uncle Norman" whose brother, "Uncle Nick," had died. For reasons I still don't know to this day, my mother and I were the only people at his funeral.

The moment came afterward, while my mother and I were walking back to her car. I don't know what motivated me to purge my thoughts, as though there would be some prize at the end, some final "grown-up" distinction I'd always desired, but while my mother opened the passenger side car door to let me in, I turned to her and said, "Mom, I don't know why I am telling you this, but I slept with Uncle Nick."

My mother calmly got inside, started the motor, turned to me and said, "So did I."

I swallowed the phlegm that was slowly rising into my throat and emotionally vomited.

The next day, I woke up as an entirely different person. My mother and I had slept with the same man. This was the moment I should have carried with me straight into therapy, but I didn't. Instead I went back into my life and experienced what I should have experienced in the first place.

My childhood.

I was still a teenager, technically. And now I would want it to linger for as long as possible. I would make friends with people at Beverly Hills High, and shockingly found that I did have things in common with them. I didn't miss the clubs. The Shermans. The star stalking. I had a crush on a boy in high school! And the best part was, we waited to have sex. Okay, not until it was legal, but hey, when you're living life in reverse, you have to start somewhere.

Jillian Franklyn *was born in Hollywood. Knowing she was conceived in the Beverly Wilshire Hotel always presented her with the struggle not to be identified as a princess. After realizing that acting was not her calling, she began to take the practice of writing she started at thirteen seriously. Her first job was the "Yada Yada" episode of* Seinfeld, *which earned her an Emmy nomination. Her feature film* My First Mister, *starring Albert Brooks, opened Sundance Film Festival.* Gravity, *starring Krysten Ritter, aired on the Starz Network and was her first Producer/Writer credit. She continues to sell pilots and features every year and recently had her first magazine article titled, "My First Fat Man," published in* Glamour.

BRIGHT LIGHTS, B-CITY

by Bruce Ferber

"I don't want to live in a city where the main cultural advantage is that you can make a right turn on a red light."

—Woody Allen

THIS PITHY, YET POINTED, indictment of Los Angeles would be granted its formal place in the zeitgeist with the 1977 release of *Annie Hall*. The sentiment behind it, however, had long been entrenched in the mind-set of anyone who considered himself a sophisticated New Yorker. The City of Angels was a cow town. Duluth with smog and avocados. No Guggenheim. No Frick. Want a decent bagel? None to be found in West Bumfuck, my friend. Feel like seeing a basketball game? You'll have to head home at the end of the third quarter to beat the crowd—which cuts out at the start of the fourth. And, let's be honest. Who in his right mind would willingly choose to live in a city without a Dakota or an Elaine's?

As a twenty-two-year-old film and TV graduate of NYU's School of the Arts (pre-Tisch, no less) who needed a job, I made it my business to find out. What was it about this place that was so goddamn loathsome? I had heard all the bad-mouthing from my peers, but secretly, I didn't think it made much sense. Didn't every kid who grew up in New York dream of going to Disneyland and wearing shorts in the winter? Was I the only erstwhile eight-year-old sports fanatic who watched the '61 Yankee-Dodger series on a neighbor's color TV, and needed to see, up close and personal, the tropical paradise that was Chavez Ravine? Hell, the town was good enough for Koufax. Come to think of it, it was good enough for many of the filmmakers we New Yorkers (presumably Mr. Allen among us) had studied and emulated. Not to take anything away from *Bananas*, but it seemed to me that Preston Sturges survived quite nicely in a land without Zabar's and egg creams, managing to make *The Lady Eve* and *The Palm Beach Story* long before the advent of turning right on red. Somehow, Billy Wilder and I. A. L. Diamond were also able to make great art in a bagel-challenged universe. Three thousand miles from the Metropolitan Opera House, Howard Hawks found a way to throw together some decent stuff, too.

I suppose Woody's point was that if one were to choose a coast on which to make a living, the East, and specifically New York City, was the winner, hands-down. All well and good, but when one didn't have the means to be a snob, the default was an open mind. Which not only seemed appropriate, but imperative for a kid coming straight out of college. My westward migration, in the winter of 1975, followed the exodus of a myriad of NYU grads. Marty Scorsese had famously gone out to LA to make *Boxcar Bertha*, his first Hollywood film, for American International Pictures. Rising stars Marty Brest and Amy Heckerling enrolled at the American Film Institute to study directing. The rest of us, who weren't yet in any semblance of demand, banked on the theory that Hollywood was still the Wild West. There was a ton of work, and you were only one break away from becoming a major player in what would be a new Golden Age in American Film. Any one of us could wind up making the next *French Connection*, *Godfather*, or *Last Picture Show*, we just needed jobs that would give us the opportunity to hone our skills. Fortunately, Hollywood in the seventies had a farm system, a de facto graduate school comprised of independent studios and producers that made low-budget B-movies, shown in drive-ins and small towns purported to be even more Bumfuckian than Los Angeles.

AIP, New World Pictures, Crown International, Cannon Films, and countless others needed fresh, inexpensive blood to churn out their discount goods. As a result, the B-movie world became the training ground for soon-to-be mainstream directors. Ron Howard would ultimately reinvent himself as an Oscar-winning producer and director who'd give us a movie about Formula One racing, but not before laying a very different road trip on us in *Grand Theft Auto*. Joe Dante's *Gremlins* were cute before midnight snacks, less so after, but his *Piranha* made no such time-of-day distinctions where dining fare was concerned. And Jonathan Kaplan would eventually explore the perils of a pinball machine for Jodie Foster, but his titular *Night Call Nurses* were immune to the dangers of multi-platform sexual surfaces. My introduction to the delights of bargain basement cinema began with an exploratory trip to LA, and a meeting with director Paul Bartel, the son of my father's colleague in advertising. Bartel, who was about to begin a picture for Roger Corman, summoned me to the Magic Pan in Beverly Hills, where he was dining with his sister, Wendy, the production secretary, and Tina Hirsch, the film editor. Much to my surprise, I was offered a job on the spot. All I needed was a car, and I could become a production assistant on what would become the international cult classic *Death Race 2000*. Oh, and there was one minor catch—they couldn't pay me. Obviously, I had no choice but to cancel my return flight and borrow money for a Thomas Guide and a '66 VW bug, which would soon be used to transport the likes of sexy female lead, Simone Griffeth, male lead, David Carradine, and an up-and-coming New York actor named Sylvester Stallone.

Over the course of the two-week shoot, I learned my way around town, apparently doing such a stellar job that the production manager decided to pay me a salary for week two—forty dollars. Los Angeles seemed less like a city than one giant suburb, and the sheer amount of territory to explore was exhausting, but exhilarating. I'd pick up wardrobe at Western Costume in Hollywood, drive to location in Malibu, and go for burritos with the other PA's at El Tepeyac in East LA. It was a quintessentially un–New York experience that, despite my metropolitan roots, begged further investigation.

In fact, it was so intoxicating that it made me forget to pine for the Whitney and some cliquey restaurant I'd never visited on the Upper East Side. I had become friendly with some of the employees at Roger Corman's New World Pictures, who'd given me the lowdown on how his company worked. Evidently, Corman's frugality knew no bounds. He would think nothing of having his secretary dash off the first draft of a screenplay over the weekend, so he would only have to pay a "real" writer for a rewrite and polish. Corman was also a big believer in the power of the press release, and would regularly place random blurbs in the trades, regardless of whether or not the information had any basis in fact. One morning, I was excited to read that a friend of mine who worked at New World was prepping *The Casey Stengel Story*. Excited, I gave her a quick call, only to find that the enthusiasm was completely one-sided as the news item was a bogus plant, engineered to plump up the appearance of the company's development slate. I also learned that there were lots of players, and sub-players, in the low-budget world, and I endeavored to meet as many of them as possible. I had figured out early on that no matter how schlocky a film might seem, chances were some really smart folks were behind it—writers and directors who were paying their dues before moving up to the next level. If I could move up with them, so much the better.

I spent a couple of weeks in the editing room on a sequel to the soft-porn/hard-R hit, *The Cheerleaders*, written and directed by an avant-garde filmmaker and a documentarian from Berkeley. The production offices were in the BBS building on La Brea, home to the Schneider brothers, Bert and Harold, who, along with Bob Rafelson, had produced *Easy Rider*, *The Last Picture Show*, and *Head*, the movie that had brought the prefab, post-Fab Four Monkees to the forefront of American popular culture. Also in the building was filmmaker Henry Jaglom who, then as now, is known primarily for being a confidant of Orson Welles. On lunch breaks, and whenever possible, I chatted up Jaglom's attractive assistant, Laura, who was considerably older than I and had a kid to boot, until she finally agreed to go out with me. Then, during dinner at the classic Hollywood haunt, Port's, she casually dropped the bomb that she had once slept with Jim Morrison. After nearly choking on my sand dabs, all I could think about was how my tongue would stack up against the Lizard King's. Sadly, the Fates (okay, Laura) never afforded me the opportunity to find out.

My life began to take on the character of the city—a dreamy, jasminey, carbon monoxide haze. Personal and professional adventures seemed to be inextricably entwined in a Los Angeles primer that was being written specifically for me, with each new chapter a revelation, and each new, often odd, adventure seemed to be perfectly scripted around this colorful world of sub-denizens in which I found myself ensconced. Determined to mine every contact thrown my way and see if I could improve upon the life-imitates-something-short-of-art dynamic, I decided to look up a friend of a friend, a mysterious fellow named Frankie who was supposed to be "well-connected." Apparently, Frankie didn't have a phone, so if you wanted to reach him, you had to call the Beverly Wilshire Hotel barbershop and they would give him the message. One day, he returned my call and invited me to a house in Mandeville Canyon, where, supposedly, there would be lots of industry types with whom I could network. Frankie's friends were throwing a lavish thirteenth birthday party for someone named Max, whom I assumed was their son. I showed up, only to learn that this was a birthday party for…well, not their son. Standing in the backyard was a sleek Peruvian Paso, adorned with a tallit and kippah, prepared for what Max's owners had dubbed his Horse Mitzvah. I would have thought, *Hollywood, baby,* if not for the fact that life and B-movies had officially converged at the warp speed of a cheesy *Forbidden Planet* knock-off.

I continued to mine the subterranean depths of the low-budget world (most of LA was barely at sea level, so it wasn't all that hard), gleefully discovering that there were C- and even D-quality movies whose production "values," for lack of a better word, made Corman's movies look like *Lawrence of Arabia.* As luck would have it, black exploitation films were still alive and well, and I was introduced to a niche of pictures that would take a successful, Caucasian-starring title, like *Shampoo,* and stick the word "black" in front of it, resulting in a dirt-cheap clone with an all–African-American cast. Indeed, I got to experience, firsthand, one of the most deliciously awful pieces of work in American cinema, *Black Shampoo.* Its director, the white-as-rice Greydon Clark, whose artistic range would grow to encompass everything from *Satan's Cheerleaders* to *The Forbidden Dance is Lambada,* would never see the mainstream career of a Ron Howard or a Joe Dante, but would, nevertheless, go on to attain cult status at fan memorabilia shows he probably never knew, or hoped, existed.

Shortly afterward, I was hired to write a treatment for a film to be directed by the ubiquitous Chinese character actor James Hong, who, at the time, was best known for his role as Faye Dunaway's butler in *Chinatown*. Hong had previously directed a soft porn flick called *Hot Connections* and was looking to make another movie for the same production company. This particular outfit, run by Edmund Goldman and son, appeared to be several notches below the Corman operation, and boasted a moniker very much in keeping with its lurid titles: Manson Distribution. I found it a bit odd that with the Tate-LaBianca murders still echoing in the hills and psyches of Hollywood, the Goldmans couldn't come up with a slightly less creepy name. But what they called their company wasn't for me to decide or judge; I needed to get busy writing *The Beast of Boa Island*, the tale of a half-man, half-monster who terrorizes scantily clad coeds. Not totally convinced of the idea's brilliance, I pumped myself up by thinking about all the other ridiculous sounding low-budget titles that had landed in theaters: *Mission Batangas, Dracula's Dog*. Hey, why not *The Beast of Boa Island*? I would have the answer soon enough. My suspicion that I had single-handedly invented the D-minus—or, as was probably more appropriate, the DD-minus—movie was confirmed when the nice Manson folks informed me that my script wasn't up (or down—I was never sure which) to their standards.

Things on the personal front, however, were looking up. I rented a guesthouse in Santa Monica Canyon, two blocks from the beach, for $150 per month. (Zip Code 90402 median home price in 2016: $3.5 million.) In the seventies, Santa Monica was a charming small town, with a retro outdoor mall that stood on the current site of our shrine to income inequality, the Third Street Promenade. My hometown mall of the seventies housed a Newberry's, a Woolworth's, a J. C. Penney, a Sears, and, just for good measure, an independent low-level department store called Henshey's. There was an awesome Latin record shop, where I purchased the Ray Barretto classic *Acid*, and the Hennessey + Ingalls Bookstore, where I browsed after sampling the inspiration for Baretto's LP. Santa Monica had maybe two upscale restaurants, which, somehow, seemed like plenty. Montana and Seventh, still in its glorious, ungentrified state, was home to Jack's Fluff 'N' Fold Laundry, where I and a young actress named Jessica Lange brought our dirty clothes. While my prayers that Jack would one day mix up our orders were never answered, I was able to console myself by running on the beach every morning and walking down the block to what was then Gladstone's for All-You-Can-Eat Shrimp Night. On many an evening, I'd repair to O'Mahoney's Bar on Main Street to hear the kick-ass house band, Hot Lips and Fingertips, play Celtic fiddle tunes and Bob Wills swing. No cover. No minimum. Cheap beer and free pool and, as should be clear, good times aplenty.

Meanwhile, I hadn't forgotten my responsibility to flex my New York superiority muscle. But there was no hiding the truth. My resolve was being eaten away by balmy sea breezes, cheap rent, and unavoidable, beautiful women. I made a conscious effort to regain some of my strength by conjuring up images of autumn in Central Park, the leaves turning their magnificent shades of auburn and chestnut as lovestruck couples strode hand in hand along Fifth Avenue. But then I drove up the Pacific Coast Highway, saw Big Sur, and it all vanished in a proverbial New York minute.

By then, I'd found a new groove in the professional arena. I would take a job in the editing room of a movie for six months, then, once the picture was finished, I'd collect unemployment insurance for the next six months and work on my screenplays. I viewed the money as an NEA grant, back before Jesse Helms made them feel pornographic, and wrote prodigiously until the government funding ran out and I needed another gig. This balancing act went on for a year and a half, until I was presented with a concrete offer to advance my editing career. I could become a member of IATSE Local 776, the Film Editor's Guild, and collect union wages and benefits if I agreed to sign on to Paramount Pictures as an apprentice editor. This entailed taking a step back in terms of the actual work I had been doing, and serving as a gofer in the studio's shipping department. On the days when a Paramount movie or TV series needed an additional assistant editor to help with the workload, I would get sent up to the show and make full assistant's wages for the day.

Paramount revealed itself to be an entirely different sort of adventure, providing me the chance to help out on wildly different types of projects—features, TV movies, *Laverne & Shirley*, even an episode of *The American Sportsman*, directed by the legendary John Frankenheimer. One day, I was sent to work on a feature that would become yet another cult classic: *Citizens Band*, later retitled *Handle With Care*. This tongue-in-cheek ode to the CB radio craze was directed by Jonathan Demme (who, just a few years prior, had cut his directorial teeth with Corman's *Caged Heat*), written by Paul Brickman (who would go on to direct *Risky Business* and *Men Don't Leave*, the latter of which starred my onetime laundry mate, Jessica Lange), and produced by former über agent, Freddie Fields. I found both Demme and Brickman to be extremely talented, and together with Fields, gracious toward a lowly temporary assistant editor. Inside the brain trust, however, there existed no such cordiality. Demme and Brickman had strong disagreements about the editing of the movie and would recut scenes without the other knowing; the arguing had gotten to the point where the actual film editor threw up his hands and let them do whatever they wanted. Eventually, Fields wound up siding with Brickman, and Demme was banned from the editing room of his own movie. When I ran into him months later on the MGM lot, I was struck by the fact that he seemed to have taken it all in stride. The director was focused on his next project and would, soon enough, be on his way to joining the A-list.

As enlightening as it had been to observe these talents and egos at work, the defining epiphany of my Paramount tenure took place in the sound effects department, where I had been enlisted to assist a sound editor on a movie that was a month behind schedule. Studio Sound Effects had its own building, replete with a head-shaved foreman named, what else? Baldy. Baldy's job was to roam the halls, making sure the employees were hard at work, slaving over their moviolas and not cheating on their time cards. The sound editors would get an hour for lunch, as well as union-stipulated breaks, where they'd peruse the latest *Playboy* and estimate how much they were going to drink once they clocked out. Suddenly, it seemed as if I had been transported to another time and place. Having come to Hollywood to practice the art of filmmaking, I now felt like a machinist at the Hormel Factory. The guys I met in sound effects (yes, they were all guys) were working Joes, who might as well have been making bacon. The takeaway: when it came to below-the-line work, Hollywood was a solid blue-collar town, filled with the kinds of characters who, in their spare time, would likely enjoy checking out one of the B-, C-, or D-level films on which I'd worked during my first few months in Hollywood. It made me feel as though I was on some kind of trajectory, albeit where to, exactly, I had no idea.

The epiphany occurred when I happened to walk by one of the cutting rooms and heard the sounds of an editor working on his moviola. I looked inside, saw the editor asleep in a chair, and realized that he was playing a sound loop of an editor working on a moviola so that Baldy wouldn't be inclined to peek in and catch him snoozing. This was the moment in which I came to understand class distinction in Hollywood. Most picture editors, as well as the sound guys, were treated like assembly line workers—"cutters," who were nothing more than a pair of scissors for the director, and had little motivation to do anything beyond what was required of them. There were a few elite editors who had managed to earn the ear of their directors and offer artistic input, but for a young person trying to map out a career, the numbers were not in my favor. I realized that if I wanted to have a more creative impact in film, it was essential to get myself above the line. So I continued to put pen to paper. Eventually, I made the transition from Editor's Guild to Writer's Guild, but in a completely unexpected way; after years of churning out spec screenplays (scripts that hadn't been commissioned, but rather were written on speculation, or "spec"), my ticket out of the factory wound up being situation comedy. It wasn't anything I'd had a burning desire to do; I just happened to know people who were having success at it, I thought I was funny, and it seemed a hell of a lot easier than breaking into feature films. At that time, there weren't eight thousand film schools, and *The Simpsons* hadn't yet been created to lure Harvard's best and brightest away from the East Coast's finest law schools. According to everyone I'd met, all you needed to get a shot was a good sample script. I proceeded to write one *M*A*S*H* spec, and managed to have it read all over town.

The next thing I knew, I had teamed up with a friend, we were hired to write two episodes of *Bosom Buddies*, and I became a working scribe, never to return to the editing room.

Concurrently, the seventies had ended. Black exploitation films were a memory. The massage parlors started disappearing from Western Avenue. A few more good restaurants popped up in soon-to-be-hot Santa Monica. Bands like Los Lobos, X, and The Blasters were fashioning what was to become the new LA sound. I was spending some blissful evenings at the field of my childhood dreams, soaking up the Chavez Ravine vibe, and witnessing the start of Fernandomania. As far as what was coming out of New York, Woody Allen had recently released *Manhattan*, a film in which a middle-aged, Upper East Side writer sleeps with a seventeen-year-old. There were many reviews lauding the film's Gershwinesque romanticism, but none that dared to challenge the decidedly icky pedophilia infusing the story. I had to wonder: was this the coveted urban sophistication to which Woody thought we should aspire?

Something was off here. The zeitgeist needed a rewrite. It had been five years since my move west, three since *Annie Hall*, and I could no longer find a reason to pine for the ostensibly superior metropolis I had left. I also realized that Los Angeles was growing up, and that by having opened my heart to what it was I was able to witness, and participate in, what it would become. In 2016, the inarguable fact is that we are no longer the American International Pictures of cities, and our scenery doesn't have that washed-out look the B-movie mavens so patently perfected. Los Angeles, with its groundbreaking right turns, is A-list all the way.

Bruce Ferber, *before publishing his debut novel* Elevating Overman, *built a long and successful career as a television comedy writer and producer. A multiple Emmy and Golden Globe nominee, his credits include* Bosom Buddies; Growing Pains; Sabrina, the Teenage Witch; Coach; *and* Home Improvement, *where he served as executive producer and showrunner. In addition to being recognized by the Television Academy, Ferber's work has received the People's Choice, Kid's Choice, and Environmental Media Awards. After the publication of* Elevating Overman, *Ferber toured extensively with his novel, delivering the closing keynote speech at the Erma Bombeck Writers Workshop.* Overman *was recently released on audiobook, recorded by Jason Alexander, and is being developed for the big screen. Ferber's second novel,* Cascade Falls, *was published in March 2015 by Rare Bird Books. He lives in Southern California, with his wife, large dog, and assorted musical instruments.*

LAST BUTTON ON THE LEFT: THE LATE, GREAT Z CHANNEL

by Matthew Specktor

N OTHING SHOCKS ME ANYMORE, or at least, not much. Meteorology, death, the outcomes of elections: life might get weirder as we age, but I wouldn't say it gets any harder to process, especially when it comes to culture. Movies, like bands and books, were once amazements, little bridges between wonder and trauma; now, it seems, they're just blunt force repetitions, sequels to things we've already seen even on those increasingly rare occasions they're literally otherwise. Tell me the last movie that you saw that didn't feel reheated. Even, say, *Mad Max: Fury Road* (to name one picture lauded recently enough for its invention) which merely breathed gassy life into the bloated corpse of a franchise thirty-years dormant. When was the last time you saw something unprecedented, that set the world on its side for an hour and a half? The movies, in 2015, may or may not be a dead art form—I certainly don't give a fuck about them, myself—but all this dyspepsia melts away when I consider the Z Channel, one of those LA-specific conduits (like The Source or Hamburger Hamlet, like Rodney's English Disco or the Germs) melding art and gaudiness, and a little bit of sleaze. It's difficult to imagine, now, a moment in which "cable television" was an invention, but it was. In 1975 my parents joined the lot of our friends and neighbors by augmenting their regular, good-old network TV (rabbit ears, *The ABC Sunday Night Movie*, Marlin Perkins, etc.,) with a small brown box that offered, if I recall correctly, twenty-four channels in lieu of the ordinary thirteen. I don't remember what other wonders our provider, Theta Cable, offered besides (there was, I believe, a dedicated weather channel and such like; things we didn't otherwise encounter on telly), but I do remember the Z Channel, the alpha and omega, bringing as it did actual movies, uncut and without commercial interruption, into my house. Even the location of the channel's portal itself—a button all the way over to the far left of the other channels, right at the very edge of the brown box—hinted at pleasures heretofore unseen, physically unfelt, yet strangely, if our parents' permissiveness in allowing us virtually unlimited access to the channel was any indication, not unwarranted.

I grew up in a typical louche seventies household, assuming "typical" included the constant presence of working actors and directors and musicians clustered around the dinner table, which in Los Angeles it certainly did. Bruce Dern and Beau Bridges and—very occasionally—Clint Eastwood, Judy Collins and, much later, Jerzy Kosiński: these were the people my parents hung out with, and if that sounds a little glamorous, well, all it meant to me at that impressionable young age was that the border between life and the movies was porous, and that the skin of an icon, or more often of an actor who showed up third-billed in a raucous comedy that wasn't even a hit, was no more otherworldly than the scent of hamburgers cooking on the patio grill. My parents were not cocaine cowboys or closet pornographers. All I remember are bottles of Beaujolais nouveau and copies of *Playboy*, things that were as typical of the times as my father's thumb-wide mustache and driving without a seatbelt. The Z Channel thus cruised into my life at nine years old, of a piece with all these other things: it brought to my doorstep the life that was already on my doorstep, or rather brought it into my living room, that dusky green chamber in which I ate my mother's spare ribs and argued with my kid sister, even as our parents contended with it in the dining room next door. I watched *Thunderbolt and Lightfoot* for the first time

there, as I watched *The Sting* (which I'd seen in a theater with my dad)
for the second, fourth, and tenth. The Z Channel's programming,
as anyone who's seen Xan Cassavetes' excellent documentary on
the subject (*Z Channel: A Magnificent Obsession*) also knows, was
superlatively curated. Charles Champlin and F. X. Feeney were
involved early on as columnists for the channel's weekly magazine,
and Jerry Harvey, the programming director who took over in 1980,
had his own magnificent and dismaying story—it's worth watching
Cassavetes' documentary just for that—but all I knew, when I was
a boy, was that the movies were now available without a parent or a
friend's parent to take me to them, back when an "R" rating was very
much the equivalent of a velvet rope or a "must be sixty-five inches to
ride" sign for a nine year-old boy. Which meant that, I dunno, *Death
Wish* (to name but one film I remember being hot and heavy currency
among the under-ten set, despite—or I should say because of—its
R-rating) could be viewed without much difficulty. If I recall correctly,
afternoons tended to huddle in the slightly-more-family-friendly
range—which, back in the days, as it was, of Disney's "dark years,"
meant that fare like *Pete's Dragon* was viewable more times than I'd
like to think was acceptable under Geneva Code stipulations—while
the R-rated programming (and, now-and-again, beyond) was pushed
back into the evening. Eight o'clock or even ten on a Wednesday was
a perfectly fine time to watch Charles Bronson mete out a little street
justice, but sometimes, if I hung on a little longer, I'd catch sight of
something that really moved things around. I don't remember exactly
how old I was when I first saw *A Clockwork Orange*—young enough
that it was the first time I caught sight of a woman's pubic hair, for
sure—or *Lisztomania*...or *Rosemary's Baby* or *Don't Look Now*; in
a strict, developmentally regulatory sense I was nowhere near old
enough, and yet each and every one of these movies came to me via
the Z Channel, and all of them...well, they shaped my imagination,
by which I mean my sexuality, among other things, for sure, especially
when Mssrs. Champlin and Feeney would hold forth on whether
Sutherland and Christie were, y'know, "doing it" for real. These
films shaped my sense of the world, and my burgeoning aesthetic,
and if loosing these things upon a child well below the threshold of

adolescence seems a little, uh, risky, I'd argue that's the nature of art. It certainly didn't bring me anything that didn't already exist, and in fact it didn't bring me anything that wasn't already present in the room, the house, or the neighborhood next door, especially given that, after all, it was the seventies and in LA to boot. No, the Z Channel's numerous libertine pleasures merely codified life in all its oddity and brought it home for me to look at, in a space where I could still, if I wanted to, tiptoe into the kitchen to grab a glass of milk before I resumed viewing. Which I did, through all my adolescence: through *Heaven's Gate* and *Apocalypse Now* (the latter, as I recall, transferred from the Z Channel to Betamax cassette, the better to watch at will, rather than waiting for it to spin up again on the wheel of Theta Cable's recurrence), through all the Altmans and Aldrichs and Alan Rudolphs (and, less displeasingly, through Helen Mirren's full-frontal nudity in *Savage Messiah* that practically catapulted me into puberty in five awestruck minutes). God knows what else, really. There was a time in which the Z Channel was basically a synonym for my own developing cultural vocabulary, when it was, in essence, my lifeline to the outside world: a world that existed both within and without, which seems a reasonable definition of both the movies and reality.

I don't have a lot more to say about the channel itself, beyond that. I could go on and on, listing the exhaustive titles and categories, eras and nationalities, and high and low artistic distinctions the channel brought, if not exactly to light, then certainly back into circulation, yet to do so would be simply to valorize a time and place—a canon, I suppose—that is now lost; it would be equivalent to blathering on about Haight-Ashbury, or Paris in the twenties, succumbing, on however small a scale, to nostalgia, which forever dictates that the watersheds and inventions of the past (even something as humble and suburban as a cable television network) tower over the diminished grandeur of the present. Fuck that. Los Angeles in the seventies was a queer and crooked place, furtive and anxious, fraught with all the ambivalence—divorce, drug abuse, political panic, and extra-cinematic scandal; the Hillside Strangler and the Energy Crisis—that haunted everywhere else in whatever regional form. Tempting as it is to renovate the memories, to reconstruct Scandia or Osko's Disco on a room-by-room, fabric-by-fabric basis, the fact remains, the era's power derives from the fact it is gone. Were its structures still present, we'd probably be as eager to tip them over and tear them down as we are—or, at least, as I am—those of the present. And yet the Z Channel, long before HBO or Showtime or even revival house programming (as I encountered it later, in the eighties, at places like the Nuart Theatre, the New Beverly Cinema, or the Vista, places that deserve their own valentines within these pages) brought me a sense of the movies not as byproducts of the deal—for, believe me, no matter how we imagine those days were the last Golden Era of Cinema, to the people making them, the films of the seventies were as pressurized by commerce as they had been from the beginning—but as, well, art. Not just me; the truth is, if you want something more than my own personal testimony, filmmakers like Paul Thomas Anderson, Alexander Payne, and Quentin Tarantino have indicated that the channel did as much in shaping their cinematic sensibilities as well. But I suppose that's neither here nor there. Those of us who grew up in Los Angeles in the seventies—some of whom went on to work in entertainment, others of us (like myself or Bret Easton Ellis) disposed to critique it and embrace it, with whatever degree of ambivalence ourselves, still others not so much connected with the industry at all, but every last one touched by the movies, just as every native New Yorker has ridden in a cab and every Chicagoan has most likely met a man with a Polish surname—all of us, thus, owe the Z Channel a debt. Like all such debts, it arrives already forgiven. All it asks is that we close our eyes and remain ready to see, that we clear away the cobwebs of the present and stare across a gulf that feels, at times, only centimeters wide, after all, on the opposite side a small screen, glowing vibrant and gray, a chromium radiance in the dark.

Matthew Specktor *is the author of the novels* American Dream Machine *and* That Summertime Sound, *as well as a nonfiction book of film criticism. His writing has appeared in* The New York Times, GQ, Harper's, The Paris Review, The Believer, Tin House, *and numerous other periodicals and anthologies. He is a founding editor of the* Los Angeles Review of Books.

HEART OF DORKNESS: HOW DR. DEMENTO SAVED MY BONY, WHITE ASS

by Michael Lazarou

ERHAPS IT'S BECAUSE I recently celebrated yet another birthday with a great big five in front of it, or maybe because I'm witnessing my oldest kids entering adulthood, but when I think about the linchpin moments in my life, many, if not most, of those moments were an expectation that was violated—bashed like a piñata is more like it, and not always, but usually, in a good way. This pattern of expectational smithereens began at a specific time and place. It even had its own music to properly underscore the mood.

I was down to my last two days. Forty-eight hours before I was to start junior high. It was a reunion of sorts with my same public school cohort from nearly four years earlier, most of whom I hadn't seen since third grade, the year I was asked to leave (more about this later). You didn't have to be Dr. Joyce Brothers—Dr. Phil's female ancestor— to see that I was wound tighter than a monkey on barbed wire over the prospect of being "mainstreamed" back into the public school system. Honestly, I had all kinds of good reasons to feel like Caryl Chessman after blowing through his final appeal. As was often the case in the LA area during the first week or two of school, the weather forecast called for "blast furnace with continuing blast furnace into the early morning hours, blah, dee, blah, blah." In other words, the Santa Ana winds were blowing hotter than Nick Gilder's child in the city, which as anyone in the Southland can tell you, tends to make people twitchy. Don't believe me? Take a peek at LA County's violent crime stats. Reads like a demon's honey-do list.

The Spivey brothers from down the block and I picked up a batch of twenty-gallon Slurpees (I'm bad with weights and measures—sue me!) and we rode our bikes to the top of Mar Vista Avenue, the highest point in the Whittier hills. The same Santa Ana winds that were whipping the temps up to triple digits also blew out all the smog. We could see Downtown LA in a way that we'd never quite seen it before…which is to say that we could see it at all. We couldn't stop looking at it. Didn't say a word. Nobody. For like, twenty minutes. Three preteen wing nuts who couldn't go three seconds without belching, farting, or having to pull a PF Flyer from their soft palate, silently taking in that moment for twenty minutes. Truth be told, we were all dealing with a fair amount of shit. So was the country. The last of our soldiers who served in Vietnam were home, sleeping in their own beds, but between the failure to adjust to changing markets and a serious economic downturn, tens of thousands of LA-area aerospace workers—including the engineer father of my two bike-riding, Slurpee-hauling buddies—were on unemployment for the first time in their lives with no prospects in sight. A summer earlier, we had watched the 1972 Olympics and Mark Spitz, as he won seven gold medals and broke seven world records, yet wound up being only the twelfth most famous Jew in the Games of the XX Olympiad. Closer to home, the Senate Watergate hearings took over daytime television, followed by the House vote on impeachment, but not before our nation watched the President of the United States, (a Whittier boy, no less) declare "I'm not a crook!" with all the weighty gravitas of a Cheez Whiz daiquiri. Bombs were going off in America's streets on the regular, but terrorists didn't put them there—worse. The Ford Motor Company did, and they were collectively known as The Pinto. The really sketchy part, of course, was the moral calculus in which the corporate Titan that built this bomb determined it was more cost-effective to settle lawsuits from victims of what they knew to be a subcompact Hindenburg than to recall the vehicle and make the unsafe safe. Speaking of cars, who can forget that seventies classic, the OPEC oil embargo? And on the B-side—purchasing gas on odd or even days based on the last character on your license plate? Unfortunately, lines to gas stations would often snake for blocks and frequently run out of fuel before everyone queued up could finally make their way up to a pump.

Even little things went comically awry. Take the leisure suit, which did for men's fashion what Lt. William Calley did for the thatched hut. Their ubiquity made them seem all the more grotesque, as the leisure suit swept America seemingly overnight, well before the CDC and NIH could possibly develop a working vaccine. But, hey, even a white guy from Duluth could look like a poorly dressed pimp and there's real value in that somewhere. (Mine was powder blue, by the way. Thanks, a bunch, Mom.) While we had certainly (okay, maybe?) been through worse times, it was, for most of us, a period that had its fair share of pain and uncertainty, and we were certainly coughing, if not outright choking, while trying to suck in a little air through the clouds of cynicism and smog that hung over us. We needed to heal. We needed to laugh. We were a nation desperately in need of *more cowbell*.

If you were lucky enough to live in Los Angeles, you had your clinician. And this badass doctor even made house calls.

It was a Panasonic, it had AM and FM, and I couldn't even remotely tell you the model number, but it had those digits that would flip over. In the early seventies, a clock radio with LED digits was some serious NASA shit; maybe Buzz Aldrin's kid got one of those, but my dad was no astronaut. I got the clock with the flippy digits, and though I got it around my eleventh birthday, trust me, it was no birthday present. My parents and I didn't speak much and when we did, explosions usually followed. My mom was the one who was tasked with waking me up in the morning for school and getting my breakfast on the table. We'd invariably be at each other's throats within seconds. My dad was usually at work before I got up; I suspect because he still wanted a voice and a little sanity left when he got there. After months of ugliness and punched-in drywall, it was mutually decided that I should wake myself up, make my own breakfast, and we could avoid each other entirely in the morning. As fucked up as that may sound, at the time it was the right play and it brings me back to the aforementioned clock radio…well, the radio part, anyway.

There's this wonderful scene in the movie *Almost Famous* where eleven-year-old William is gifted his older sister's sizable album collection—everything from *Get Yer Ya-Yas Out!* to *Cheap Thrills* to *Crosby, Stills & Nash* to *Blonde on Blonde* to *Tommy*. This scene particularly resonates for me because not only did my sister leave me her albums when she went off to college, she left me the exact same albums William's big sis left him. So if your tastes ran along those lines, and you happened to live in LA in the 1970s, there was, in my opinion, one choice when looking for a radio station to satisfy those urges: KMET, aka the "Mighty Met." KMET's format was known as "Freeform Progressive Rock," which was a ginned-up way of saying their DJ's could play whatever the fuck they wanted. B. Mitchel Reed, "The Burner" Mary Turner, Jeff Gonzer, Raechel Donahue, and, of course, Jim Ladd, who had the unmitigated sack to play entire sides of Bob Marley and The Wailers, "Burnin'" and "Catch a Fire." I didn't know what I wanted to be when I grew up. But I knew I wanted to smoke some decent shit, spend some time in Jamaica, and marry a girl who looked like Judy Mowatt. (I would ultimately go three for three!) KMET was the top-rated station in LA with a format that was considered manifestly irresponsible by nearly every station manager in the business even then. As much as I bowed down to the station's signature upside down bumper stickers, the best was yet to come, albeit totally and completely unexpected.

Which brings me back to Sunday night. Junior high now exactly fourteen hours away. The bags of Ruffles and box of Kit Kats at the ready. I tune in, expecting the aforementioned Jim Ladd. I did not find what I was looking for but oy-to-the-motherfucking-vey, did I find what I needed. His name: Demento. Dr. Demento.

A cacophony of horns, then brass, then congas. Congas?! You didn't need to be the editor of *Crawdaddy!* to know that this was not

side one of *Live at Leeds*. Honestly, I thought somebody had messed
with my parent's tuner, but I was the only one who ever so much
as touched the thing. I checked and rechecked. I was on the right
station, but what the hell was this driving Latin rhythm stuff? I was
about to shut it all down when the opening chorus exploded: "Pico and
Sepulveda! Pico and Sepulveda! Pico and Sepulveda!" Then the featured
vocalist did his thing, the lyrics to the song consisting almost entirely of
the names of well-known and not-so-well-known LA streets. It was as
if Desi Arnaz and his orchestra had gone on a gargantuan molly bender
and written and arranged a song based on a Thomas Brothers Guide.
I was laughing so hard my ab muscles were getting sore, and I wasn't
even smiling much those days, much less laughing.

I was sold. Immediately! But who was this act, and more
importantly, who would put it on the air?

"That was Felix Figueroa and his Orchestra and 'Pico and
Sepulveda.' I'm Dr. Demento, your happy host of the *Dr. Demento
Show* here on KMET."

The voice was possibly Midwestern, not particularly polished
by DJ standards, and it was jovial. This Demento dude was clearly
having a good time. He had the most ridiculously transcendent and
unique record collection on the planet and he just couldn't wait to
share it with his friends who, and I didn't know it yet, numbered into
the hundreds of thousands. For the next four hours, he played song
after song that ran the gamut from the near subversive to the *oh, no
he didn't!* naughty. After the second hour, I started taping the show.
Yes, this was a habit of mine and I wanted to hear this again later, but
mostly I rolled tape because it all seemed too good to be true. There
was a part of me that wondered if this was some strange one-off that
I'd never hear again. In a way, that was a legit concern; just like no
two Dead concerts were alike, no two *Dr. Demento Show*s were either.
But it was the last hour that turned me from instant fan to obsessed
devotee, when Dr. Demento would play his Top-10 tunes of the week
as determined entirely by listener requests. Dr. D would even give
a generous portion of shout-outs to many of his petitioners. These
shout-outs mattered. They mattered a great deal. In addition to giving
a rapidly growing and loyal community of followers skin in the game,

the request-driven Top-10 gave a very old technology a rather ahead-of-its-time element of interactivity. But the Top-10 went well beyond community and interactivity. In fact, it was downright revolutionary, and the revolution was definitely not being televised. For perhaps the very first and only time—and in the second largest media market in the country—a large and very young demographic that invariably had to bend over and listen to what industry grown-ups said they were going to listen to were decidedly in the driver's seat. Not only were mostly middle school and high school kids doing the programming, they were choosing music—novelty records mostly—from which the major labels were seeing little if any bump in their revenue stream.

What were the top three tunes that night? The number three was a song by Tom Lehrer, a guy who got sidetracked from his day job as an MIT mathematics professor to become perhaps the greatest musical satirist of the twentieth century. His offering that night was a sardonic and riotous ragtime send-up of Vatican II entitled, most appropriately, "The Vatican Rag." And Professor Lehrer would go on to influence other luminaries such as Mark Russell, Randy Newman, and a kid who was growing up only a few miles away from me in Lynwood, California. Just like me, this kid was listening to those very same early seventies Demento shows…with a twist. Demento shows were far more than just a big giggle to this kid. These Sunday night soirees greased his impulses to a much higher calling. By the late seventies, Dr. Demento would be instrumental in helping break this kid's career wide open. In fact, Weird Al Yankovic and Dr. Demento were, and still are, a match made in demented heaven.

Number two (Do You Like) "Boobs A Lot" by the Holy Modal Rounders. The title pretty much tells you everything you need to know. Like many songs played on the *Dr. Demento Show*, this one had a little-known nugget behind it. The Holy Modal Rounders' drummer would, six years later, go on to write a Pulitzer Prize–winning play and would become one of the greatest American playwrights of his generation. Oh, and, this mammary-loving percussionist—known to most of us as Sam Shepard—would also earn an Oscar nomination for Best Actor in his spare time.

Number one "They're Coming To Take Me Away, Ha-Haaa!" written performed and produced by some guy calling himself

Napoleon XIV. The character in the song is some poor schmuck who describes his obvious descent into madness when the love of his life—presumably his wife or girlfriend—has kicked him to the curb and left his sorry ass. Nap XIV describes how he cooked his love's food, cleaned house, and yet this was how he was paid back for all his magnanimity: with a trip to the loony bin, at the hands of "those nice young men in their clean white coats." Then comes that great reversal when we discover that the object of the narrator's obsession has four legs, a tail, and barks when she has to pee…although to be fair, the gender of the cavorting canine is never revealed. One of those timeless mysteries. Hilarious…and thank God, I got it on tape! Ah, that tape! That tape would prove to be coin of the realm before long and I didn't even know it!

The following morning, I was sitting in my homeroom when the tardy bell rang. Zero hour. I recognized maybe half the kids from my previous stint in the public school system years earlier. The good news was, everybody else seemed pretty damn nervous, too. The bad news was, they weren't on de facto probation the way I was. I had been pulled out of public school shortly after starting third grade because the wheels had fallen off the wagon. Reading was an enormous challenge, but writing was damn near impossible. Frankly, I don't know how I lasted as long as I did. I assumed what I'm sure some of my peers and teachers assumed, that I'd fallen out of the dumbass tree and hit every fucking branch on my way down. When we were taught cursive by transcribing the exemplar that was displayed over the blackboard… well, I couldn't. I wanted to. More than anything, I wanted to. The worst students in class could handle this with facile aplomb. I couldn't manage a single uppercase "A". I may not have shown it, but I was absolutely gutted. Finally, I was tested, and I was found to be both dyslexic and dysgraphic. Back then, school districts lacked the know-how and resources to deal with this, so I was sent to a school for kids with "special needs" in Anaheim, a good hour's bus ride from my house. I'm not sure how they work with kids with these sorts of issues today, but they knew little about it then. The school I went to for nearly four years had kids that ran the gamut from Asperger's to the hearing impaired to the high-functioning autistic. While little was known about dealing with my kind of learning disabilities, I had one very enterprising young teacher who came up with a great idea: she sold me on the idea of learning enough cursive to have a "cool signature." It took me two months, but sure enough I had a signature that looked like a signature. Miss Reed, my teacher, was so stoked she suggested I design some "cool signatures" for my classmates, and I was totally game. I didn't know that I was acquiring a skill that would serve me well a few years down the road.

In the early seventies, physical education was required. You wore shorts, your reversible T-shirt, did calisthenics, a fast lap. And mine was fast; I was a track guy, and I liked to show off. It was Friday of that first week of school. Since I'd been faring well enough in my classes—and by well enough, I mean remaining in them, period—it had qualified as a pretty good week. It was about to take a great turn. I was headed for the shower when, from one of the stalls, a kid named Richard Rodriquez started singing "Boobs A Lot" at the top of his lungs. Much to my surprise and delight, three or four other guys started singing it with him. Well, shit! I wasn't about to let my mellifluous tenor go to waste. I ran my bony ass into the shower and started singing. Clearly, there were a fair number of kids who were already seasoned listeners of Dr. Demento, but many weren't. That was changing. And fast. By our third a cappella number, everybody in that locker room who wasn't wise to things Demented wanted to know more about this very cheeky radio show and the man who played these records. I knew I was on to something when I mentioned in passing that I had a tape of the previous Sunday's Top-10. Why, of course I'd make copies for my new pals. *That's just the kind of guy I am!* But it wasn't just tapes and it wasn't just me.

By the third week of school, every Monday morning Hillview Intermediate was an eight hundred–student water cooler confab and it was *all* about the batshit crazy tunes that had made it on to Dr. Demento the night before. Making Demento tapes and sharing them was a thriving cottage industry. Hillview had a pretty diverse ethnic and socioeconomic mix, but Demento was something everybody readily agreed on. After a month or two of tape-swapping and hours of debate on who put together the best Top-10 mix tape, a few of us Mighty Met–heads decided that our school should start flexing its collective muscle and make a serious run at getting a song played at the number one spot, which would get us an on-air mention from the Doctor himself. A song called "Friendly Neighborhood Narco Agent" was the song we chose.

On Monday at 8:00 a.m. we started circulating a petition. By the following morning, we had over seven hundred names, which was easily ninety percent of the school. There was fear that seven hundred wouldn't be enough because of those damn junior high and high schools in LA Unified and Long Beach which were "freakin' huge, dude!" Dr. Demento would often admonish his listeners not to forge signatures on request petitions because, "We check them all *very* carefully and we have ways of detecting malfeasance, my good friends." Fuck that! I had spent three years learning how to write signatures for my classmates in special ed. I had a talent and I would be damned if I was going to waste it. My brother and sister Hillview Huskies had a need, and I was uniquely qualified to fill it. Within twenty-four hours, there were nearly 1,200 signatures on the petition (I'm proud to say that no two looked remotely alike), which was soon in the mailbox and en route to the KMET studios on Wilshire Blvd.

That Sunday night at 9:53 p.m., and with seemingly every tape in LA radioland rolling, Dr. D gave us our shout-out and played our song. Effin' epic! Perhaps too epic, as it caught the attention of East Whittier Intermediate, our hated rival. East Whittier wanted some airtime of their own and on the following Sunday, those sons of bitches got it. This touched off a full scale war of sorts, and for the next couple of months or so, two junior high schools in Whittier, of all places, were getting song after song deep into the Dr. Demento Top-10. Lest anyone assume the *Dr. Demento Show* didn't enjoy broad appeal across the extensive social fabric that is the Southland, one experience sure clued me in.

After getting waxed by East Whittier two weeks in a row, we discovered that our rivals had altered their tactics. While sending in a petition under their school's name, they sent in some smaller ones with names like "Future Moonshiners of America", etc. In short, we were afraid that maybe our one gargantuan petition was looking a little undersized. Luckily, dyslexia and dysgraphia do not effect one's foot speed. My father worked with a gentleman who happened to be the highly respected coach of a youth track club. For two months I had been a member of the Compton Striders Track Club. We trained at Compton College and Dominguez High School. Not only was I the only white kid on the team, none of my teammates had a white classmate, knew a white person, or, I was pretty sure, even had a white pair of sneakers. Stupidly, without asking, I forged a petition with bogus signatures, but under the name Compton Striders Track Club.

That Sunday, Hillview was back in the driver's seat and in the same breath our school was mentioned, Dr. Demento gave a booming shout out to the Compton Striders Track Club. There were only twenty-two guys on the team and I assumed none of them listened to the *Dr. Demento Show*, if for no reason other than nobody had ever mentioned it before. I got to practice a few minutes late and I noticed all my teammates were huddled together and talking about something that looked important. Jamie, coach's son, team captain, and the kid I knew best, walked up to me.

"Laz? Did ya hear? We're famous!"

"Huh?"

"I ain't lyin'! You ever check out the *Dr. Demento Show*? The show with all those crazy-ass songs? Somebody asked to hear a song and said it was from us! They mentioned Compton Striders T. C. on the radio! On-the-radio! You believe that? You gotta listen to that show!"

I nodded my head and never said a word. From that point forward, the Striders would sign a Demento petition every Monday after practice—after, of course, critiquing the previous night's show. In fact, if you go to YouTube, you can actually find Dr. Demento's Top-10 from August 18, 1974. Dr. Demento doesn't mention who requested the number ten song, but he does say, "My, what a classy request! 'Cab Calloway' and 'Minnie the Moocher'!" I couldn't tell you everybody who requested that song that Sunday night, but I can tell you that twenty-two were members of the Compton Striders Track Club, including their bony-assed, white sprinter from Whittier.

While Dr. Demento was, and remains, an original, perhaps the biggest reason why he had such a hold on so many of us was his all-too-rare authenticity that was so clear and resonant to those who listened in. It wasn't as though other LA stations weren't fighting to take back some of that young demographic he so successfully amassed from his earliest days, to the late seventies, and beyond, when he would introduce us to the aforementioned Weird Al Yankovic and the likes of Barnes and Barnes who, among other wonderfully demented works, gave us their anthemic "Fish Heads" (which remains the most requested song in the history of the *Dr. Demento Show*). As hard as those other stations tried to yank back that audience, they mostly failed. Before long, the *Dr. Demento Show* was syndicated and went national. This was no longer a strictly LA phenomenon. My future wife and her friends made it their business to tune in to the *Dr. Demento Show* every Sunday night from their homes in Chicago's South Side. Still, I think back to the early seventies and one specific occasion when an expectation of mine was blown to bits in a way that was profoundly personal, and, of course, it was a song on a radio show that would make it possible.

My father was born in the south Bronx, the son of a waiter who came to the States from Greece in the twenties. My mother came to this country from England by way of Czechoslovakia, a country she and the rest of her Jewish family had fled in the late thirties as it came under Hitler's occupation. I always knew my mother, an only child, lived with her parents in London and miraculously survived many terrifying close calls during the "Blitz." There was more to the story that nobody ever told me. A lot more. One Sunday I was listening to the *Dr. Demento Show* and an old song called "Der Fuehrer's Face" by Spike Jones & His City Slickers came on. It was a parody of the Nazi anthem, "The Horst Wessel Song," and was written, recorded and released in 1942. "When de Fuehrer says, we is the master race, we Heil, Heil, right in the Fuehrer's face!" with a Bronx cheer following every mention of the word "Heil." My mom burst into the room when she heard this. I assumed it was to yell at me about the music being too loud, the growing pile of dirty laundry in my bedroom, something. But she wasn't yelling. She was—and this was novel—smiling at me. She told me how she and her parents listened and laughed when they heard this song on the BBC almost exactly thirty years earlier. Mom told me she had an uncle who would sing a song similar to that one and throw in the exact same funny sound effects, while breaking up the entire room.

I asked her what ever happened to him. She took a deep breath and told me. As it turned out, my mother and her parents didn't just leave Czechoslavakia one day. She, her parents, and thirty aunts, uncles, and cousins left in the middle of the night with little more than the clothing on their backs and headed up and over the Tatra mountains toward Poland, where they would take a boat to England if all went according to plan. The party of thirty-three made it to a ski lodge near the summit of one of the mountains and stayed there for the night. Because my grandparents had an eleven-year-old daughter, and the chambermaid was off for the weekend, they were put in the chambermaid's room. The next morning, my mother and grandparents woke up and discovered that, during the night, a contingent of Gestapo and SS had arrested all thirty of her family members, but didn't check her room because they didn't want to disturb the chambermaid. Those thirty relatives were never seen again.

My parents and I had a very tenuous relationship. It would remain that way for many years before we'd turn the corner and things would get better. But because of a song that made her laugh that she heard on the BBC in 1943, and me on KMET in 1973, I was given the gift of a critical piece of my mother's history, and as difficult as our relationship was, I could never think about her quite the same way again. It would be years before we actually started to like each other, but a seed of understanding was planted that night. Talk about a violation of expectation.

Sure, we could easily dismiss the *Dr. Demento Show* as just a humble show, albeit highly original and perhaps a once and forever happening. But ask anybody who was a kid and who regularly danced his or her way into Dr. Demento's ticklish world of dementia in the seventies to talk about the show and the things they remember most, and you'll get one hell of a smile, at least a couple of badly-warbled novelty tunes, and a surprising number of very old and very well-preserved tapes.

"Crank up those radios, friends!"

Michael Lazarou *is a graduate of UCLA and AFI. He has written for motion pictures and television in half-hour comedy, one-hour drama, and long form. Lazarou received the WGA's Honorary Paul Selvin Award, the youngest recipient ever of an honorary Writers Guild award. He was nominated for a WGA Award for his teleplay for* Heat Wave, *a fact-based film about the 1965 Watts Uprising. Lazarou is married to former NBC and Lifetime programming executive Charisse McGhee. They have four children.*

FOR NOW

by Lynell George

B Y THE TIME I was eight years old, I yearned to drive a car. A longing that first, I'm certain, manifested itself as envy. My brother, Rocky, younger by two-and-a-half years, had been gifted a set of plastic car keys that looked authentic enough to covet. I'd abscond with them for part of the afternoon and mimic the "going out" motions my parents performed—patting pockets, checking "handbags"—before they stepped into the vastness beyond the heavy front door. Where I might go hadn't occurred to me. I just wanted to move—explore.

Los Angeles had a particular scent back then, a residue that clung to my parents' clothes. Whenever they returned, I'd breathe it in when they held me close. Was it smog? Exhaust? The crumbling ozone? It registered as a worldliness that I wanted in on. That was 1971. It was also the same year that I first felt the earth pitch and roll—huge, wild, uncertain—beneath me. That quake (6.5, Sylmar, the biggest one in the century in LA proper until Northridge's 6.7 in 1994) shook me awake in a way I couldn't quite describe for some time.

When I think about *that* Los Angeles, that big city rolling and unfurling beneath me, it felt both more vast and mysterious than it does now. Not just because I was a child, but because it simply *was*.

For natives of a certain age, the ground one walked on and the territory one passed through were seldom what they first seemed. Those fold-out gas station maps we'd kept stuffed in the glove box, "in case," revealed little about the spaces that we, over time, dreamed of, occupied, then shed. "Turf" was something that didn't exist officially on a map, but rather in one's head. It needed to be negotiated, memorized, and updated frequently.

In the seventies, those words—*turf, territory, enclave*—circled through our language; they found their way into street slang, news reports, and family conversation. Power wrote and erased borders and dividing lines, and power—in politics or population—was always shifting. Those memorized maps provided an overlay—temporary, always fluid—to the official city grid. Truly knowing Los Angeles meant putting yourself into it, giving yourself over to it.

We moved only once in that span of a decade; in that time I lived in several distinct territories, both physical and of the mind. Los Angeles could be this way. Worlds unto themselves, side by side, veiled only by star jasmine hedges or hastily erected privacy fences. Mostly they were invisible dividing lines you'd come to know only if you stumbled across them.

The first streets I had begun to memorize—Arlington, Normandie, Denker, Florence, Hoover, Twenty-Fifth—shifted. For a time it was Hyde Park, Crenshaw, West Boulevard, South La Brea, Centinela. Later it would be Jefferson, Overland, Venice. Slauson, for all of its unglamourous heavy industry, the zipper of railroad ties, I realize now was the only familiar and dependable through-line linking those many chapters.

I started school with almost all-black classmates. Then, for a time, predominately white. Then black, and by the end, tipping toward mixed again.

Over that time, through all of those shifts, I always resisted—no, bristled at—the term "melting pot." It sounded like a cartoon cauldron. Relatedly, in the seventies, each time I heard the term "white flight" floating out from the TV, I imagined a set of wings—not the entire bird, just one detached span of wings. Aloft.

At any given time, some groups were fleeing as others were arriving. It was about the time that I realized that there were "many" Los Angeleses swarming, each with stories that tended to remain in the margins, territories that could only be accessed by someone familiar with its history and layout. So many neighborhoods seemed to have holdovers—that house in the center of the block whose owners refused to budge, who still put their laundry on the line and had blue bottles planted in the garden to ward off bad spirits. The hope was that that "placeholder" ensured that what *had been* before informed what it would be.

What I saw on television or in the movies didn't gibe with what I encountered daily, no matter where I lived. The black LA I grew up in in the seventies was a territory built of dreams and defeats. A work-in-progress that was still being shaped by the unrest of the sixties and the outsized dreams of our forebears. Impatience and disappointment created a generational dissonance that played out differently on this turf—from block to block.

My family was tugged by its own particular countermelody: in the early fifties, my parents, who had yet to cross paths, migrated to Los Angeles from different spots on the map. My father from the east; my mother from the south. Their specific experiences—southern de jure segregation versus northern de facto—provided distinctive prisms for addressing the present and anticipating the future. Their notion of "more" was determined and calibrated by what their access had been.

They both traveled here for "opportunity." I see it in their smiles in the deckle-edged snapshots from that time. That sense of optimism lingers in their expressions in images from later in the decade, by which point they'd learned that that word, which *felt* expansive, took on a different shade of meaning here. In spite of it, within those enclaves, they created communities. They created emotional safety nets. They created big worlds—study groups, community organizing, social clubs, Pokeno nights—in those narrow margins.

If segregation in Los Angeles didn't resemble its counterpart in other cities—restrictive housing covenants, whispered demarcations—so, too, would integration. In the seventies, the same year of that earthquake that rocked me, we moved to a house with a wide view of the city. A cinematic establishing shot on the southeast edge of Culver City. There, I began to get a different lay of the land.

A new neighbor, an archaeologist, with whom my mother had struck up friendly driveway conversations, brought over a fossil in a plastic box as a gift for my brother, who had been showing interest in history and science. She also brought with her stories of cross burnings in the hills just west of where our house stood, and violent incidents marking territory not so long ago. My parents had been tipped off. We'd purchased our home from a Jewish couple, who'd sat with my parents on the half-circle, olive-green sofa negotiating a plan: it was suggested that we keep the sign up on the lawn until we'd moved in, to keep questions to a minimum. They'd had "a time coming in" themselves, they'd confided to my parents. It was familiar territory. This would be the second time in my young lifetime that a household move would involve an intricate plan and a surreptitious arrival.

In the weeks leading up to moving day, I had been consumed with reading and rereading *Mary Jane*, one of those books you'd order at school that would arrive in a stack with a rubber band cinched around it. The novel was about a black girl who was integrating into a white school in some unnamed city. In the cover illustration she had a ponytail like mine, tied tight and high with a red ribbon. I have no memory of the plot turns, just her face and how set apart she appeared on the cover.

I began to obsess quietly about students carving *epithets* on my wooden desk. "Epithets" was one of the words my eye kept landing on in stories I'd been reading about the era, and the Civil Rights Movement in particular. That word sounded more dire than whatever specific invective might be hurled my way. I wanted to know everything that was possible about crossing lines. I viewed my new environment in the context of the not-too-distant past. It was difficult not to. With Boston and its operatic busing crisis erupting on the TV nightly, it still very much seemed to be part of the present. People were holding the line, securing their territory. Not braving, but enacting violence to do so. How could *skin*, and proximity to it, be so terrifying?

Our old block had seemed to me an idyll—aprons of green lawns, bountiful shade, and fruit trees, a row of homes of stucco and red tile—but much later I understood that we were living in the heart of the Rollin' Sixties Crips territory. Gang turf. These streets I knew. They were streets I skated and biked and lingered on past sundown. It seemed beyond imagination that something bad could happen, but that's what folks from out of town always used to say: "Where are the bad parts? Have we gotten to the bad part yet?"

I would repeat, for decades, "Inside, it's different."

In response to the moment, I watched my older male cousins' hair bloom from brushed-back waves into beautifully shaped spheres. Crowns. Six foot four and six foot five, they were royalty of LA High. At home, they were soft-spoken, pulled out chairs, walked on the outside of the sidewalk. Sunday dinners in Chinatown to accommodate family and extended family ringed around an enormous lazy Susan. Outside of their familiar blocks—our territory—they were seen as "radical" or "angry." I wondered at the use of that word: did radical mean that you liked to read, that you looked people in the eye? That you knew your history and spoke your mind, as they did? Context, I would learn, in the seventies, was everything.

In the early seventies I sometimes slept with a transistor radio under my pillow. My mother, a teacher, did so too. I found music, Motown and Stax and Philadelphia International, other-city sounds that opened up vistas. My mother was transfixed by news and talk radio. Headlines and talking points she'd weave into classroom lectures. The destabilizing pitch and roll was happening across the country; it was reimagining the notion and composition of neighborhoods. As with Boston, Los Angeles schools were just beginning a round of mandatory busing, but unlike Boston, it wasn't so much violent as it was dislocating. There was a current of worry. I recently found a diary entry of my mother's from that time: "Went to Area Integration Mtg w/ team. Stopped at Kaiser Emergency. Blood pressure was up 170/108."

In my new neighborhood, first day of school, no one carved any epithets on my desk. I was relieved. But at recess, the neighborhood girls with the butter-colored hair would play "horse." This required that the participants get on all fours in the grassy area and crawl around and neigh. There were four or five other black girls in my class that year. A couple of them crawled around too. I watched for awhile, then drifted away. I couldn't imagine coming home with grass stains on my white knee socks and having to explain why. "You let someone do *what*?" It would be one of the first lines I drew, one border I would not cross.

I longed for the "geometric gym" of our old all-asphalt playground at Forty-Eighth and Wilton, hearing the over-the-fence fender benders, the muffler shop's alley laughter, and windowsill radios tuned to Sly & the Family Stone singing "Everyday People." Some days we'd replay scenes from last night's episode of *Mod Squad*. Heads or tails: who gets to be Linq with the righteous 'fro? I missed the air raid horn from the old neighborhood, even then a relic. The danger it was there to warn us of had evaporated. We were now more concentrated on the danger at home.

From time to time, we'd circle back to the old neighborhood for church. Or when my parents had plans to be out for the evening. They trusted only family or friends of family to watch us. That meant a trip back through those old memorized streets, a recitation of names I'd perform aloud. Our babysitter wore gloves—kid or cotton depending the season—when she got behind the wheel to ferry us, even if it was just to make a quick stop at one of the few markets still left in the neighborhood after the riots of '65. Her house was a neat white-and-yellow bungalow, run through with wall-to-wall shag carpeting that was a shocking shade of Christmas cranberry. Her husband was always dozing, drifting in a big leather La-Z-Boy. A cutout in his slipper revealed an open sore near his heel that never seemed to heal. She cared for him with a warmth and efficiency that propped up his dignity. If she was worried or sad, she didn't reveal it; that pain perhaps located in some zone, blocked off, deep inside her. This was time slowed down, protected. I can still smell the tea cakes baking in the oven and the sweetness of the south that had come here to South Los Angeles. But we didn't call it that then. We just called it "home."

And a tangible sense of home was necessary whenever some destabilizing affront would occur, like the welcome-week salvo I had in our neighborhood park when a little girl I was playing with informed me, without prompting, that she was smarter because she was white and I was not. Or the time my sixth grade teacher in my new school pulled me aside to tell me that she wasn't happy with a poem I'd written because it was "too angry." But she didn't phrase it that way, instead she framed her distaste thusly: "*Dr. King* wouldn't like it," spoken in a tone that should have shamed me for life.

Like our parents, we were creating and charting our own worlds. Hierarchies came with them, too, as it happens. They had to. Rumor was winding around was that one classmate's mother was dating a Temptation. It sounded like a poem to my ear. I knew better. Of course, she was dating a *Temptation*. One of the singers, from one of the many iterations of the group. Sometimes, while waiting for the bus to carry us to school, we could catch a glimpse of him—Afro, flared pants, and platform shoes, standing in front of some shiny sedan in the driveway. It gave an already popular girl teen-magazine status.

In these moments, what I began to translate was that turf and territory weren't simply about race; rather, the place to which one was condemned or elevated was also bound up in status. Again, hierarchies. If you were impatient, you could force a crossing in creative or canny ways. One Monday morning, my best friend arrived at school and announced that she had gone to see *The Exorcist*. Masses, it seemed, crowded around her. Gaining access to anything outside the confines of our neighborhood's closely knit network of Lanes, Courts, Ways, and Terraces registered as seismic. *The Exorcist*'s run at the National theater in Westwood had been an event for weeks. People camped out on sidewalks. Lines looped around the block. Even full-page ads in the newspaper fanned at the phenomenon.

Her parents, like mine, were protective; they tended to keep a short leash. They were religious—Black Southern Baptists—so I couldn't imagine that she'd be greenlighted to see an R-rated movie that essentially handed Satan a starring role. I didn't believe her. It set my stomach in a spin that my best friend had told me something that I knew to be patently untrue. I felt something move inside, sever. I knew she wanted to fit in with the other, older-appearing girls. I knew she wanted to cross over a line and into territory it would take me a decade or more to even understand; a blasé, LA sophistication. Moving outside of those borders lent her gravitas, a worldliness. Now I understood the idea and power of spectacle as only Los Angeles could play it.

Still, I wanted to match her, to claim my own place on her turf, despite its dubious form. I begged, but my mother wouldn't allow it. I sat mesmerized by TV news reports about the pandemonium that now seemed to take place nightly. It was reported with a sensationalism and frequency that suggested a natural disaster. Protesters with placards and rosaries lined Lindbrook Drive. Grown men fainted. Audience members threw up in the aisles. I begged some more, to no avail.

I knew not to push it. My neighbor—part Mexican American, part Black—was in the same boat. Her father had also issued a non-negotiable, "No—you are far from grown." Our borders were firmly in place. We'd groused about it over homework one afternoon with her father in the background. By now he was fed up with the histrionics on the TV screen, the daily reporting stand-ups from in front of the theaters. "Foolishness!" he muttered to his wife. "You see? That's why they didn't want us too close. We'd see a little bit too much." As quickly as his appraisal greeted air, I could see the regret pass over his face. He'd forgotten my presence, an extra set of ears that weren't within the family's. He apologized, then picked up another thread of conversation, as we were all supposed to be integrating nicely without much editorializing from the grown folks. No matter; I knew we were deep into the wilderness by now.

I began junior high school with boys named Keith, Kevin, and Kenyatta. By high school I knew an Aristides, Imtiaz, and Ephrahim. Our campus breezeways buzzed with an intricate lacework of foreign languages, strategically unleashed in the presence of teachers, narcs, or anyone who should be viewed cautiously. It was a moment to test and usurp boundaries, to shift power. My Persian and Arab friends struggled under the weekly headlines of the gas crisis and images of the Ayatollah Khomeini staring back at us all with stormy eyes in dinnertime news clips. Sometime around then, the city's department of transit abruptly halted the bus service that loped up into our neighborhood. The bus driver claimed he was afraid of us. *Us.* It took a contingent of parents doing double shifts of carpool duty and city council meetings to reinstate our branch of service on the line. No, we weren't melting. We were bumping around for some sort of way to be.

Between the end of junior high and the beginning of high school I became obsessed with a boy named Erick. Even if there were seats, he always chose to stand in the middle of the aisle of our morning bus and not hold onto the rail above. Essentially, he would "surf" the curves that the bus took as it wended its way to our school. It took me months, maybe years, to realize that it wasn't a crush I'd had, but rather an obsession, to watch this Mexican American boy—with liquid brown eyes and "Jesus hair," as one of my bus mates put it—defy what box anyone chose to put in him. His OP cords and two-toned, mismatched Vans moved him out of easy categories in which anyone might foolishly try to place him. He seemed to run with no one. No crew, clique, or tribe. He seemed to float above their territories.

As they do, lines that seemed indelible eventually wear, or sometimes even wash away.

We had seasons of rain back then. Flooding. In 1977 we watched the La Ballona Creek rise higher and higher. There was a line painted on a paved creek wall. Campus lore had it that both the junior and senior school campuses would be dismissed if the water crawled above it. One magical morning it did. Teachers rushed us home under a bruised sky. I couldn't remember being set free to explore. Ad hoc carpools were set up to ferry those of us home who had working parents. I got into a car of an upperclassman neighbor, a Japanese American boy who was remote, but not unfriendly. I'd seen him daily, but we'd never exchanged more than a couple of sentences. Maybe his silence was simply about brokering distance, creating a space for reinvention. Was he embarrassed of those streets of which I was so proud? I wouldn't ever come to know. That day, instead of taking the most direct route, he chose a longer way home—Sepulveda to Slauson, looping back to La Cienega, then Stocker, which edged past the old oil wells. We rode in silence in the rain for some time, emboldened by this freedom time that could be left unaccounted to roam.

I knew by now I needed to draw maps of my own. During summer school, I enrolled in driver's training. The car to which we were assigned always faintly smelled of weed. My driver's training teacher wore his blue-black hair hanging free, falling just past the collar of his bright blue windbreaker. He was easy to talk to in a way that was comforting and yet not over-the-line creepy. I shared the car with two boys, Jeff and Rob. Surfers. Not part of a tribe, just devout "water babies." The four of us would slide into our seats early in the morning, heading south along the S-curves of Sepulveda Boulevard. Some mornings the socked-in fog added extra intrigue to our journey. Our instructor always referred to the sleepy suburb of El Segundo—where we did most of our street driving—as El Stinko because of all the industry chugging away nearby. I never went to El Segundo with my family; someone told me years later that they thought it was a sundown town, a segregated city where people of color were aggressively—often violently—kept out of their boundaries, especially after sunset. I'd never heard that confirmed. But Culver City was indeed one.

I wish I could better remember the constellation of protected places. The rise of wall on the junior high school quad. The area off to the side of the portable classrooms near the playing fields. There was a nook, somewhere in front of the high school, where one of the car clubs (Cuban?) would collect before school. That spot where the surfers would congregate after the beach, just as first period was ending. Constant assessing: "Which lunch table could you sit at?" "Which one should you avoid at all costs?" All of it vague or gone now. But all of this was so essential to know, to commit to memory. It took up so much brain space. The whole campus was marked with invisible designations, places you were not to cross, pause, sit, or stand for fear of repercussion. Long after the bus driver expressed his fears, the Crips made their way to campus, too. Boys stepped on the bus in puffy blue jackets with orange lining. The last row of seats was left open expressly for them. By then, most times, we had a black driver.

Some weekends, the grown-ups' conversation around the garage bar at my new junior high school friend's home tended toward bawdy. The jokes snaked with innuendo as the adults leaned over card games of risk. Her father's friends were studio craft guys—carpenters, gaffers, prop men and women, etc. All white. Most were polite, some even friendly, but there was always one. Just one. He'd sidle up and let it drop: "There was a club on Jefferson, in Culver City, called the Plantation." Not quite a statement, not quite an open question either. "Your family? Where'd they come from, Watts?" Hostile? Certainly. I knew to look him in the eye, as if to say "I *see* you. I do." Such focused resentment in his prodding. Though he never arrived to the point, I knew precisely where he was headed. He was put off by having to share personal, sacred space…with *me*. Finally, I explained to my new friend that I would no longer be stopping by if he was ever part of the mix. She never told me if she'd mentioned my line in the sand to her parents, but shortly thereafter, Rob vanished.

I'd won.

But what, exactly?

I put my hands in masa for the very first time during a Christmas season in the late seventies. I listened to instruction about how much to spoon onto the cornhusk and how to arrange the delicate package in the pot for steaming so as not to harm it. My friend Rita's grandmother was leading us through this journey, but she was speaking carefully, dotingly, in Spanish. Later, I understood that I had begun to comprehend more than I realized, the result of proximity and will. This is how so much came to us if we allowed it to happen, were open to it. While we marked our turf in language, in clothing, through slang, we moved in and out of circles, taking pieces of the old with us, making something new. I used to think we found common ground, but no, better; we made common ground when need be.

By seventeen, I'd failed my driving test twice. News I shared with no one. In Los Angeles, this ignominy was almost worse than being held back a grade. So as not to feel so marooned heading into my senior year, I bussed it or caged rides from friends in their Pintos, Corollas, and Fairlanes. It was 1979. College lurked, and I was still eleventh-hour practicing; my father's urgent directives to "cover the brake!" ratcheting up my nerves. Third time was a miracle. And though I'd botched the three-point turn, the test administrator showed mercy. Maybe had once been me. Perhaps knew what it was like to be just so close to being independent, to moving into and defining your own space.

Back then, after nightfall in some parts of the city, the air was redolent of the ocean—sharp, brackish, and vivid—even if you were miles away. That scent traveled like radio signals did at night—beyond specific borders. I always took that phenomenon to mean that all of

Los Angeles was ours if we could reach it, unlock it. That evening
of my triumph, the first place I drove to on my own was the ocean.
Out to the very edges of discernible land. This strip of unremarkable
beach had no associations, no history for me. It wasn't a touchstone.
And that, I learned, was immeasurably powerful. It was the first pin
on a new map.

It's dangerous to deal in nostalgia. Especially here. Change is rapid
and it's seldom kind. Though I know this, sometimes the awareness
alone doesn't keep me from trespassing territories of time. This all
sailed back recently when road work forced me off the freeway three
exits too soon, and the GPS attempted to correct the error and push
me back on course, its testy voice hectoring: "Resume route." I want to
tell it, as I always do, "Excuse me, but I think I know my way around
this territory by now."

Because I had some time to spare, I made a detour to the detour.
Pulled by some old strain of wistfulness, I wanted to loop, if briefly,
through those old memorized streets—the places hard won, the places
we'd always called home. I parked and, moments out of the car, found
myself at a dead stop in front of a house. An old neighbor's stately
California craftsman, now painted charcoal gray with a chartreuse
door, the planks of its privacy fence turned horizontal. History turned
on its head.

My thoughts came fast, but were tripped up by movement in a
neighboring yard. I saw just the top of a man's watch cap and a plaid
shirt. I heard the blade of a tool he was using to chop away at a tangle
of morning glories. A gardener? My eye moved back to the cartoon
house across the away. So sad. Who would do this? Why?

Before I spun too far into my questions, my protestations were
interrupted by a sneeze. "Bless you," I said reflexively, turning into the
sound. The man in the watch cap looked up. No. Not the gardener:
he was my age, graying around the temples, his eyes the same blue
as my driver's ed teacher's windbreaker. It wasn't a plaid shirt he was
wearing, but a bathrobe, hastily tied, his coffee cup balanced on a
weathered fence post. He was not on the job. He was home.

"I'm sorry," he said gently. "Did I startle you?"

"No," I responded. Quickly. The crispness in my voice surprised me.

But really, was that true?

He *had* startled me. But not for the reasons for which he was apologizing.

What did it mean for me to feel startled, to be so tangled in the push/pull of emotions that it was simpler, but certainly not easier, to lie?

I lingered on the sidewalk for an extended moment, not just without words, but disoriented. Uncertain.

An old sensation passed through me, a feeling linked to childhood: my body being pulled and released by the ocean, and how the echo of that sensation would linger for hours, well into the evening, even as I was settling down to sleep. The pull and release of something far bigger than me was what was pushing through me.

This acquiring and ceding territory, it's the same to be caught up in motion that never ceases—a tide that drags in, drags out. Lines etched and erased with time. It keeps you uncertain. It whispers: *for now, not for always.*

From where I stand this spring morning, this place—the territory that has most felt like home—is still not so fully transformed that I can't feel its old rhythms, breathe in its familiar scents. But how much longer can I call it mine? Maybe it never really was. Like Erick on the bus, maybe I've always floated over it. Ridden its curves.

Place is tangible—navigable, yes—but place is also time. Moments, collected and protected: that late-night radio transmission, that air raid horn, that blue bottle garden, the fierceness of a hug— that's part of me. All those points leading from here to there. It's deep inside. And that's the territory that most matters. That's the territory that can't be mapped, breached, renamed—or erased.

Lynell George *is an LA-based journalist and essayist who covers the arts, culture, and social issues. She's a former staff writer for the* Los Angeles Times *and* LA Weekly *and a current columnist for KCET's* Artbound. *She is also the author of* No Crystal Stair: African Americans in the City of Angels. *She is a native of Los Angeles.*

BORROWING SUGAR

by Susan Hayden

I used to borrow sugar,
or try to.
Not from just anyone;
from "entertainers"
in the neighborhood.
They lived
in sprawling, ranch-style homes
with aerial views,
front yard aquariums
and life-sized statues.
Leon Russell, on Woodley
The Jackson Five, on Hayvenhurst
Tom Petty, on Mooncrest.
Affluence and intimacy—
a false sense of security:
That was the real Encino.

Never had a strategy,
only an impulse.
I wasn't even developed.
Was nine/ten/eleven—
playing house with
a Betsey Clark folding scene

and Hallmark reusable stickers,
the inspirational kind
that said things like:
"Every Day is a Gift From God,"
"Showered with Blessings,"
and "I Believe in Miracles."

I was an anomaly
in the West Valley.
A trickster
with a two-spirit nature,
a Technics turntable
and a Barbie suitcase,
jam-packed
with personal belongings—
a sheltered freewheeler,
seeking access
and the thrill of the hunt.
And I was a bolter,
always running away,
just for a little while.

Mostly I was
a New Romantic,
the sameness of my fate
as yet to be determined.
Love was someone else's story
carved in a spiral groove
on a vinyl platter,
and so I borrowed sugar
or tried to
but instead
dogs barked, alarms rang out
and I was escorted off Private Property,
released back into
"The Ranch of the Evergreens"

—Los Encinos—
encircled by the Transverse Ranges,
surrounded by the nouveau riche.

For months, years,
my measuring cup stayed empty;
roaming the streets of the 91316
where *It's a Wonderful Life*
was shot
long before anyone was ever
borrowing sugar.
South of Ventura,
Liberace had a piano-shaped pool.
Let me swim in it once.
Called me "Sweetie."
North of Valley Vista,
the gulleys and ditches
connecting flatland to hillside
were hideouts,
wishing wells of early faith—

Faith in the power of Everything
canceled out by a voice saying,
"You're nothing."
Words of my brother,
brazenly dealing weed and coke
from his bedroom window,
dispensing insult and harm
to the one most in need
of protection.
He tried to teach me
that Goodness was impermanent,
on loan
but I had my stickers to remind me
of another way of thinking;
I had love songs in my head

that gave fair warning
but made Big promises.
When the lunatic moon
touched my brother,
converting him from a tender boy
into the Opposite of Sugar,
it was songs and sweets
that pulled me across.

When not borrowing,
I was busy eating:
Hostess cupcakes, fruit pies,
Sno Balls, Twinkies,
Zingers, Donettes.
I was addicted to sugar.
It made me bold and shy.
Empowered me.
Sedated me.
Borrowing sugar equaled escape
from an unsafe home.
Fleeing risk by risking
was better than staying put.

The in-crowd lived elsewhere,
that much was clear.
Over-the-Hill,
in woodsy canyons
with more shade and less heat.
Jackson Browne was on Outpost Drive;
Joni Mitchell, on Appian Way.
I wanted to be free and in the clouds
but was relegated to Royal Oaks
with its lion's head door knockers
and central air conditioning
and I learned how to work my way in
by saying things like:

"Lend me some sugar,
I am your neighbor."

It was my only way around
a set of circumstances:
In search of the sweetness
from someone else's life
whose whereabouts were hidden
but known to me.
That's how it started,
this borrowing sugar.
That's how it started,
this running away.

Susan Hayden *is a fiction writer and poet. Her essay "The Soul Section" was published in the critically acclaimed anthology* The Black Body *(Seven Stories Press, edited by Meri Danquah.) Her short story "You Are What You Drive" was published in* Storie: All Write, *an Italian/ American literary journal based in Rome. She is the author of a novel set in the San Fernando Valley in the 1970s. Her poetry has appeared in numerous publications, including* Areté, Hollywood Review, Venice Magazine, *and* Atlanta Journal, *and can be heard on two spoken word CDs,* Innings & Quarters *and* DisClosure: Voices of Women. *She is the cofounder of LA's first performance fiction series,* Gas/Food/Lodging, *where writers, actors, and directors would come together to dramatize short stories. Most recently, she is the creator/producer of* Library Girl, *a monthly literary series at the Ruskin Theatre in Santa Monica.*

IT WAS FUN WHILE IT LASTED: SCIENTOLOGY, est, HIGH TIMES, AND HIGHER LEARNING AT UNI HIGH

by David Kukoff

CALDWELL WILLIAMS (FOUNDER): I was a teacher at Uni High, and had worked with Senator Alan Cranston on a plan to open an alternative school in South Central. The plan didn't go through, but it got me thinking in other terms, closer to home.

In the spring of 1970, there was a teachers' strike. During the strike, a woman named Naomi Childs hosted a meeting and wanted to know which faculty they should invite to discuss doing something innovative at University High. I walked in and saw an articulate, highly educated group of parents with high intentions.

Kato Pomer was at the parents' meeting. She'd been a proponent of an innovative school in Philadelphia. I saw the potential for a school within a school.

Fred Holtby (rhetoric teacher/codirector): To my knowledge, we were the first public school, maybe the first school period, to have a school-within-a-school. It got started with one parent who had a daughter who was unhappy.

Karen Pomer (filmmaker): My mother was involved in the founding of IPS. I had visited the Philadelphia Parkway School, which had a no-wall policy and was extremely racially integrated. *TIME* magazine called it the most innovative school in the US. I think their policy was that fifty percent of the student body had to be African-American.

CW: I only knew Fred Holtby by reputation, until that meeting. Upon hearing what people were talking about, he practically jumped out of his seat and called me into the kitchen. He proposed that he and I be the nucleus of the team, and I agreed. I went back into the room where the parents were meeting and told them that we had a plan. The parents cheered.

KP: I was very excited at what they were offering, and talked about it with my mother, who was a child psychiatrist and had, along with a few other parents, been exploring the idea of an alternative school on the Uni High campus. At the same time, Caldwell Williams and a few other teachers had gotten involved. I'm not sure which came first, or how it all came together, but that was more or less the beginning of IPS.

CW: We were ready to march on the principal of Uni High, Warren Juhnke, and make demands. I called Warren and told him we'd have a proposal tomorrow.

There had been a number of headlines about affluent, Westside kids involved in drugs. People were freaking out about it, and I had a program (DAWN, Developing Adolescents Without Narcotics, a nighttime counseling group founded by Williams) that dealt with it.

There were people in that room who wrote checks to the Board of Ed. So when my people called over there, the Board told the Superintendent to let me do my thing at Uni. And when we showed up in Warren's office as planned, Warren preempted everyone and said that he was ready to go.

Stephan Michaels (music supervisor, writer): I think the music scene in LA greatly contributed to the city's free spirited vibe and social mores. Weed, acid, cocaine, and quaaludes were prevalent everywhere you turned, public beaches were allowing nudity, and even our parents were wearing bell-bottoms and torn Levi's and mimicking hip lingo. IPS mirrored that mind-expanding cultural hipness, and could probably have only thrived for as long as it did in the liberal clime of West LA circa 1970s.

CW: Two weeks before school started, there was a mailing to all the Uni High students that there would be a possibility of an innovative program. Eleven hundred out of three thousand total families showed up. On the spot, the administration put the students' names on slips of paper and drew them. The district gave me permission for one hundred and fifty.

KP: I put my name in randomly, just like everyone else. And I was the first person drawn! Since everyone knew my mom had been involved, I could imagine people thinking, "Oh great—the fix is in!"

Elizabeth Warner (talent booker): There was a random lottery that took place a few months before the school year. My name was picked. I really had no idea what I was getting into except that IPS was a "free" school where you didn't have to do any homework, or go to class. My mom really had no idea what IPS was, either.

Robert A. B. Sawyer (poet and former adman): I believe my brother Charles may have attended. In any event, I was bored and underachieving in "regular" school and was looking for something less "ordinary." I suspect it was a case of the grass was greener.

Glenn T. Morgan (sound editor): IPS was known for being a dumping ground for a lot of neglected children. High-end families. There were a lot of affluent people going through there, plus parents who wanted to be part of the trend but didn't want to be involved.

CW: We had a mix of bored, brilliant kids and stone-cold stoners.

Paul Roessler (musician, music producer): The image of the IPS students to the rest of the school was that we were weirdos and drug addicts, and they were intimidated by us. A lot of their judgements sprang not from the whole, but from the few loudest outliers.

Pat Smear (musician): The IPS kids were misfits, but they weren't stupid misfits like the people in continuation school. Everyone was really smart and savvy; they were usually in IPS for disciplinary reasons, or that they were too bright for the regular classes. A school like that would never be allowed to exist now.

Michael Apstein (entrepreneur): I had done my freshman and sophomore years at Beverly Hills High School, and I was skipping school, failing classes. I was a hot mess. My mother, who was a psychologist, knew another psychologist—an IPS school parent—who suggested it. I'd grown up in Beverly Hills, and when I heard that IPS was in a public school located by Barrington and Wilshire, I thought it was the barrio. That's how sheltered I was.

Laurie Marks Wagner (writer, writing instructor): I had been a student at Crossroads, a private school in Santa Monica, and a friend told me about IPS—how kids were free to do what they wanted, and I guess that appealed to me at the time. Not my mother though, who said, "Over my dead body you'll go." I must have worn her down; I went.

Phillip Van Allen (professor, artist): Overall, IPS kind of saved me. I was disillusioned with school at the time, and even though I could be a good student, I was not getting great grades and was totally bored. That, plus my father had moved to England and then died while I was in junior high. I wasn't really conscious of being down, but looking at the pictures of me in the first year of IPS I clearly was.

SM: I was in the regular school at University High for the tenth and eleventh grades. Played on the JV baseball team and was a rock drummer. Was a fairly disinterested student and didn't know where or even if I'd go to college. Felt pretty sure that music would be my career.

Most of my friends were in this "school within a school" called IPS, the Innovative Program School. It was more free-structured than the traditional school, and the curriculum was anything but traditional. On the surface it seemed like the high school equivalent to UCLA's University Elementary School (UES)—a celebrated laboratory for research and innovation in education. Some of my friends who had attended UES were now in IPS. But I think that in order to get into UES, kids had to be gifted or possess fairly high IQs. No such prerequisite at IPS.

RABS: IPS offered a carnival mirror of the lifestyle of a certain class of people living in West LA. Men and women who wanted to live without restraints or discipline. These people wanted to be safe to experiment with drugs, with sex, with danger. Men who wanted to take off their ties. Women who wanted their orgasms. They thought IPS would prepare their children for the world they would create.

Joel Drucker (author, journalist): Let's begin by acknowledging that adolescence is a time of tremendous self-absorption, of all sorts of tumult—emotional, physical, intellectual. All concur on that. The conventional approach has been to take you away from that, to get you out of yourself by exposure to math, science, literature, history, and other topics.

IPS went in the opposite direction. You want to understand yourself? You want to understand yourself? Well, here you are. Have at it.

CW: Westside kids not only didn't know what they were interested in, they didn't know who they were. They'd say what they were interested in, and we'd let them explore that.

PVA: This was a group of kids who, on the one hand, were just your average high school kids. But at the same time, we were in the intellectual and entertainment locus of Los Angeles. Our parents were mostly professionals, liberal, often divorced, and completely out of their element in terms of raising kids. So it was possible for all kinds of shit to be going on, and our parents either didn't know about it, or chose to look the other way. And on the whole, this wasn't really a bad thing.

RABS: IPS placed a special emphasis on critical thinking. In particular, it encouraged a range of reaction to the "system"—from a healthy skepticism to repudiation. IPS expected a lot from its students, in particular, that they be willing to reject received wisdom, and hierarchical structures.

We were taught as a whole—the lack of physical structures, i.e., desks, encouraged a genuine mingling. What's more, the Socratic manner of instruction practiced by Caldwell and Fred made clear there were no geniuses and no dunces among us.

PR: Fred Holtby's post-modernist critical theory background, combined with the thread of openness to eastern philosophy gave the school an almost mystical feel. For me, this gave it a very energized "wide-awake" atmosphere. There was a feeling that we were all participating in something important, even revolutionary. As a young person, this was a sort of continuation of the social exploration embodied by The Beatles and other musical groups of that time; the anything-is-possible side of the sixties filtering out into the educational system.

Sharon Weil (author): We were trying to delve into what was good for education, and what education was good for. We were turning things inside out, upside down. IPS was the first school within a school, as well as the first alternative school. Nowadays, you have magnets, etc., but that didn't exist back then.

They would remind us that the teacher was working for us. You had to come to the teacher and discuss your interests, and their job was to show you how their discipline worked with those interests. Say I'm a surfer and the teacher is going to teach me about wave motion. Or I'm interested in music and the teacher would put me on a path to learn about American folk music.

SM: The first incarnation of IPS embraced the notions that personal growth and academic achievement were integral, that students should be actively involved in shaping their education and that mistakes were to be valued as a source of learning. But by the time I got there, something new was happening.

CW: In our second year, we looked at classes as frames of reference. We viewed the world through the frame, but they still correlated to the basic subjects. The premise to the student was, find yourself. Find your frame.

Once a week was frame day. In addition to how you handled your subject matter, once per week was a day that everyone was focused on a single frame. Guest presenter, or all of us together interacting, or the students in our frame sat around us while we pestered the presenter with questions or comments, or we could have a field trip.

RABS: I mainly remember long conversations, loosely following the Socratic tradition of inquiry. I remember a lot of play and an impression I hold to this day that every woman had a little drawing book and a fistful of Rapidographs.

SM: Each instructor had their own individual gifts at getting us to examine our thinking and our prejudices. Don was great at prodding us to question our assumptions. You would say something about a subject, and he'd ask you to look at the exact words or concept you had just uttered, to examine the entire notion behind what you had said and see how it influenced your understanding of the subject. One of my favorite classes with Don was Taoism. We would each read aloud from the *Tao Te Ching* by Lao Tzu, and then collectively examine and interpret its possible meanings.

SW: Don Chronister was a real socialist. Radical politics were accepted in the classroom, and we were encouraged to question them. Why do you think what you think?

PR: There was a frame taught by each teacher and it would last several hours. You would focus on one subject at a time for several months. If you took Caldwell's frame, the focus would be relationships: Fred's was English; Don and Bill, social studies; Patty, art; Jerry, math. Some of the classes were taught with the kids sitting in circles on beanbag chairs.

PVA: IPS gave me the space to explore and do what I was interested in. That meant doing advanced math with Jerry, a brilliant but insane grad student from UCLA, science with Mike, reading hard books with Fred, debating politics with Don, and reading Robert Burns and talking philosophy of life with Seymore. Academically, it was very idiosyncratic, and I missed huge chunks of the normal curriculum. But clichéd as it may sound, I learned to think and learn in a very real way.

SW: By the third year, things had changed so much that the tenth graders weren't getting the basics. When I was there, it was elevated, and most of the kids there were working at a very high level. But if you weren't self-motivated, you could drift off and not be heard from.

LMW: If you left IPS and you had a pretty good sense for how to read and write you could get through college. Still, I didn't read the classics and I lacked some writing skills some of the regular school kids probably got, but academics weren't on our mind.

MA: I was lucky that I'd had a strong basic education at Beverly High, but I got little to no high school education at IPS. I already had the ability to research, write a paper, understand grammar. I knew enough to transition to college. But a lot of people who didn't have the basic ed I had came out of IPS, had a hard time because they could not write a paper. The education side was really bad there.

RABS: I played more than I studied—I stopped studying German. I stopped studying math. I can't remember a single book I read.

EW: We were responsible for our own education, getting to class and learning. There were no rules. There were lectures by the teacher, but you could walk in and out whenever you wanted to. We called our teachers by their first names. No one took attendance. There were no rules, no homework. We did not have to read any books. I don't think I read a book the whole year, except for books that I was interested in. We gave ourselves our own grades, which was on the "honor" system. I think I gave myself As and Bs at random.

LMW: I remember going up to Bill, one of our teachers, and him saying,
"So Laurie, what do you think you deserve in history this term?"
"An A?" I answered. "How about a B," he said. "I've given out too many As today."

PR: I took Jerry's calculus class, which left me with a very tenuous grasp of calculus but which fulfilled my college requirements for math and allowed me to focus on music when I got to CSUN. I'm not sure

I would have acquired any better understanding of it had I taken it in regular school anyway.

GTM: You were "shared" information. Not "taught." How you chose to use it was your business.

PVA: Mike, the awkward, geeky science teacher, arranged for a bunch of us to go out on the "Vantuna" science vessel that was used to study oceanography. The ship went out to the open ocean, and we participated in all kinds of experiments over the day-long trip. We dropped containers to capture water from various depths, trawled for fish, etc. Inside the cabin there were microscopes and other gear for analyzing the "catch." I think I got sick at one point, but it was still a great day.

SW: My mom taught a cooking class at the house. There was this idea of using the resources in the community. You were asked to identify an interest, and pursue it, and let the teachers bring their disciplines into your interest. Andy Lipkis started a project at IPS where he planted trees on the hillside. He just kept at it until it evolved into Tree People.

CW: The move at your own pace thing caught on. Those throwaway kids did work at their own pace, and in the half-year they had left, they passed enough to be certified as mastery. We agreed that mastery was a criterion, so that warranted an A. Fill out your report card, have your teacher sign it, and return it. Doing their own grades based on their mastery.

That set off a hellfire of reaction in the system. The district controls when report cards go out, but some kids were getting their report cards six weeks after the course began. I would postulate that some got it and some didn't. Some no doubt saw it as an opportunity to slip by. But that's life.

EW: I would get to school at around 9:00 a.m. I would walk into a classroom and kids would be milling around. I guess there would be a class that would start, but I don't remember ever sitting through a whole class. There was not a lot of structure. As a fifteen-year-old, for me, I think some structure would have been a good idea.

LMW: Every morning we started out on some empty basketball court doing tai chi for an hour. The regular school kids were in their first periods, sometimes even watching us from the windows of their classrooms. And there we were—150 of us all lined up doing tai chi.

Michael Bright (Retired Navy Chief Petty Officer): It was called "Body-Mind." We met in the morning and took attendance as we arrived and when we formed up in a big group we got real quiet and began moving to connect our intention on focusing our minds and bodies.

Frame was at the end of the day when everyone would get together in one classroom and we began to open up and share. We could say anything on our minds. After one person shared a thought or feeling, that person would be acknowledged by a rousing round of hand-clapping. It was incredible to feel so valued by friends and the staff. Upon my senior year we were relegated to snapping our fingers as clapping was too loud for the regular school kids to hear it from our distant bungalows.

PR: There would be announcements from staff, and, as I recall it, sometimes, certain thought exercises, exploring the philosophical side of things.

LMW: The group huddled on the floor of a school room, raising our hands to speak and sharing about how we were doing for an hour. We were encouraged to share deeply and some kids did. Some kids had some serious issues too. There were gay kids, depressed kids, rich kids, poor kids.

The level that we shared at—you would never, ever see that now in school. Kids weren't sharing that they were super happy because they got a new car. They shared about feeling lonely or abandoned by their friends, or fighting with their parents or how maybe they'd hurt themselves.

SM: There was lots of hugging and emotional reinforcement. Caldwell once demonstrated the difference between the guarded, protective hug that he dubbed the "A-Frame" where two people met at the shoulders with lots of back patting. He contrasted that with the real hug he called "The Surrender." We were directed to go around the room, warmly embracing each other until we'd hugged everyone. Depending on whether I cared for the person that I was all but obligated to hug, it could be a little awkward.

JD: One Caldwell-created process: you'd stand in front of three to four students and utter these words: "I will make my life work. I am a totally able person. My friends, family, and countless others out there all love me, and want to fully participate in my life. And all I have to do, is nothing." But did the students feel and believe the sincerity of your conviction? Any of them could say, "I don't get it," in which case you would repeat. Thinking back, it was very Hollywood: selling the line.

MB: We were allowed to express our feelings in every class, every group gathering, and express ourselves we did! Clothing, ideas, dreams, ambitions, love, sex, desires, drugs, etc…after all it was the seventies. We were uninhibited in our expressions of politics, parents, and teachers.

RABS: In regular school pain was simply not discussed, it was a private matter and irrelevant to one's academic performance. At IPS pain was public, out in the air. We were exposed. Naked. Of course, some handled this better than others.

LMW: At the end of the week on Fridays, we'd have a final Friday share and then we were to go up to three people who we had "withholds" with—something we wanted to tell them that we hadn't. Sometimes that meant you liked someone and you wanted them to know. Maybe a boy. Or maybe something had happened that had hurt you and this was a chance to tell that person.

I remember it always being very intense and loaded. People might come up and tell you that they judged you for something—the way you dressed, your body. And when someone told you something you just took it in and said "thank you." So people took a lot of risks in communication—they were very up front.

FH: The one thing we all agreed on was that we didn't want a completely free-form school, although we certainly wanted a lot of input from the students.

SM: I gravitated to the rhetoric frame where Fred approached the idea that our assumptions influence our perceptions by saying, "believing is seeing." Fred often referred to East Coast philosopher and rhetorician Kenneth Burke, a poster of whom was on his classroom wall. Fred was clearly a devotee of the man he called "KB" and we read from his books *The Philosophy of Literary Form* and *Language as Symbolic Action*. We were being exposed to collegiate-level material, and we were up to it. Fred would also read eloquently to us from Hemingway to Thurber to Salinger, prompting us to think about subtext, symbolism, and meaning.

SW: After a while, we didn't write English papers, we wrote letters to Fred. He was really into Kenneth Burke. So you'd be using Kenneth Burke's critique style but as a letter. He would respond to your comment with "wow" and "whoa" not necessarily the in-depth analytic response that another teacher would give you. We didn't learn classic composition, but we were very schooled in analysis. And that was true in history as well.

PR: As I recall, I was pretty fascinated by Fred and took his electives mostly. I took his Taroom-Lit, where I remember we deconstructed the Bible and Salinger. Also his music appreciation class, where I remember listening to Stravinsky's "Firebird Suite." The "ah ha!" moment was Fred making us listen closer and closer till we suddenly noticed that we could hear the musicians shuffling and breathing a little, as well as the bowing of the strings; tiny sounds that weren't really part of the composition but were part of the actual acoustic experience.

PVA: One of the most fun things was a listening session class we invented with Fred. We'd bring in albums to play on his very high quality stereo that he had locked up in a cabinet in his classroom. A few of got really into progressive jazz like John McLaughlin's Mahavishnu Orchestra, Chick Corea, and even Frank Zappa's jazzy period. We went to see these and other bands locally. It was exciting.

GTM: Fred wore glasses and decided to train his mind and his eyes not to need them anymore. He went through a period where he didn't wear them. Did he really not need glasses from that point on? Who knows.

PR: One day, Fred had a stack of Bibles, and he was throwing them to the kids in the class. He'd throw one to a guy and say, "Here, Cock!" Then he'd throw one to a girl and say, "Here, Cunt!" Here was this freaky old guy with gold hair, throwing Bibles, going, "Here, Cock! Here Cunt!" I just thought, *Cool!*

MA: The training routines in Fred's class were, I'm pretty sure, taken directly from Scientology. I actually think Zero through Four were incredibly valuable (I did Five through Eight, and that got weirder). Four was known as Bull Baiting. One person would try to stay present with your words and not be sucked in by whatever outrageous behavior was going on outside the words. No reaction, just be present.

One time, I sat there with a jock, a big guy who I think had come over from regular Uni, and started doing this routine which was designed to make him laugh. I kept trying different things until finally I stood up in front of him, grabbed my crotch and yelled "suck my dick!" and kicked his chair. And he just lost it—cracked up, probably more out of embarrassment than anything. It attracted the whole room's attention, so Fred came over and watched, and just sat there, laughing. So that was a pretty strange thing to have happen in high school.

SM: Fred offered that our experiences and memories were stored like stacks of dishes in a greasy spoon restaurant. Apparently, we were all going through life, perceiving and responding to the present based on decisions we'd made from past experiences. Fred sometimes used the term "ulcerating beliefs." We were encouraged to reexamine unresolved experiences and decisions buried in our "stacks," so that we could be free of the emotional charge they had on us and make our lives work.

Karen Hampton (artist): Fred had a saying on his wall that said "think for yourself; your teacher could be wrong."

***

From a *Red Tide* article, entitled "IPS Reality is not Reality:"

> I was in an IPS class a few weeks ago to bring up the idea of IPS people going down to picket Nixon Headquarters to

protest the escalation of the war in Indo-China. Since almost all IPS people say that they are against the war and because we don't have to worry about ditching, I thought that the response to my suggestion would be greeted warmly...

I explained how a paraplegic (paralyzed from the chest down) Vietnam vet named Ron Kovic had been thrown out of his wheelchair and beaten by police for no apparent reason... However, when I asked for a reaction from people, all I got was "how do we know that this really happened?" and "how do we know that this is reality anyway?"

PVA: Throw all these kids together, and mix in the long history of cults and religion in LA, and you get IPS. A rebellious place of privilege and contrast, on a continuous quest to figure itself out. A place where the *Red Tide* radical newspaper was supported and normal.

SW: The *Red Tide* was started while I was there. We used to joke because whether it came out of Mark Harris' mouth or if it was in the paper, "fuck that shit" seemed to be a common refrain

KP: *Red Tide*, the newspaper, started in November 1971. A lot of IPS students worked on it. Then it moved up to Northern California and became a regional newspaper, before ultimately going on to Detroit. It lasted ten years, which was longer than IPS itself lasted. It had a precedent-setting case about student newspapers and censorship.

JD: IPS mirrored the shifts in American society. Its first three to four years had more of an external focus on such clearly news-oriented, civic events like the Manson trial, Watergate, and left-wing politics. Consider the avatar of that first phase to be the politicized Jane Fonda.

KH: The *Red Tide* brought Jane Fonda to campus, produced women's week on Uni's campus, sued the school board (and won in the State Supreme Court) on free speech, and led walkouts on campus.

RABS: What made the strongest impression on me regarding IPS' pedagogic philosophy was its compelling Question Authority doctrine. I can discuss this in greater detail by telling the story of Jane Fonda's visit and a visit from a local branch of the American Nazi Party.

IPS had a sizable and active anti-war constituency. Fonda's presence was more significant than anything she actually said. There was a serious uproar from parents and the community, veteran groups, when they learned "Hanoi Jane" had come. She was not necessarily revered by the IPS community, but her visit, as Fred or Caldwell might say, mattered as an exercise in free speech.

Of the two, the Nazis left a much greater impression on me. First, because they were obviously so sad: working class men, dressed in improvised uniforms, gray pants and shirts, which I thought were bought at Sears. Second, because individually and collectively they lacked charisma, good looks, or charm.

I don't remember anything in particular that they advocated—the rot Jewish conspiracy line, the necessity of white people to stand together to protect themselves, the need to honor and respect one another, etc. They were heckled by students and outside the gates parents and members of the community tried to shout them down. They spoke in a classroom, four or five men, cropped heads or cheap haircuts, uncomfortable while trying to assert discipline and authority.

After they left, Fred held a lecture. What I remember to this day was that he drew a vertical line. He then created a list of attributes. On one side of the line he wrote: "wants community," "wants justice," "wants freedom of speech," and the list of admirable attributes went on. On the other side of the line he wrote: "intolerant," "bigoted," "rude," "dismissive," and the list went on. Then, after soliciting our thoughts, and when the list filled the blackboard, Fred, with a flourish, wrote Nazis over the positive attributes and IPS over the negative.

LMW: Our guest speakers, the people who they brought in to talk to us, were people like Sly Stone. Or maybe it was Sly Stone's producer, but still it was all about being who you were.

EW: The actor that played Billy Jack came to visit us one day and did a talk, and that made a big impression on me. Here was a big movie star coming to visit us at IPS.

JD: In the fall of 1976, LA school board member Kathleen Brown—sister of one governor, daughter of another—visited IPS. Since I eventually wanted to be in politics, I made it a point to spend a lot of time with her that day. She loved IPS. And so I wondered: when would Jerry visit and bestow his blessing?

PVA: In spring of '74, a few of us decided to go streaking through the campus. It was happening around the country, and we just thought it would be a kind of outrageous thing to do. So we got some big masks to hide our identities and stripped in the bathrooms that were in the bungalow area where IPS was centered (next to Barrington). We took off running down to the main girls field across campus.

When we got there, it turned out the school was taking the Senior Class picture (of about a thousand people). The students let out a huge cheer for us as we ran across the field in front of them. It was a complete rush, and it looked like we completely disrupted the photo shoot.

The only problem was, we hadn't quite planned the return trip. We got to the other side of the field and hid behind the band room and caught our breath (this was famously the location where everyone smoked pot). Realizing there was nothing else to do, we ran back the way we came to much less fanfare. We went across the field and back up the hill to the IPS area where our friends were keeping an eye on our clothes. It was fun, and there were no consequences.

LMW: In the Death Game you would lie on the floor and kids would surround you—teachers too—and tell you things they never told you while you were alive. You'd lie there with your eyes closed listening to kids tell you all sorts of things; how much they really liked you but were intimidated by you, or maybe they always felt guilty about something a friend of theirs had done to you. And you'd just lie there listening.

In Deep Dark Secrets, kids had to get stuff off their chest. Masturbation, stealing, drugs, suicide, lying. It was endlessly fascinating and very real. It was a chance to find out who you were in this circle of people. A chance to understand who you were in the scheme of things, and maybe feel less alone because you weren't the only one having trouble.

We also used to have these group picnics where there were only two rules. The first one was, you couldn't talk. The second was, you couldn't feed yourself.

CW: My students wanted to see *Deep Throat*. I told them to ask their parents, and if they supported seeing it, I'd allow it. There was a lively discussion between parents about appropriate material. My contention was, these kids are sixteen, seventeen years old. They're curious about everything. The end result was, they agreed to show the movie at a parent's home. We also agreed to have an evening where we discussed homosexual sex and sexual deviance, and open up the conversation.

RABS: The philosophy of IPS also acknowledged that teenagers were sexual beings and sexuality was not avoided nor sexual relationships discouraged. "Rights"—women's liberation, civil rights, human rights, and anti-war sentiments—were all part of the ongoing dialogue.

Of course, all this must be understood in the context of the times—the mid-seventies—and place—West LA, when a large proportion of students' parents were divorcing, experimenting, swinging, men marrying girls half their age, gay parents coming out, both voluntarily and involuntarily. There was no war on drugs, no, "just say no" campaign.

JD: The focus on sex was beyond significant, beyond a clinical education. It was sizzling. Everything from the weather to the era lived in to constantly put sexuality into the stew. Sharing any sexual thoughts—from the loss of virginity to telling fantasies to declaring one's homosexuality—was just about certain to captivate and raise one's credibility.

CW: A tenth grade student's brother jumped off the Palisades and killed himself. Every night the girl had nightmares about him. She asked me for help. I found everything Kubler Ross had written at UCLA. The class ended with a mediation in which I invited each one to approach their own dying moment and see where they got. Then we had a discussion about it. Her nightmares stopped. Word got out, and the rest of the students wanted to do it. Parents asked, too.

This led to a discussion about birth. So we ended up creating a birthing experience. Everybody got to experience being born; the person being born would direct the pressure, the hands on the body, when they wanted to be born. I played midwife. Some loved it there;

they were not ready to be born. Some came right out. They went right home to talk to their mothers about their birthing experience, and every one of those mothers confirmed that this had accurately reflected their child's birthing experience.

The next question was, what about conception? So we did a conception exercise—when were you conceived? One boy broke into tears. He said he could only see violence, it was unpleasant, painful, upset him. He reported, after talking to his mother, that she was divorcing his father and the father had raped her, which led to the kid's conception.

Parents wanted part of the experience. They did it with the same result. So that was the kind of community we became. Our monthly community meetings filled UCLA's Melnitz Hall.

SM: I attended one of those seminars, where Caldwell led us through a simulated rebirthing process. It was akin to what Vital Spark describes: "rebirthing is both a simple physical breathing technique and a profound emotional cleansing tool." It was powerful stuff.

***

Lemme get control I've got your minds / now I want / Your souls, lemme get control / I've got your minds / Now I want control, I need control...
—Germs, "Shut Down (Annihilation Man)"

PR: Perhaps the single most influential experience that happened to me there was meeting a kid named Paul Beahm who later went on to become the lead singer from a punk band called the Germs, using the pseudonym Darby Crash. Ferociously intelligent, mysterious, and charismatic, his personality stood out in a school full of personalities.

Paul Beahm (Darby Crash): People thought it was a really weird school. Like one of the teachers was a convicted child molester. Carole King's daughter went there with us, too. And Jeff Bridges used to visit us all the time.

PS: We'd heard stories like, "the IPS teachers take acid with the students!" We thought, "Cool! We've gotta get into this school!" That was really our motivation, and it turned out to be true, at least about the math teacher. IPS was the ultimate rebellion. We decided to get into it so we could rebel against it.

PVA: My vague memory of Paul Beahm's (Darby Crash's) personal life was living on the Westside, but in an apartment with his mom and without much in the way of resources. And so he exemplified in a much stronger way than most of us, a kind of suburban malaise.

PR: Paul dressed differently, he wore strange hairstyles. He looked unique in a school of three thousand students. And he gave off a distinct impression that he was the center of about eight or ten other kids. There was a Manson Family aura about it. Before I ever met him, I was warned not to talk to him, that he would brainwash me. That would have delighted him.

Fred called him a "rhetorician" and Jerry said he was the most brilliant math student he had ever worked with. But he could never stand a rival and the guru side of IPS became something that he had to set himself in opposition to. If you recall being dressed down in high school by a teacher, you may recall their utter power and your own inarticulateness arguing with an adult in front of a class. And yet, Paul Beahm was able to hold his own against the teachers in a verbal battle.

PB: Teachers got mad. And the parents got upset because we went to this other school and caused trouble. And one of the teacher's sons was hanging around with us, and we were taking acid, so he was pretty upset.

PR: His tactics were impeccable. Among the recruits for his personal cult were Fred's son Doug and IPS wondergirl, Liz Belzer. Paul would use hallucinogens, Bowie, and his own brand of rhetoric to "deprogram" IPS kids. He would take us on "field trips" to the Scientology Center to take personality tests (he scored perfect and was asked to come teach); to the Hare Krishna temple to chant and eat their fruit and nuts and yogurt; to the West LA underground reservoir where we swam in pitch black darkness in the middle of the night.

PVA: One of the first meetings at IPS was on the bleachers of the girls Field. We were asked if we had any interests we'd like to share, and I said I was building a recording studio in my garage and if anyone was interested in recording there they should get in touch. Gary Baker came up to me and said he was in The Big River Band (BRB) and wanted to see what I was up to.

The bass player in the BRB (Grant McDonald) worked at Peaches Records in Hollywood and introduced me to Chris Ashford who was the producer of the Germs in their early days. It turns out that Paul Beahm (Darby Crash) was also in IPS, though a year behind I think. So Chris brought in the Germs in late '77 to record several songs that were released under Chris's What Records? label. While I was not deeply into punk, I appreciated the rebellion, especially in contrast to the Bee Gees and other pop bands of the time.

PR: Eventually, IPS rightfully saw him as a threat and kicked him out, giving him all his credits and straight As. He had earned them.

CW: In the entire time we were up and running, Paul Beahm was the only student we ever asked to leave. I'm no clinician, but I'm fairly certain he was schizophrenic.

PR: Perhaps this story would give the impression that I would see IPS as diminished. But Paul Beahm was IPS, a fully realized and unique entity. His sad outcome had nothing to do with IPS and everything to do with things that had happened to him before he got there. After creating one of the greatest albums ever recorded by an LA band, he committed suicide at age twenty-one.

***

"Each of us must come to the realization that we can function and live at the level of vision rather than following some great leader's vision. Instead of looking for a great leader, we are in an era where each of us needs to find the great leader in ourselves."

—Werner Erhard, founder of est

JD: To innovate meant a consistent emphasis on change, on trying new ideas. The early years of IPS, what the staff often referred to as "a free school," were massively deregulated. For every student who indeed took to independent study and could engage in self-regulated coursework, many, many more were hardly doing much more than going to the beach and doing drugs. Soon enough, in '73–'74, there became much more emphasis on self-awareness; and so, yes, ideas from est were wholesaled into IPS.

SM: Caldwell Williams had done the Erhard Seminar Training, and I vaguely recall his telling me he had spent about twenty hours with Werner Erhard. IPS philosophy was suddenly infused with est concepts and jargon. Slogans like "what you resist persists," "take responsibility for your experience," and "see yourself as the cause of your experience" now permeated the daily school experience. IPS was becoming an alternative program school modeled within the framework of est.

CW: In the summer of 1971, I took my wife and kids on vacation in Vancouver Island, BC. We spent five days of that week at Fritz Perl's Gestalt institute. Fritz had died that summer, so I didn't get to see him, but the young people he had trained were skilled and sensitive. That fall, in moving toward the concept of frames—that we could teach them to discover themselves and their interests—I proposed that Fritz's Gestalt Institute be the focus of our frame day. There was no opposition from the parents.

By the end of the second year, we instituted basic training for the kids. We got lecture hall space that would accommodate the entire student body. In the summer, before classes started, the first five days—all day, from 8:00 a.m. to 3:00 p.m.—was basic training where we introduced students to our psychology and methodology.

At the end of the week, we were filling the ground at Royce Hall with our students and parents and faculty for a four-hour testimonial. Kids talking about insights, transgressions committed secretly they hadn't told their parents about, making commitments for the upcoming year.

There were tears all over the place. This happened simultaneously with the administration dumping students on us. We had doubled, to two hundred and fifty students. And basic training handled it.

SW: Caldwell brought Gestalt in. It was new to involve emotional intelligence in the educational space. You were taught to speak from "I" instead of rejecting "you" or making it all about "one."

MA: I have one memory of Basic Training, but it's one I've never forgotten. When I got there, people were standing up and sharing stories. I thought "this is bullshit; they're all lying. They're telling the teachers what they want to hear." On the very last day, a girl talked about a court case in which she was the victim and she had testified as a victim. Then it hit me like the second ton of bricks "holy shit—this entire thing was real. These people are telling the truth about the difficulties of being a teenager." There was no denying the emotion of it.

I went home Friday and lay in bed all weekend, just absorbing it. I came back to school Monday and it took me a long time to come out of the intensity. I was in a shell for the first few months.

PR: They'd have you look at the person next to you, just stare into their eyes and just "be" with them for about ten to fifteen minutes. You weren't supposed to laugh, or joke, or say anything; then they'd ask you, "Notice what your brain is doing right now?"

You'd get down on the floor in front of everyone, and the boys would have to act like girls, and the girls would have to act like boys. If you had a headache, they'd make you describe what color it was, or how much water it would hold.

SM: I distinctly remember standing up and complaining. I offered that the est exercises seemed like mind control and worried that we were being brainwashed. Fred swiftly discounted my concern and volleyed that I was free to go back to the regular school any time I wanted. Caldwell added that we were not to believe what the staff was telling us and to "check it out" for ourselves. We weren't even allowed to go the restroom until the official break. And that could be for hours. The rationale was something like "don't be at the effect of your bladder." That no going to the bathroom bullshit was straight out of est.

CW: Basic Training signified that we weren't a dumping ground, even though by the third year we became a repository for every mental case, criminal case, and academically-doomed student at Uni.

The whole staff was a support team, with everyone focused on the presenter. First it was Fred and me, then eventually everyone else joined in. And kids got it. No matter what an adolescent's act is, it's not permanent; you can bust it if you don't give in and you're clear and make sense. So we'd win them over. Sunday was their celebration. We'd have parents showing up to see their kid in a community of other kids celebrating.

JD: Caldwell liked to let people know how he perceived them. Sometimes, he would bluntly say things, such as telling some rich boy, "You're more than your body and your BMW" or to an attractive girl, "You're more than your ability to give men erections."

Another time, he took an entire room—twenty of us—and shaped us each into sculptures. He had me with an arm touching two different students. To my left was a boy, sitting in the classic Rodin's thinker pose. To my right, a girl, her arm flexed and bumped akin to a bodybuilder with a classic "don't mess with me" look. So there I was, poised between tender thought and brazen action. It's actually a pretty good concept for much of how I've lived my life.

RABS: Caldwell probably saved my life. He was my first adult friend. No, we did not have sex. Yes, we could sit together for an hour and not say a word. Once, he gave me a massage and commented that I was perfectly proportioned. Today, he would be lynched for "exploiting my vulnerability." To me it was another IPS experience, like an encounter, where we were encouraged to embrace, hug and kiss each other. Men and women, women and women, men and men. And, yes, I know some people are, to this day very angry with Caldwell and IPS. Many blame him for this or that unfortunate event, or for their own hurt feelings or shame.

SM: Caldwell sermonized and condescended and sometimes assumed a dismissive tone, notably with some of the female students in class. I clearly recall his aiming a rather invective laden barb at two young women for talking during his frame group. I felt badly for them and admired those girls for being mature enough to shrug it off. Were a teacher to utter that kind of pejorative language today, it would likely invite severe repercussions. But these were the seventies, and that sort of display somehow flew below the radar.

PVA: On one hand, the faculty would really get into your head, and I think for some students this was almost abusive. And on the other hand, I'm pretty sure Fred and Caldwell had sex with students. There was one student I was aware of who was clearly very close to Fred, and to those of us around her, it was uncomfortable. Now perhaps she was just a fan of his, but there was talk amongst the students and it seemed like something more. There are other classmates who simply will not talk to Caldwell to this day because of what they believe he did. I've never heard the details, but the anger is palpable.

JD: Parents in '77 were also casting a closer eye on IPS's practices. For years, Basic Training at UCLA had concluded with a mandatory meeting for staff, students, and even parents that took place on a Sunday. It was called "The Sunday Meeting."

I'd skipped it my first year to attend a tennis tournament—and the next day, Fred confronted me and told me I was now in "limbo," that I might in due time be dispatched from IPS. I was reinstated, but made darn sure to attend the subsequent Sunday Meetings. But in other cases, certain parents and kids began to wonder: Why must I attend this meeting on a Sunday? What's that all about?

SM: Not surprising that student frustrations mounted in the spring of '75 and became manifest the day a handful of us literally commandeered the staff into an emergency meeting. About half a dozen of the older pre-est students had grown frustrated with the constant drumming of Erhard's jargon and the direction in which the school was headed. They felt the staff was being autocratic and that students weren't being listened to. A few of us decided we'd make the teachers listen and hatched a fairly lame-brained plan we called Free IPS, or FRIPS.

One morning, several of us entered each of the frame groups and theatrically took each teacher into custody. We essentially told them they were going with us to another classroom for an emergency school meeting or something like that. It was more theater than an actual kidnapping. No physical force was used; no threats were issued or anything radical like that, but we were insistent and tenacious.

Once in the other room with all the staff and most of the students present, one of the FRIPS read a list of complaints and demands. The staff, however, quickly derailed our agenda and proceeded to make us to feel foolish for our tactics. We spent most of the morning examining our behavior and our issues more than anything else.

The crux of the staff response was "haven't we taught you anything?" But as one of the coconspirators recalls, "In some sense, we did what the school had taught us: to think for ourselves and speak up for what we believed in. I'm not sure that Fred and Caldwell believed that anymore by then—power and ego had gone to their heads. But at least we spoke up."

***

> "Scientology does not teach you. It only reminds you. For the information was yours in the first place."
>
> —L. Ron Hubbard, founder of Scientology

CW: I learned that on two or three occasions, I was subject of discussion of executive sessions of the board who said that this man was doing illegal things out there, violating laws, perhaps committing felonies. The intent was first to destroy my reputation, then destroy me.

The local administration unilaterally changed the procedure from a lottery to assigning students to us. One year, in the middle of the school year, we had sixty seniors dumped on us who weren't going to graduate. The administration told me it was an administrative decision and asked if I was going to be insubordinate.

A former student of mine had a friend, Amanda Ambrose, who taught illiterate USC football players how to read. That intrigued me. Her office was on the USC campus. Fred and I went to meet her. Amanda was a Scientologist. She told me they had a Hubbard technology that taught people how to read. If your English teacher says that this could be helpful to kids that are struggling, in my universe, that's useful. So we introduced Study Tech. Remember, this is all in the context of us being a dumping ground.

When parents raised questions, I invited them to a meeting, and I invited Amanda Ambrose so they could all interact. It was one of the few times in my eight years where some people in the community were so adamant that this was bad that they were unwilling to hear. I didn't know what to do with that, except to say there was something amiss if so many people had such strong feelings.

PR: I couldn't follow IPS into its exploration of Scientology. At first I was willing to examine it based on my faith in Fred and the other teachers, and some of its methods seemed like they might be useful. But when IPS gave me an ultimatum to choose between Paul Beahm and the IPS which was no longer the anarchic experience it began as, and which seemed poised to slip into a questionable dogma, I chose to leave.

MB: IPS turned into a Scientology experiment after 1977 and I did not like it. But I was tolerant of it. I wanted to complete my time in IPS and felt like I just could not reenroll in regular school. We were est-oriented prior to 1977. I attended an actualizations workshop in 1976 so I was familiar with Werner Erhard's est philosophy.

PS: The teachers were attempting to brainwash us, while teaching us brainwashing techniques. We were rebelling against that—on top of the acid.

CW: We found usefulness and validity in some of the Study Tech, in terms of some of the kids getting reading skills. A kid named David Hirsch couldn't read. Fred taught rhetoric, which is very different from teaching people how to read. David had no mechanics. Using Study Tech, he learned how to read.

The stuff we presented to students were study techniques that had nothing to do with any beliefs. For example, don't skip over words you don't understand. I had no bias against Scientology, or basis for judgment. I grew up curious; as a marginalized, excluded minority, I've been curious and eager to explore.

JD: For all the people who whine about Scientology marking the trigger point for IPS' demise, I can guarantee you there were many enrolled in that last year of '77–'78 who got tremendous value from those ideas.

SM: In Fred's frame, there was less emphasis on the reading and analyzing of literary works and more focus on self-exploration. He eventually stopped offering the music appreciation class that he also taught, which I loved. Increasingly dedicated to the idea of self-realization, Holtby announced that his bungalow-style classroom was to be called "The Truth Room."

I think the transition from Kenneth Burke to L. Ron Hubbard is a good analogy for how IPS digressed. If applying the est philosophy to IPS was questionable, it is my own contention that introducing the doctrine of Scientology into the public school curriculum was patently inappropriate. I know of at least one IPS graduate who became a dedicated Scientologist, along with Fred, who I believe is still active in the church.

CW: Fred immersed himself in one of their processes. And I respect that, because I had already seen him as having some real mental health issues. And as far as I was concerned, he was trying to address them. The controversy came when Fred became completely immersed in it. Students frequently follow teachers' examples, especially if they're in similar struggle points. Kids close to Fred were going to the Scientology Center to take classes.

Scientologists have never called or rung the doorbell, and the same is true for my particular students.

JD: I doubt that it was the use of ideas from Scientology that led to the downfall of IPS. As one of the staff pointed out to me years later, once Paul Godfrey took over as Uni's principal in the mid-seventies, IPS failed at building a smooth relationship with the Uni administration. IPS became more insular, not good at maintaining a functional connection with Uni and the LA school board.

CW: The school district had been run since 1900 by Methodist men from USC. They ran it until the civil rights movement busted their monopoly.

I was fighting daily battles with the administration, who charged our school with sixty-three charges of asserted felonies. Which later became charges against me. They sent a team of evaluators to our campus to take our school down. The team was blown away by how welcoming and friendly the kids were. To this day, we've never seen the evaluator's report.

JD: There had been rumors in the spring of '77 that IPS was going to end. But that didn't quite happen. Still, there was a strong sense through '77–'78 that the school was being watched by the LA school district officials more closely than ever.

Perhaps one subtle change was when we went from clapping after sharing to snapping our fingers. IPS was being slowly muzzled and the staff was a bit less unified and productive. Caldwell was spending a lot of time dealing with the school district people. Fred himself was getting more zealous about Scientology. Bill Greene, the sensible social studies teacher, retired in the fall of '77. The new science teacher brought in that year, Lynn, had minimal affinity for IPS's cozy humanism.

SM: By the time I had departed IPS, Fred was making and wearing his own homemade clothes, bead necklaces, and leather sandals. Caldwell was driving a sporty new car, and Don was also wearing beads but still wearing button down shirts and driving his old Datsun B-210.

MB: The school changed course when Uncle Bill (staff member) retired. Uncle Bill had a great deal of power with the Uni principal and shortly after Bill's retirement Caldwell Williams represented our IPS program to a less than lukewarm reception by the Uni principal. Bill's retirement would determine the ending of IPS.

We had many restrictions placed upon us. Mostly we had to have desks and chairs in classrooms instead of couches and large pillows to sit on. Massage class was banned. Frame became a very quiet event; in fact it, too, was banned, but we continued in a cloak and dagger manner. Math classes were mandatory, no more tai chi. We were not as fun or liberal as we were previously.

KH: I remember that the administration from Uni's regular school wanted to end IPS for many years. They felt that we did not do any real work in IPS.

GTM: The school was pulled away from Caldwell, but Uni wanted to continue it under a more controlled environment. Tom Anderson, Roberta Yutan, who were put in charge, they were PE coaches.

CW: They tried to put it in the hands of a PE teacher, but it takes much more than putting it in the hands of a different person. Don Chronister, before he died, contacted me and said that after a year trying to duplicate what I did at IPS, they weren't able to do it.

SM: The new principal at Uni High—a former US General, I think— was very suspicious and critical of what was going on at IPS. There was definitely friction between him and Caldwell. I also think some parents had complained about the program. One former IPS student chimed in on the IPS Facebook page that Fred and Caldwell had charged parents for their weekend seminars, and that was the last straw. Apparently, teachers aren't supposed to take money from parents.

Initially, I was angry at the conservative hard-liners in the school administration and the LA School District. But I also shook my head at Fred and Caldwell for pushing the envelope, and lamented that the other staff members did not rein them in. I think they were asking for it, effectively leading with their chins.

RABS: I have no doubt that many former students, in retrospect, or under the influence of current modes of thought, think some of Caldwell's and his colleagues actions and relationships were wrong, if not criminal. But again by the standards and hopes of that time, everything was appropriate, if the motivation was appropriate.

KP: From my perspective, it was a disappointment because it wasn't like the Parkway school—not community based, more navel gazing. Not activist enough.

PR: A truly revolutionary system embedded within a larger reactionary system is likely to be killed like a virus eventually. IPS had no wiggle room for mistakes, and there were no doubt plenty of those.

PVA: From what I heard, IPS started requiring that parents attend workshops, and they charged for it. So parents complained because that goes completely against the idea of a free public school. This led to the shutdown of IPS. I think there were lawsuits, etc., but I don't have personal knowledge of that.

RABS: I heard of scandals and improprieties. Tales of abuse. But what I heard were echoes of echoes. Everything third or fourth hand. But I was not in the least surprised. The truth was even when I was a student there were tensions between IPS and the administration. IPS had its critics, and as some say today, its "haters."

EW: I heard rumors about inappropriate behavior, but I don't know what happened. I think times changed, and people realized that having structure as a teenager is important.

MA: By today's PC standards, there was all kinds of outrageous behavior. There are a whole host of things that I could critique, but you have to start by putting this in context of the mid to late-seventies because it was just a different time.

JD: By 1977–78, IPS wasn't the only place starting to feel a bit weary of the time period's earlier hopefulness. In their own way, albums like *Rumors* and *Hotel California* revealed much of that disaffection and world-weariness. Meanwhile, all that hippy-dippy vibe was proving far less important than raw economics and resistance to government intrusion in the form of everything from alternative schools to ill-conceived busing to rising property taxes.

It's interesting to note that the last month of IPS—June 1978—was also the month Proposition 13, bugle call for the tax revolt, was passed. For all the Cat Stevens songs we sang, the revolution came from the right, not the left.

SW: A lot of us went to schools that allowed us to continue innovative models. At that time, Santa Cruz was the hardest UC to get into because people wanted that model. Then came the eighties, and people wanted stability and MBAs. Within a few years, people were applying to Berkeley and UCLA because people wanted more conventional approaches.

LMW: I was already an artist, a musician, a writer, and a meaning maker when I got to IPS. I had been practicing self-expression in some way since I was a young teenager. My parents let me draw on my bedroom wall. I illustrated and wrote comics, wrote poetry, wrote music, and performed. So I think the way they encouraged us to express ourselves to one another—to become curious about ourselves and who we were and how we met the world—was instantly exciting for me. It was deep. You could sink your teeth in.

EW: When I tell people about my crazy tenth grade, it is with fond memories.

RABS: An IPS education, as I believe Caldwell and Fred saw it, was really about preparing young minds to think, think for themselves, and to challenge assumptions. To be prepared to repudiate privilege and prerogative in order to find their true selves. It was a learning process that is antithetical to today's result-oriented education.

IPS taught me to look at what I describe as "bright perishables" with, as Yeats wrote, a "cold eye." I discovered I was unwilling to violate my principles, my sense of honor, for love or money, let alone fame and fortune.

CW: A former student of mine, Scott Kornberg, told me, "My mother is still the only person who hates you. What I learned from you is self-reliance. While I was an undergrad at Santa Cruz, deep in the Sequoia forest, we grew a pot farm. That's how I paid for college. That's how I learned horticulture, and I now own my own company in Washington. In my daily prayers, I thank you."

Our students are a testimony as to how IPS worked. And the answer is, ask them. In eight years, I never got one administrator willing to hear our results.

PS: Yeah, I'd say that IPS definitely affected me, sometimes to the present day.

KH: I think that IPS taught all of us to think for ourselves, to trust our own knowledge, and if we need to learn something, to conduct research. I think the most important thing IPS left me with is a sense of responsibility for my own decisions, being clear about my values, and wanting to make the world a better place.

LMW: I'm completely relationship-oriented. Communication is essential to me. I continue to be a meaning-maker. I am curious. I ask questions and I dig deeply into myself. I also teach authentic writing, creating safe spaces where people can tell the truth and reveal themselves. This aspect of my work can easily be tied to IPS. I was the right person to go there. It served me.

MA: The lesson is real. I can sit in a meeting where somebody loses their shit and I can pay attention them and say, "well you're angry, but let's talk about it," and not get distracted by someone calling you any name in the book. Anyone trying to keep you from communicating. I walk into meetings with clear objective of what I'm trying to accomplish and don't get distracted from that objective. And I learned those techniques at IPS.

I'm fifty-five, and thirty-seven, thirty-eight years later, most of my friends are IPS grads. I was married to an IPS grad for twenty years. I have five children, and I looked for an IPS-style school for four out of five of them. Couldn't find it, but for four out of five of my kids, I would have accepted IPS had it been available.

PR: I think it's safe to say that I learned more things that I can remember in that year than any other year in school. Taoism, tai chi, and rhetoric (Fred close reading the Bible: "In the beginning was THE WORD..." and looking at us significantly) are obvious. P. D. Ouspensky's *Tertium Organum* was a book recommended by Jerry as the greatest book ever written and I tackled it, and I daresay it permanently altered my view of reality.

IPS taught me that what I saw as "the world" was actually a projection of my consciousness on...something. The est-ian "Drop Your Act!" in other words being genuine and spontaneous. Functioning with others by agreement and participation. And many other things.

EW: I am a celebrity talent producer for television shows. I guess because I was not in school very much in tentth grade, that allowed me to watch as much TV as I wanted. So in a strange way, I guess that year of doing whatever I wanted helped me to get the pop culture background.

SM: I can trace the notion of having an impact back to Don Chronister. And also to Buckminster Fuller and his ideas about personal individual integrity, which dovetail neatly with what we learned early on at IPS. (Interesting to note, Werner Erhard and Bucky Fuller were also associated in the 1970s.)

PVA: On an emotional level, I learned to be more self-reflective and honest with myself. Even if the est stuff was kind of fucked up, the basics of therapy and group encounter was a good thing. Amusingly, years later, by complete coincidence, I ended up going to a therapist, who I realized was a fellow student in IPS. She was a year or two ahead, and while I was in IPS, a bunch of us went to her house in Topanga Canyon for a massage workshop or something.

JD: IPS had a dramatic impact in fueling my ambitions. The biggest lesson of IPS was that each of us was in control of our own destiny, that we were the "cause" rather than the "effect." So concepts like intention and desire put us each at the center of universe, leading anyone to think they were the spiritual epicenter of IPS. You could feel that way if you were a Bowie wannabe, a Manson family renegade, a Joni Mitchell poetess, or, in my case, someone obsessed with John and Bobby Kennedy.

In college, this sense of personal destiny fueled in me a certain passion. In many ways thanks to IPS, college—that is, coursework— to me wasn't something I viewed with the kind of ironic, mild level of engagement typically seen in privileged West LA kids. College to me was destiny, a high stakes game where I wanted to excel and bring my great ideas to the world. IPS infused me with that spirit to the point where one of my professors told me she thought I was, in her words, "pathologically subjective." So be it.

MA: On the main office bungalow, there was a board with wooden letters that said "IPS." Right after our graduation, I took it down and handed it to Caldwell.

RABS: As a character in a play I wrote taunted another: "It was fun while it lasted, but had it lasted it would not have been fun."

David Kukoff *has eight produced film and television credits and has sold dozens of scripts to every studio in Hollywood. His acclaimed first novel,* Children of the Canyon, *the story of a boy growing up in the midst of the Laurel Canyon counterculture in the 1970s, was published in 2014 and is being adapted for television. He is currently at work on a second novel, as well as on a number of film and television projects in various stages of development. He has also taught film and television writing at Northwestern, NYU, and Cal State Fullerton and has been featured as a guest lecturer for UCLA's Lake Arrowhead Faculty Lecture series. Kukoff is a lifelong resident of Los Angeles.*

CRUISING VAN NUYS BOULEVARD

by Rick McCloskey

CRUISE NIGHT WAS EVERY Wednesday on Van Nuys Boulevard from the early 1950s through the 1970s.

Gasoline was mighty cheap, and new and old cars were surprisingly inexpensive as well. The San Fernando Valley was home to, what seemed like at the time, a million teenagers, and just about all of them spent many a wonderful evening endlessly cruising from one end of Van Nuys Boulevard to the other, and then back again.

Popular stops along the way were Bob's Big Boy, June Ellen's Donuts, A&W Root Beer, as well as many lesser known spots. "The Boulevard" was where you went to see and be seen, and to meet new friends, show off your ride, grab a milkshake or a "Double Burger," and just have an all-around great time.

The images in my photographic essay were made during the summer of 1972, almost ten years after my own high school cruising days in the early 1960s. Cruising was such a terrific and pervasive past time of growing up in America during those years, it is difficult to imagine that the world has so changed, has moved on, and that cruising the boulevard, any boulevard, has all but vanished.

Rick McCloskey *was born in Hollywood, then moved to Sherman Oaks in 1957, only a few feet from the city of Van Nuys, and from Van Nuys Boulevard. His images of Van Nuys Boulevard were featured in a one-man show at California State University at Northridge's Art Department in 1973. He has worked at the* Maui Sun *and has done photo work, etched glass, and taught photo at Maui Community College. Today, he lives in Lakewood, Washington where his main line of work is building new wood bodies for 1949–51 Ford and Mercury "Woodies." He still shoots photography and paints.*

THE NOTRE DAME KILLER

by Anthony Davis and Jeremy Rosenberg

THEY CALL ME "AD"—NOT the world's most creative nickname, but it stuck back in 1972 and it's been mine since.

When I played football at the University of Southern California, we had a great left tackle, Pete Adams, later a first-round draft pick of the Cleveland Browns. Adams was the craziest white boy on the team. He played guitar and he used to walk around everywhere with this old, white, mangy dog named Turk.

At the time, Adee Plumbing in Los Angeles was running commercials. The announcer said something like, "Who fixes your plumbing and drainage problems? Adee do!" Pete Adams heard that and started calling me "AD-Do."

The "Do" got axed pretty quickly—it would have been redundant.

AD wasn't my only nickname. Later they called me "the Big Sexy." A Japanese woman I met in Hawaii at an NFL event gave me that name. USC baseball coach Rod Dedeaux called me "Tiger"—but he called everybody Tiger.

***

ABOVE ALL THE OTHER nicknames I've had, there is one that I'm best known for. It has endured in Southern California, across the Midwest, and in the news media, for more than four decades.

That nickname? The Notre Dame Killer.

In three college football games against Notre Dame, I scored eleven touchdowns. Six of those came in one game at the Coliseum in 1972. Four came in another in '74. The year when I only scored one touchdown, and we lost on the road, I was on the cover of *Sports Illustrated*, same as the two times that I dominated and we won.

During these USC years, members of the Nation of Islam asked me to change my name, like two of my heroes, Kareem Abdul-Jabbar and Muhammad Ali, had done. I declined, out of respect for my mother. If Davis was her name, then Davis was my name.

Speaking of Ali, in '72 a message was relayed to me that I should come meet him, at LAX. You better believe I said yes. The Champ shadowboxed with me and told me he liked how I'd told the world in advance what I'd do against Notre Dame, then gone out and done it. I bet you he liked my famous "knee dance," too, that I'd break out after a big TD. Meanwhile, over in South Bend, Indiana, home of Notre Dame, they actually burned me in effigy. A woman held up a crucifix. A doll of me was hung from a tree. I'm not making any of this up.

***

LESS THAN A YEAR after my third and final Notre Dame game, I was playing pro ball on a $1.5 million contract in my LA hometown, driving a Rolls Royce, and wearing a fur coat.

Back on October 28, 1972, though, I was just a guy sitting on a bench in Eugene, Oregon, a third-string tailback who picked up occasional carries on what would soon come to be known as the greatest team in the history of college football. I was a SoCal guy getting soaked in a cold northwest rain.

I was wrapped up in a big rain jacket. I was closer to where coach John McKay and offensive coordinator John Robinson were standing than I was to my teammates on the field. Truth be told, I was maybe one-third focused on the action on the field, and two-thirds focused on staying warm.

What was I doing on the bench? In high school, I had been the most accomplished athlete in Los Angeles. I was the city's coplayer of the year in football. The player of the year in baseball. A city high school wrestling champion.

Everyone knew I was going to the major leagues. I was going to be a baseball star. That was my true love, my true game. I was a switch-hitting center fielder. The Baltimore Orioles drafted me and tried to sign me out of high school. Their front office pegged me as the next Reggie Jackson. Yeah, *that* Hall of Famer, Mr. October, candy-bar-named-after-him, Reggie Jackson.

Both my mother and I wanted for me to earn a college education. I had a 3.2 grade point average at LA's San Fernando High, but when the Orioles wouldn't offer to pay for my education, I accepted an athletic scholarship from USC.

I had considered attending Arizona State, which at the time was known for being both a baseball and football powerhouse. I had considered Oregon, where soon-to-be NFL Hall of Famer Dan Fouts was the quarterback. I took a campus visit to Midwestern football behemoth Nebraska, a place I only considered because my mom thought Coach Tom Osborne was the nicest of all the men who came to our house to recruit me.

I never responded to Ohio State's initial recruiting letter, for both football and geographic reasons. The same went for Brown of the Ivy Leagues. I also rejected going to any school in the south, because my mom told my high school football coach that life was hard enough in the relatively liberal West and she'd prefer if I didn't get lynched. The only place I wanted to go that wouldn't have me was Stanford; they said if I didn't have a 3.4 GPA, I'd need to go to community college first.

Freshmen were ineligible to play varsity sports, a nationwide rule that changed during my junior year. So my sophomore year, 1972, was my first crack at playing big-time college baseball and football. During the six seasons that followed—three baseball, three football—I was a member of *five* national championship teams. Good luck duplicating or beating that in big-time sports.

***

THAT DAY IN OREGON was our eighth game of the season. We'd romped over all of our opponents, week after week, winning by twenty-one points, forty-five points, thirty-five points, forty-five points again, nine points in a game that wasn't really as close as the score indicated, twenty-eight points, and twenty-seven points.

Many of these games were against highly ranked opponents. I'm pretty sure we were never behind once during that entire season, and I know we never once trailed during the second half of any game in what would end with an unblemished 12–0 record, Rose Bowl win, and the launch of my collegiate career.

Against Oregon, we were slogging our way through an early 0–0 deadlock that, to us, was the equivalent of a three-touchdown loss. It had been raining for days and the artificial turf field was a slick mess. You couldn't cut properly—I would have been better off if I'd brought water skis and our fullback, Sam Cunningham, had pretended to be a powerboat.

There would be nine fumbles between both teams and fourteen total turnovers before the game ended. Fourteen turnovers are good if you're a bakery, but something quite the opposite of that if you're a college football team.

Our starting tailback that day, the extravagantly talented Rod McNeil (also a local—from Baldwin Park, California), went down with a leg-related injury. Almost immediately after that, our number two tailback, my roommate Allen Carter, from San Dimas, California, went down with shin splints. Now, Allen was a *fast* man. He'd won the state hundred meters when he was seventeen years old, when he ran a 9.3. And Rod played in the NFL; I missed being his Tampa Bay Buccaneers teammate by one year.

So there I was, sitting on the bench, borderline shivering, probably daydreaming about playing center field at Yankee Stadium, when I noticed our running back coach and offensive coordinator John Robinson grumbling and kicking at the turf. Before I knew it, he was standing next to me.

"Hey, AD, you ready to go?"

I said to myself: *Well, that's awful.*

"Anthony, you have to go. McNeil and Carter are down."

I was looking at John like: *What the hell are you talking about?*

Remember, it was cold, I was pretty far from loose, and…well, that center field fantasy on a New York September afternoon was looking pretty good from where I was standing.

Our quarterback, Mike Rae, called out the plays. We had a quarterback option play called "Haw. Forty-eight Option Left." Rae would take the snap, move laterally down the line, and if a lineman came at him, he'd pitch the ball to the tailback.

In the huddle, Rae called out, "Haw. Forty-eight Option Left."

I thought, *Hell, that's my call.*

Wanting no part of any of this, I said, "Mike, that's a terrible call!"

Mike said, "You S.O.B., this is what coach said to run. Run it!"

So the first time I was going to get the ball. All I was thinking about was how badly I was going to get creamed, and how Willie Mays didn't have to face this problem.

The ball was snapped. We ran the play. Rae saw the linemen converging on him and lateraled to me. I got blocks from Sam Cunningham, Charles Young, and Lynn Swann—all names football fans know well—and forty-eight yards and a couple of seconds later, we had our first touchdown, as well as our first lead of the day.

I came back to the sideline, accepted some congratulations, and figured, *okay, I escaped.* I thought one of the guys, Freddie or Allen, would be ready to go back in after Oregon had the ball for a while.

Instead, Oregon fumbled. We got the ball back at our forty-five yard line.

We had a couple of basic calls designated: "Haw" and "Gee." "Haw" means power pitch to the left. "Gee" means power pitch to the right. The "power" designation mans the side of the line where the tight end lines up; this gives the tailback one extra blocker to follow. The outside world knew these plays as "student body left" and "student body right."

I went back out on the field. Mike Rae called "Haw, twenty-eight pitch." I took the toss and off I went. I had another great block from Sam Cunningham, the all-world fullback who would become the New England Patriots' all-time leading rusher. I cut back across the grain—just instincts at work—I broke into the open field and then got picked up by Edesel Garrison, a split end from Compton.

Now you have to understand that Edesel ran a 10.2, the equivalent of a 9.2 hundred-yard dash. I mean, Edesel was *flying*. When I was running, you could tell I was working because my knees would chug up-and-down like pistons on my Lincoln Continental. Edesel didn't even look like he was breaking a sweat, just gliding down that field, blocking some hapless defensive back. I was a 10.5 man—fast but not like Edesel. As I far as I was concerned, the man was part panther, and I'm not talking about the social activist kind.

Edesel was talking to me as I was running. "Come on D! Come on D!" Edesel eased me to the end zone. Touchdown again. Fifty-five yards. Two plays, two touchdowns, 103 total yards.

We went on to win what for us was a close call, 18–0. I ran for 206 yards on 25 carries. And from then on, games nine, ten, eleven, and twelve, and throughout 1973 and 1974, I was the starting USC Trojan tailback.

By the time I was done, three years later, I became the first ever Pacific-8 Conference player ever to rush for more than one thousand yards in three different seasons. I scored fifty-two touchdowns in my college career. I held more records than a DJ. When I left 'SC, I had accumulated two-dozen school, conference, and NCAA records combined. One of my records—my average of 36.6 yards per kick-off return—wasn't broken until 2009.

***

ON CAMPUS I USED to sit on what we called the ghetto steps, located at the Von Kleinsmid Center. I would sit alongside some of the handful of other brothas who attended 'SC back then, and watch the world go by.

This was the era of H. Rap Brown, Stokely Carmichael, and Harry Edwards. USC wasn't nearly as radicalized a campus as UCLA, where Angela Davis was rockin' her 'fro and forcing major change. Still, every traditional role in American culture and society was being questioned and recalculated back in the early 1970s, from Black

Power to Women's Liberation to citizens rethinking their relationship to the President and military.

Don Quarrie was even faster than Edesel Garrison. Don was the world's fastest man. He won the gold medal in the 200 meter in the 1976 Olympics. He added two silvers and a bronze during the next two Olympics.

Don, who was born in Jamaica, went to 'SC and used to hang out with a couple other Jamaicans. These were all great guys, but when they got here, they were naïve about life in the US.

We were all sitting one night on the ghetto steps. Don and his boys were planning on going out in South Central. We told them, "Okay, man, make sure you have your ID." We said, "You ain't going to get by as someone from Jamaica. The cops are going to think you're making all that up."

Sure enough, later that year, they got stopped in the city, and one of the guys didn't have his ID. He said, "I'm from Jamaica." And he said the cops said, "Don't lie to me. You're as South Central as they come. You're going to jail tonight."

Growing up in San Fernando and spending time in nearby Pacoima, I could drive around and hang out all day with my white friend Kenny Brock. They used to call Kenny and me the "*I Spy* boys"—like Bill Cosby and Bill Culp, stars of a groundbreaking interracial buddy cop TV show in the sixties.

Kenny had a '67 Camaro four-speed with a 454 engine. Kenny and I could hang out, but we knew we couldn't go to certain areas together without taking a risk. San Fernando was primarily white, with Latinos residing on the other side of the wash.

That meant if you were a young, black male, you weren't going over to this particular part of Pacoima. You weren't going to Glendale, to the south, without risking being pulled over. You weren't going to Arleta, three miles southwest. Same for Sylmar, to the northwest. At best you could roll through Granada Hills, Reseda, and Chatsworth, but you risked being stopped and harassed by the police—the same folks paid by all of us to serve and protect all of us.

Remember those Freedom Riders who were murdered in Mississippi in 1964? Rest in peace, James Chaney. Rest in peace,

Andrew Goodman. Rest in peace, Michael Schwerner. Southern California wasn't Mississippi, but, still, whether a white kid and a black kid were hanging out unconsciously for social purposes or consciously to advance the cause, you just never knew what a bigot would say or do.

Most white guys, they couldn't even talk to a black guy in those days without taking serious crap from their friends and families. That's just males I'm speaking of. When it came to females, the tension was greater. I could not drive around with a girl the way I could with Kenny. Too many bigots with guns—and, sometimes, badges.

When I was sixteen, I was getting a ride home from a girl. We got pulled over by the police for no good reason. The officer put me in the back of the girl's car. Right in front me of, he said to her, "Hey, what are you doing with this nigger? You need to be with a white boy."

***

WHEN I WAS AT 'SC, lacking a father figure, a man introduced himself to me after a game. He lived just off campus. I'll give him the pseudonym "King." King drove a brand new '72 Cadillac, white with red interior. He was a stylish Korean War vet, a suave-looking man with straight brown hair. King was a hustler. King was a pimp.

King wanted me to get in his game. He told me how he'd been watching me and saw how women of all colors gravitated toward me. He told me I would be a great pimp. I turned him down, cold. I respect women. I told him I would never do that to a woman.

Truth is, women have never been shy with me. I've always said that even if everything else in my life went wrong, I could get a hot woman before I could get a hot meal.

At 'SC, I openly dated the roommate of Coach McKay's daughter. She was great, outspoken, and white. Later in the seventies, playing pro football in Tampa Bay, white women down there would give me their number, but tell me that we had to go to St. Petersburg, the next city over, to go on a date.

***

As a kid, living on the wrong side of the tracks, I'd been shot at twice and stabbed once. The stabbing? I was just grazed. The shootings? I was in the wrong place at the wrong time. The first time, some cats thought I was someone else. We were in South Central, at Jack in the Box. This one thug shot at me and my friend. A bullet went through the middle of our windshield and into the car. It landed harmlessly between us.

During the seventies, living the life of a well-compensated traveling gladiator, I broke three bones in my back in Toronto; cracked my fibula in half in Houston; hurt my shoulder so bad in Tampa Bay that for a month I couldn't reach up to comb my hair; smashed my hand and fingers many times; cut my palm so badly it looked like I'd been crucified; mashed up my knuckles; had cleat marks permanently etched on the back of my left hand. A Hall of Fame Oakland Raider intentionally stomped on me, then helped me up and asked me if I'd seen his role in the movie *North Dallas Forty*.

I suffered non-sports related injuries, too. I was in a car crash—hurt my Achilles heel and my knee when I hit a telephone pole while driving my brother's girlfriend home to Inglewood in his 1969 baby blue Triumph. Of course, as a running back and kick returner, I'd been in thousands of car-crash equivalents.

I retired from football in 1983—I'd played in four different professional leagues, always pursuing the better paycheck whether it was in the National Football League, Canadian Football League, World Football League, or United States Football League. I should have played baseball. I made a big mistake.

Before I bowed out from football, I suffered at least three concussions. Two were diagnosed at the time. I have a book out now titled, *Kick-Off: Concussion*. It's in part about my work to help former and current athletes heal from the brain traumas so many of us sustain, and a guide about how to make football safer at all levels.

When I was fifty-five years old, I had my brain scanned. The results showed I had the brain of an eighty-five-year-old. I'm sixty-three years old as I tell my story today. Thanks to a great doctor, visits to hyperbaric chambers, a strict daily regiment of supplements, and other hard work, my brain age is now close to my true age.

Not everybody I played ball with made it out alive and well into senior citizenry. You've all heard about suicides and CTE.

***

NOT EVERYBODY FROM THE old neighborhoods made it out alive and well from San Fernando and Pacoima. Pacoima today has something like twenty active street gangs. Pac-Town—or, *Pacas*, has changed dramatically. Like so many areas in and around Los Angeles that used to be populated by blacks, Pacoima and San Fernando are overwhelmingly Latino. Seventy percent of Pacas' population originally hails from Mexico, according to the 2010 US Census. And, yes, I realize that nobody should be surprised that a place named San Fernando has so many Spanish-named businesses and people.

***

THE 1974 USC–NOTRE DAME, where I scored four touchdowns, is forever referred to as "The Comeback." As perfect as a name that is—we came back from 24–0 deficit to win 55–24 in front of 88,552 ecstatic fans—these days, when I think of a comeback, I think of my own return from the hazy depths of bad decisions and bad results to the clearer heights of a sharper mind and sounder body.

During the 1970s, I gave everything I had to football. My body, my brain. Now, I'm ready to take something back.

Adapted with permission from Kick-Off: Concussion. How The Notre Dame Killer Recovered His Brain, *(2014) by Anthony Davis and Jeremy Rosenberg. Available via Amazon.com.*

Anthony Davis *is a member of the College Football Hall of Fame. Davis played on five national championship teams at the University of Southern California—three in football and two in baseball. Known as the "Notre Dame Killer" for his dominating performances against the Fighting Irish. Davis played professional football in four different leagues and professional baseball in another. When injuries forced him off the field, Davis became an actor and worked in real estate. Today, he is a pied piper of concussion studies and an outspoken advocate for victims of brain trauma.*

Jeremy Rosenberg *is a Los Angeles-based writer whose wide variety of works have appeared in dozens of online and printed books, newspapers, and magazines. His* Under Spring: Voices + Art + Los Angeles *(Heyday) won the 2013 California Historical Society Book Award. A former employee of the* Los Angeles Times *and the Annenberg Foundation, Rosenberg is an assistant dean at the USC Annenberg School for Communication and Journalism.*

THE DAY THREE CHICANOS DIED

by Del Zamora

UGUST 29, 1970 WAS the day of the Chicano Moratorium. A day of protest against the Vietnam War, the inherent racism toward Mexican Americans (Chicano/as), the lack of opportunities, the poverty, and poor education. Chicanos, like all US citizens, paid taxes to the federal and state governments, taxes which helped cover the costs of infrastructure, governance, and education. UCLA, California State University at Long Beach—state funded universities and colleges—were less expensive than private schools such as USC and Pepperdine. However, were someone to look at student rolls at UCLA, CSULB, and the like, it would have been abundantly clear that there was a paucity of Spanish surnames amongst the student population. In effect, Chicanos were paying for Anglos to attend these schools. And, yet, Chicanos have a long history of fighting all of the wars that the US has fought (Latinos have won the Congressional Medal of Honor in everything from the Revolutionary War to the recent Gulf Wars).

Chicanos for the most part, predate Anglos in the US. Many states, cities, and towns, as well as rivers, lakes, and trails have Spanish names from the time the Southwest was Mexico. Chicanos used to own much of the Southwest, and in the Mexican culture, owning land is viewed as the ultimate source of pride.

Once the treaty of Guadalupe Hidalgo was signed, however, this ownership changed forever. These newly minted US citizens were forced off land that their families had owned and lived on for centuries, dating back to the 1500s.

It is important to remember that Mexican Americans are not foreigners. Our ancestral Mothers were violated by Spanish Conquistadors, and we are the offspring of that violation. Our Mothers were born in North America, and so were we. We are not from Europe, but our ancestral Fathers are. They came here and dominated the Native cultures with their religion and culture and by fathering children with our ancestral Mothers. Eventually, all of these cultures had successful revolutions against their Spanish overlords, and we were left with the countries that currently exist.

For centuries, after the Southwest was taken from Mexico, newly minted Mexican Americans were lynched, beaten, and forced off their land. Mexico did not want them to come to Mexico; to this day, the pejorative *pocho* is used by Mexicans against Mexican Americans. "Pocho" means faded, or pale, or rotten, language that perfectly describes how Mexico feels about Mexican Americans. We are considered gringos—not Mexican at all. Yet here in the US, we are viewed through the same foreign prism as native Mexicans. "A people without a country" is what many call us.

It was against this backdrop that the 1960s Chicano Movimiento began; the Brown Berets, a militant leftist advocacy group that was considered dangerous by the FBI, were formed, and the Chicano Moratorium on August 29, 1970, occurred. The primary objections were police brutality, poor education, poverty, lack of opportunity, and, most importantly, the US government plan of tracking Chicano, black, and Native American students. Tracking was a technique utilized by the high schools, ostensibly to proffer guidance to these minority students, but, in reality, was a ploy to guide them into trade educational tracks. Thus were minority students "counseled" by their school counselors to avoid any college prep classes, as they were openly told that they were not smart enough to attend a university. In many cases, even if minority students were straight-A students, they were advised to avoid Algebra, Geometry, and American Literature and instead take classes in Auto or Metal Shop or Home Economics. The trades were seen as the only future for these minority students, for whom the default view of less than their Anglo counterparts was done under the guise of "we know better."

What was not lost on these young boys and girls was that, if unable to attend a college or university, they would be the highest percentage drafted to fight in the Vietnam War. In effect, Chicanos, African-American men, and Native American men, whose families paid state taxes, were paying for Anglos to attend these universities and colleges, while at the same time being used as fodder to fight in an unpopular war. Chicanos made up roughly 5 percent of the official population, yet represented well over 30 percent of the casualties in Vietnam. The same held true for African-American men and Native American men. Their casualties in Vietnam were completely disproportionate to their actual populations.

Thus on August 29, 1970, after a number protests, demonstrations, and acrimony on all sides during the 1960s, the Chicano Moratorium was held. Thousands attended what was intended as a moratorium on the Vietnam War. Three of them, however, never left the scene of what had started as a peaceful protest, but devolved into a veritable—in the eyes of many—police riot on the Chicano population gathered in what was then called Laguna Park in East Los Angeles, but is now known as Salazar Park.

Journalist Ruben Salazar was there to cover the moratorium for NBC, La Opinion, and KMEX. He watched as a number of draft cards were burned or torn up that day. Shortly after it began, members of the Los Angeles Sheriff's Department fired tear gas into the park, where several families had been seated on the grass in front of a makeshift stage. There was widespread pandemonium as the sheriffs entered the park, wearing full riot gear, intent on beating these upstart Chicanos down. Who were they to demand equal rights and outwardly display such insubordination?

As the sheriffs descended upon the crowd, wearing gas masks and swinging their batons, a number of the Brown Berets and other men from the community met the Sheriffs head on, swinging baseball bats, tire irons, chains, pool cues, and whatever else they'd had the foresight to fashion for any potential problems. It was hand to hand combat—batons on one side, bats and tire irons on the other. Thanks to the efforts of these young men—who'd been classified as dangerous revolutionaries by the government—many grandmothers, mothers, and children were able to flee the park. They scattered eastward, away from the tear gas. What they did not know was that the LAPD had coordinated with the sheriffs, and was waiting for the people on the East side of Laguna Park. The panicked people ran right into the LAPD, and anyone who met them head on was clubbed as they ran by. Many women and children were forced to the ground.

Brown Beret Lynn Ward was passing by a trash can right as it blew up—clearly a bomb, but the authorities later insisted it was paint spray cans that had been lit on fire and exploded as Lynn happened to pass by. He was killed in the blast.

Chicano activist Angel Gilberto Díaz was shot and killed by the authorities, who claimed that Díaz had been throwing rocks at the police and sheriffs.

Journalist Ruben Salazar, who had left the demonstration early, was seated at the Silver Dollar Saloon, drinking a beer with friends he knew from the bar. Salazar had initially thought there would be no trouble; he had no idea how much turmoil was occurring on the streets of East Los Angeles barely a few blocks from where he was enjoying his beer.

A sheriff with a tear gas gun had been told by a bystander that someone had entered the bar with a weapon of some kind. The sheriff walked to the door, and, with two women imploring him not to, fired his tear gas gun into the saloon, right through its door. The tear gas canister was a military grade projectile, not approved for civilian use; it had been manufactured from reinforced steel and had a nasty point on the end with flesh-searing barbs clearly intended to do harm. Lethal harm.

The projectile took off the back of Ruben Salazar's head. He died instantly, and the sheriff who shot the fatal shot was never held accountable. Nor was anyone held accountable for the other two deaths. Too few people remember, or even know this horrid part of US history. Just as the land had vanished from their ancestors through blood, without accountability, so did the memories of these three innocent citizens, who'd simply demanded that the ground they stood on, too, was worth something.

From that day on, the Chicano Movement was severely crippled. The Brown Berets had been infiltrated by the FBI, and the community knew that if the authorities could get away with killing an esteemed journalist like Ruben Salazar, that they would be perfectly willing to kill anyone under the guise of law and order.

But the Brown Berets still exist. Though not as numerous as they once were, nor as effective, their legacy is still strong. They continue to run positive programs for youth at risk, and much of what they and others fought for came to fruition. The universities and colleges opened their doors to these minorities in ways they never had before. The Black Power Movement, Chicano Movimiento, and American Indian Movement all affected positive change. While all were undoubtedly radical leftist organizations, it is clear that, throughout American history, change frequently requires the efforts of radicals to create, foster, and strengthen. Discrimination, police brutality, poor educational opportunities, and poverty still haunt our communities to this day, but it is clear that these radical movements of the 1960s played a major role in changing our society for the better.

They are US history, just as the Founding Fathers and settlers are US history. They should be taught, analyzed, and critiqued, but above all, remembered. A healthy society is a society that is honest about its past—good, bad, and ugly—and exposing historical injustice is a large part of what made this country great, and continues to make it great.

¡Viva La Raza! Viva Los Brown Berets! ¡Viva el Movimiento Chicano!

Del Zamora *is an actor, writer, director, producer, and journalist. Perhaps best known for his role as Lagarto Rodriguez in the cult classic film* Repo Man, *he is in the completion stages of his feature movie directorial debut* The Last Brown Beret, *based on the play* The Last Angry Brown Hat, *which played at the Smithsonian Institute, Yale, Notre Dame, USC, and UCLA.*

SNAPSHOTS: SEVENTIES PERFORMANCE ART IN LA

by Erica Lyons and Debra Wacks

"Naïve as it sounds, change was our goal."—Suzanne Lacy

WINTER, 1972. THE RATHER ordinary white exterior and mundane, unimaginative landscaping outside the home on North Mariposa Street, in a quiet, unassuming residential section of Hollywood, did little to suggest that this domicile was anything but a scene of serene suburban bliss…but for a discreet sign: *Womanhouse*, in typeface on the front door.

It started with a dilapidated house, slated for demolition, but that was ultimately transformed into the proverbial—as well as the literal—house that feminists built. Were one to enter the house, it would have become immediately apparent that this was no ordinary domestic setting, but rather a bold, consciousness-raising project organized by members of the Feminist Art Program at the California Institute of the Arts (CalArts). There, led by artists Judy Chicago and Miriam Schapiro, a group of women artists came together to question traditional concepts of middle-class femininity via installation and performance art—both relatively new and marginal practices.

Like any house, *Womanhouse* had a kitchen. But this one had been transformed into *Nurturant Kitchen* by art students Susan Frazier,

Vicki Hodgetts, and Robin Weltsch. Similar to many who might have been quick to identify the kitchen as an inherently "female sphere," these artists claimed this space, too. They coated the entire room in a hyper-feminized pink hue that paradoxically read as both ironic and sincere, replete with squishy, plastic breasts and eggs that adorned the walls and ceilings that somehow rendered an effect both menacing and pleasurable. Simultaneously, they pointed against the normative constraints of domesticity while celebrating women's traditional contribution to the twin institutions of family and home.

A woman wearing a patterned housecoat would have been carefully ironing an ordinary sheet on a nondescript ironing board. Laborious and monotonous as it would have been to watch, artist Sandra Orgel forced viewers to acknowledge the drudgery of daily housework that women were expected to accomplish without question or appreciation. Similar issues were prompted by watching Chris Rush vigorously scour the floor clean in her real-time performance called *Scrubbing*. Through the seemingly endless repetition of such mundane acts, witnesses were made acutely aware of the disheartening passage of time associated with daily chores.

Karen LeCocq and Nancy Youdelman's installation was called *Leah's Room*, a bedroom created to reflect that of the chamber in Collette's novel *Chéri*. Here, LeCocq, dressed as Leah, an aging courtesan, sat at an ornate vanity mirror, applying layer over layer of makeup to her face. Reminiscent of the pink walls of the kitchen, the artist's face became a canvas and a statement on creativity as well as artificial constructions of beauty and femininity. On the flip side of quotidian life, Judy Chicago's installation, *Menstruation Bathroom*, surprisingly still disturbed some contemporary viewers with its casual, bloodied, Kotex-filled garbage can.

***

JANUARY 5, 1973. Los Angeles International Airport (LAX). A single figure, performance artist Chris Burden, fired several shots with a pistol, at a Boeing 747 as it ascended further into the sky, unaware of the quiet drama below. This was a private performance. Like much of

Burden's work, this futile act of aggression recalled the meaningless of violence all around, especially that of the protracted Vietnam War.

Burden was perhaps best known for a 1971 LA performance in which he purposefully had himself shot in the arm by a friend using a rifle. But on this date, the shots Burden fired were entirely ineffectual. The casings fell to the soft earth of the open field with no impact. Witnesses to this event were few, and sadly, as with most performance art, there is little remaining documentation.

***

COLDWATER CANYON. THE SMOG-FILLED San Fernando Valley hosted a piece called *The Great Wall of Los Angeles*. Beneath a canopy of sycamore trees lay a colorful mural, a thousand feet long, painted in sections along the concrete walls of the Tujunga Wash. It wasn't a performance, but rather a key example of public art; the result of an on-going community-centered project that Chicana artist Judy F. Baca began in 1974 that documents the history of "California" since the age of dinosaurs.

In a painting dedicated to the 1781 founding of Los Angeles, there was an image of a missionary, Father Junipero Serra, riding his mule. School textbooks described our Los Angeles forefathers as Spanish, but this earth-colored panel portrayed those founders as they were: a multicultural group that included the city's forgotten mulatto, mestizo, black, and native Indian populations.

Also particularly striking was a panel bearing the depiction of a Chinese laborer working tirelessly on the Transcontinental Railroad. The determined look on his face, along with the apparitions of two other Chinese immigrants billowing out of the train's steam engine, were representative of a wave of Chinese immigration rendered virtually silent by many historians. Their screams, frozen on this mural, were rare reminders of the racism many immigrants endured, and their collective struggle to survive in a foreign and often hostile environment. Although Angelenos drove past this mural hundreds of times during their regular commutes, they typically gave little thought to this powerful work—until seeing it laid out before them in splendid color. This work of art began to provide some recognition of the diverse social movements and communities that contributed to California over the centuries. It was already the longest mural in the world, and, in the future, Baca's initiative would thrive and only continue to add panels to honor California's rich narrative.

***

NINETEEN-SEVENTY-SIX. IN CONTRAST TO the multicultural collaboration demonstrated by the hundreds of youths working on *The Great Wall*, the streets of East LA were the scene of an initially peaceful massive anti-war march that drew tens of thousands to these local streets. Following canisters of tear gas hurled by the police, a riot ensued that defined these neighborhoods in the earlier part of the decade. Years later, passers-by noticed what appeared to be a corpse surrounded by police flares. Artist Harry Gamboa Jr., camera in hand, photographed the body in the still of the deep, dark, quiet streets.

When he finished, the body slowly rose and strikingly seemed to face observers for a split second. All of a sudden, and with rapid fire, multiple radio broadcasts blasted forth from various speakers. Newscasters attempt to define what just played out before spectators' eyes, reporting that this was the latest casualty in the gang wars of LA's mean streets. Habitually—and obsessively—they focused on the violent spectacle, but failed to contextualize the situation. No one, it seemed, addressed the actual issues confronting the Chicano population here, like the lack of opportunity or the glaring disproportionality of lives taken from this community for the Vietnam War draft.

Gamboa and his subject, Gronk—who would later go on to become an incredibly influential artist in his own right—slowly walked away. Both were members of East LA's Asco, a Chicano artist collective whose name in Spanish meant disgust or repulsion. According to Gamboa's autobiographical writings: "I was deeply bothered and disgusted with the condition of my community and of the Mexican American people. I learned to distrust and dislike everything that was pro-establishment." For a second it seemed as though Gamboa and Gronk paused and looked back at the spot where the body just lay, perhaps in the same way an arsonist might admire his work. The artists' ambiguity, as to whether the performance was the body laid out in the street or the ensuing media frenzy reporting what was mislabeled another fatality in a gang-related crime, was intentional.

***

DECEMBER 13, 1977. THE radio announced that another body had been found, this one belonging to a teenage girl. She had been violated, sodomized, and raped, and her body was found in a perverse pose. This wasn't the first, nor would it be the last. Each sensationalized report left Los Angeles waiting for more, like a cliffhanger on some depraved show. Fear and paranoia permeated LA while the so-called Hillside Strangler and "his" sexual proclivity—as well as the juicy life circumstances of the victims themselves—became titillating subjects of media attention and public debate for months.

Directly across from the tall art-deco building that was City Hall, cameras rolled, newscasters bantered, and a hearse, followed by a motorcade, pulled up to discharge ten women robed in black from head to toe like nineteeth century mourners. Their faces were concealed, the whole image evocative. But observers would soon realize that this was a performance, not a press conference.

On the front steps of City Hall, the black-robed performers each announced a different form of violence against women, connecting these to a fabric of shameful social passivity. Like Asco's piece, *In Mourning and In Rage* was an art event specifically created for media consumption; organized by Leslie Labowitz and former CalArts student Suzanne Lacy. They joined forces with Bia Lowe, women from the LA Woman's Building, Women Against Violence Against Women, the Rape Hotline, City Councilwoman Pat Russell, and singer Holly Near to record crimes against women, but also to refuse being defined by them.

The first performer walked up to a microphone stand and stated that she was there in memory of the ten women killed by the Hillside Strangler. The second declared that she was there for the 388 women raped in LA during the same time period. After each of the ten women spoke their purpose, women from the motorcade, now arranged around the City Hall steps, chanted in unison: "In memory of our sisters, we fight back!" The tenth woman, clothed in flowing red robes, stepped forward and cried out: "I am here for the rage of all women, I am here for women fighting back!" The repetitive chant of the Greek chorus of women performer-protestors echoed away: "...we fight back!"

***

NINETEEN SEVENTY-SEVEN. JUST SOUTH EAST of City Hall, at the Los Angeles County/USC Medical Center. Viewers were rushed down the corridors until they reached a door behind which they were directed to peep. The first thing to hit them was the nauseating stench of ketchup. It took multiple hard glances for the performance to register. There were two suit-wearing men at a table. One was passively observing the other, who was wearing a freaky Eisenhower-like rubber mask and—oh—no pants. He was "playing" with some Barbie-ish dolls, but those oddities were rapidly compounded when the somewhat distraught mask-wearer climbed onto the table and began to shove the dolls into his anus.

The seemingly haphazard, masochistic spectacle was Paul McCarthy's *Grand Pop*. McCarthy proceeded to smother his penis in ketchup and squirt what might be body lotion onto the small dolls. Facial expressions in the crowd ranged from confusion, to shock, to fear, to disgust. Yet, despite their initial repulsion, it was somehow nearly impossible to look away.

McCarthy's performance spoke to violence, sex, and unchecked machismo when it clashes with commodity consumption and the heroic Jackson Pollock–esque gestures of Abstract Expressionism... ultimately, however, rendering a feeling of abject discomfort.

***

MARCH 1978. IN THE liminal space beneath the freeway overpass, Senga Nengudi, a pioneer in the Black Arts Movement, was draped in an unadorned paper tarp. She soon put on a self-made mask that entirely covered her face and rhythmically cleaned (or cleared) the area with a palm branch and water, while saying something inaudible. Unlike the drudgery linked to the common domestic chores seen in the *Womanhouse* performances, this one had a sense of spontaneous creativity and symbolism. With the rising dust, a carnivalesque scene ensued, as Nengudi danced to what no doubt sounded like an improvised soundtrack. She hypnotically interacted with a group of similarly-garbed artists that included David Hammons, Maren Hassinger, and fellow members from Studio Z, an experimental artist collective.

The title of the performance, "Fets," referenced "fetishes." It was intended as a celebration to mark the opening of Nengundi's public sculpture, which, remarkably, was funded by a CETA Art in Public Spaces Grant and CalTrans (California Department of Transportation). Nengudi's "signature" pantyhose sculpture was affixed to huge, round support columns beneath the overpass. She became associated with the use of such inexpensive materials, which were stretched and made bloated with sand to evoke the human body.

Oddly, the avant-garde dance appeared to be a mash-up of African ritual and Japanese Kabuki theater. It was as though the sound and movement of the performance drew in collective sexual energy forces, which ephemerally transformed the usually overlooked and squalid environment into something unnamable, yet dramatically meaningful. Again, sadly, the visceral quality of this experience was quickly erased, captured only in a series of stills on a single photographer's camera. The space beneath the freeway would eventually return to a resting ground for assorted litter and unpaired abandoned shoes, only to be utilized as a makeshift shelter of last resort for the city's homeless and marginalized.

***

SPRING, 1979. THE UNMISTAKABLE sound of punk music was coming from inside the feminist art and education hub known as the Women's Building, which catered to an unusual convergence of punk rockers, folk singer hippies, random curious onlookers, and feminists of all kinds.

The audience chanted "PHRANC! PHRANC!" over the thumping synthesizers emanating from the first-ever self-identified "out" punk band, "Nervous Gender." The androgynous lead singer, Phranc, was unapologetic about their confrontational demeanor and distinctly disturbing lyrics, as she brashly sang: "Manic-depressive parents is all I got from God/So mommy and I we never know what to do/So mommy and I get stoned on Librium and glue" ("Mommy's Chest").

The mood of the room was volatile; although there was an undercurrent of optimism, it became tapered by the agitation and turmoil that would soon arise from the hardcore bands—and fans— from the South Bay, whose violence and anarchic tendencies would soon lay waste to the nascent punk scene.

***

THE 1970S WERE A decade that gave rise to subversive action; where artists' bodies became canvases, where the rehearsed repetition of the norm could convey social critique, where movement and inexplicable gestures sometimes spoke in a voice louder than words, and, ultimately, where art became protest. The Vietnam War, sociopolitical unrest, and the dreaded oil crisis helped set the stage, while Los Angeles's sprawling topography inadvertently provided the space for artists to experiment.

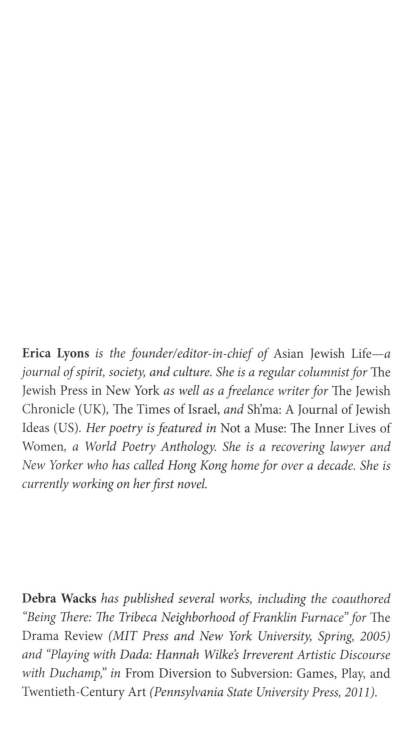

Erica Lyons *is the founder/editor-in-chief of* Asian Jewish Life—*a journal of spirit, society, and culture. She is a regular columnist for* The Jewish Press in New York *as well as a freelance writer for* The Jewish Chronicle (UK), The Times of Israel, *and* Sh'ma: A Journal of Jewish Ideas (US). *Her poetry is featured in* Not a Muse: The Inner Lives of Women, *a World Poetry Anthology. She is a recovering lawyer and New Yorker who has called Hong Kong home for over a decade. She is currently working on her first novel.*

Debra Wacks *has published several works, including the coauthored* "Being There: The Tribeca Neighborhood of Franklin Furnace" *for* The Drama Review *(MIT Press and New York University, Spring, 2005) and* "Playing with Dada: Hannah Wilke's Irreverent Artistic Discourse with Duchamp," *in* From Diversion to Subversion: Games, Play, and Twentieth-Century Art *(Pennsylvania State University Press, 2011).*

RUNNING FOR CITY COUNCIL IN THE 1970S

by Joy Picus

I GREW UP IN Chicago, in a family that was politically active. My mother was involved in several political organizations and some campaigns, and my brother planned to run for President in 1972. And yet I was thirty-five before I knew women could run for office; in the 1940s and 1950s, there were no role models of women holding public office.

I majored in political science at the University of Wisconsin. I loved it, and had no idea that among women, it wasn't a popular major. I was active in student government, the National Student Association, Hillel, and other organizations. I was married within a year after I graduated, and after my husband completed his graduate degrees at the University of Chicago, we moved to Washington, DC where we produced three baby boom children right on schedule, the clear mark of a postwar overachiever.

In the early 1960s, a new job brought us to the San Fernando Valley. I undertook the customary suburban mom activities: PTA, Scouts, Temple, and, in a nod to my enduring passion for politics, the League of Women Voters and American Association of University Women. I worked on local civic studies with the League and spent time at City Hall getting to know the players. We roamed freely in those corridors of power, schmoozing with the police officers on duty, as well as with the Council members and their staffs.

After about ten years of this, I decided it was time to stop trying to influence the decision makers and to become a decision maker myself. Even though there were scant women in positions of power, especially in politics (and all the more so in local politics), the nascent women's rights movement was filling the air with something other than the familiar smog and business-as-usual ethos. So, in 1973, I filed to run for City Council in the Third District, which encompassed the west San Fernando Valley. Not only was I a woman in unfamiliar terrain, not only did I have no access to money or power, I was a community-based, grassroots candidate taking on a one-term incumbent whose activities in local Chambers of Commerce had all but entitled him to that seat.

Taking on a one-term incumbent was then, as it is now, not the smartest thing to do, but my grassroots were deep and broad and my volunteers were passionate and numerous. In short time, I found myself appearing before the Democratic Party and unions to seek endorsement. I was asked how much money I could raise and from whom. My answer was simple: I expect to raise $25,000. I know a thousand people who will give me twenty-five dollars each. Of course, I now look back on this statement with amazement, as that sum would warrant roughly a single hour's worth of a current campaign. But back then that was how I raised the money for the rent, the telephone bill, the printer, and the postage. When we needed a graphic artist, I recruited one at an event one evening and promptly put him to work designing a mail piece.

We were fortunate in that all of the labor was volunteer-based. My campaign manager's son was the campaign photographer. Our friends and relatives posed for the campaign photos. My entire staff was comprised of friends and neighbors—capable, smart women, mostly, who knew the District and could figure out what to do and how to win.

In 1969, in an incredibly ugly and racist campaign, Mayor Sam Yorty beat Councilman Tom Bradley, and 1973 was a replay of that. The one reporter assigned by the *Los Angeles Times* to cover City

Hall handled the political races, too. Local and national news coverage was focused on the race for mayor. But local City Council government was low-key and, for the most part, ignored by the greater population. In my race, it was assumed that the incumbent would win, and those of us running against him were essentially disregarded. I had all of one paragraph in the *Los Angeles Times* and two in the *Daily News* Green Sheet, a four-day-a-week throwaway.

We had a lot of lawn signs. Someone told me I was known as the most popular real estate agent in the Valley, which I found funny, flattering, and perturbing at the same time. We sent out three pieces of mail, one of which was the piece I handed out when my army of volunteers knocked on too many doors to count. In the course of our canvassing, we discovered that walking door-to-door while pushing a stroller was a good tactic. (My kids were old enough to knock on doors, and they did.)

We had no professional campaign consultant. We got the voter lists from the City Clerk, bundled our materials, and sent out all the mail ourselves, either from the office or from the recreation room of one of our volunteer staff members (most of the time, our children helped with that). Pizza became an essential food group. We brought homemade chocolate chip cookies to the workers at the bulk mail post office. I stood outside markets and handed out my inexpensively produced cards that had useful city phone numbers on them, along with a photo of me. I soon found out that Friday evenings around five were the best time for that and can remember shoppers looking at the card, looking back at me, then saying: "That's you, right?" I acknowledged it was. More often than not, they responded: "Well you couldn't possibly do any worse than the guys are doing!"

My husband and I worked the movies on Saturday evenings. We'd figure out which movies were likely to have lines, which were a staple back in the 1970s with its stand-alone theaters. We learned how to start at the front, thirty minutes before the listed start time, and move to the back. Then on to the next theater. I did bowling alleys in the morning. Occasionally the managers would suggest that we not do this again, and we moved on. We knew better than to ask permission.

We raised money by sending letters to people we knew, all individually typed and personally signed by me! Our fundraisers were modest affairs, typically held in the homes of good friends, who cooked a dinner and served it to a group of twenty or thirty other friends, or friends of those friends, all of whom paid seventy-five dollars per couple for dinner and sangria. My artistically minded son designed the flyers for fundraisers and other special events, which were offset printed, or Xeroxed at a local print shop. If we ever got a check as big as one hundred dollars, it was time to break out into a happy dance and consider taking the rest of the day off.

I was endorsed by a group of savvy Westside women called "Women For..." They sent me $300 and even a volunteer! We had about ten car top signs, made by a neighbor, and I had a volunteer companion who drove me to all the places on my schedule on any given day. No mobile phones. I went everywhere people gathered.

On election night, as it became obvious that the incumbent was going to be forced into a runoff and I would be his opponent, the phone at our Victory Park location rang off the hook. The news folks asked "What's a Joy Picus?" They were shocked that a nobody—a woman, no less!—had fought her way to the forefront of local politics and to the point where she warranted mention on the news. In fact, Channel 2's Jerry Dunphy mispronounced my name on air (he ultimately wished me better luck in the runoff than he'd had stumbling over my name).

And there we were, more or less ready to go again, doing all the things we had done before. My oldest son and another volunteer, well-known and highly regarded in the community, went down to the City Clerk's office and hand-copied the results of each precinct. A math major computed the percentages, and my other son prepared a precinct map of the District and colored in each precinct according to how well I did in each. Red was the best, purple was the worst (Red and Blue states came decades later).

I was blocked from riding in the Memorial Day Parade down Sherman Way in Canoga Park, which took place a few days before the election. So, instead, we located a friendly businessman a few doors off Sherman Way, ordered hundreds of balloons with my name on them, and had them filled with helium at that store. Then multitudes of volunteers marched them down the block and handed them out to the folks standing on the sidewalk, watching the parade, but now distracted by their balloon take-home prize. It was over a hundred degrees that day, but the parade was a huge success (just for the record, I rode in a bright turquoise classic Thunderbird convertible in that parade every subsequent year I was in office. Suzanne Somers' *American Graffiti* mystery girl had nothing on me!)

Election night. Over a hundred of us huddled around the radio, TV, and telephone for hours. We had other campaign volunteers at City Hall where the ballots were counted, calling the results in to us. Tom Bradley was elected mayor by 10:00 p.m. The other races were settled about that time, but our race was neck and neck, with results trickling in at a tantalizingly torturous pace.

At about 2:00 a.m. it was clear that I had lost by all of one percent of the vote. We were all heartbroken. I remember looking around at my troops, all of whom had stayed through the evening despite having to go to work the next morning. And I realized that if there was ever a time to be a leader, ever a time to sum up everything I'd ever learned as a parent—and especially as a mother—it was now. I took a deep breath, stood up, and said: "Be of good cheer. We made a difference. I promise we will do it again."

In my heart, I knew these weren't just words. I knew I would run again, and I did four years later. In the interim, I went to work for the Jewish Federation, as their valley staff for community relations; along with many women of my generation, I had been out of the work force for twenty years, raising a family and keeping the community safe and informed. I went to lots of political dinners, asking for comps, or cost tickets. My staff and I learned a great deal, and we reassembled four years later, just as I'd promised.

Only this time, we were more sophisticated. We had more access to money and power. After my first campaign, a number of people had told me that if they'd had any idea I would come so close, they would have sent me money, introduced me to important people, etc… Well, I called in those chits. Technology was only slightly better, and the general outlines of the campaign were similar, only we sent out a larger number of mail pieces. We continued to knock on doors and put up lawn signs. The *Los Angeles Times* endorsed me, supporting the "peppery Mrs. Picus." There were several candidates in the race, so a runoff was required. My opponent spent about $200,000, which was the most ever spent in a Council race up to that time. I spent about $90,000, but did not have any debt at the end. At one time during the campaign, my opponent held a $1,000-per-person *luncheon*. Unheard of. I responded with a brown bag lunch fundraiser, and the press ate it up. I ordered T-shirts with the slogan "Elections should be WON, not bought!" on the back.

And this time, I won handily.

At 8:00 a.m. on July 1, 1977, I held my swearing-in ceremony in the District, at what was then Sequoia Junior High in Reseda (it's now the Sherman Oaks Center for Enriched Studies). It was precedent-setting. Newly elected Council members had never held a swearing-in ceremony in the District before. About four hundred constituents and friends joined my tired, happy volunteers. At noon, along with the other City officials, I was officially sworn in on the steps of City Hall, as Mayor Bradley began his second term.

I loved my new job. To this day, I'll tell anyone who listens that if I could write a job description for myself, this would be it!

Joy Picus, *former Los Angeles City Council Member, represented the West San Fernando Valley from 1977-1993. Her major public policy achievements were in garbage and hazardous waste, and dependent care and the creation of a family-friendly city. She is nationally recognized for her promotion of opportunities for women. Picus has continued her civic leadership as a board member of several nonprofit organizations. She has served as President and Chair of the Board of Friends of the [Griffith] Observatory. She is on the boards of Jewish World Watch, Community Partners, and the Foundation Board of California State University Northridge. She serves on the Dean's Councils for their College of Arts Media and Communication and College of Social and Behavioral Sciences, as well as being an Ambassador for their new Valley Performing Arts Center. Other significant honors include the naming of the Joy Picus Child Development Center in LA's Civic Center, and being a Ms. Woman of the Year in 1985, in recognition of her outstanding leadership in Pay Equity/Comparable Worth for the City of LA.*

JUST AN ORDINARY GIRL

by Samantha Geimer

THAT JANUARY OF 1976, the first time Dad drove me to the airport, I still remember how lost I felt knowing I'd never live in York again. I couldn't stop thinking about it as I stuffed my pet rat, Odin, into my carry-on. (I was quite a good smuggler at thirteen.)

Grim as it was, York was home—and the Pacific Palisades section of Los Angeles most certainly was not. It was beautiful, sure; I lived right near the beach where, a few years later, *Baywatch* would be filmed. But to be living in a beach bungalow covered in vines—when I moved in, one sprung out of the closet, making me scream—was a shock after the solidity of York.

More shocking, of course, was the California culture. I arrived at just about the same time the Eagles dropped "Hotel California." (*Cool wind in my hair / Warm smell of colitas rising up through the air.*) I was Aerosmith and Queen, rollerskating rinks, and bowling alleys; this was Joni, the Doobie Brothers, surfers and skateboarders, and a whole lot of drugs as a path to self-discovery. But with all the sex drugs, and rock and roll, there were the beginnings of this brooding undercurrent of violence. California, like much of the country, saw an enormous leap in violent crimes in the mid- to late-1970s. Serial killers like Herbert Mullin and Edmund Kemper—the so-called Co-Ed Killer—were still fresh in everyone's mind. They would be replaced in less than a year by the even more horrific Kenneth Bianchi and Angelo Buono, aka the Hillside Strangler. In ninth grade, we were all terrified.

Mom and Bob continued to audition for acting gigs, but, by the time we moved out to the San Fernando Valley in the fall of 1976, to make ends meet Bob had taken a job selling advertising at a new magazine called *Marijuana Monthly*. He and Mom smoked every night in their room—secretly, they thought—for the seven years they were together, and Mom's way of finally quitting was as quintessentially 1970s as the weed smoking itself. She was on a rafting trip in the Grand Canyon and met an English doctor who was a disciple of a swami; he came up to her and said, "You're searching, aren't you?" She replied, "Yes," and he said, "I'll give you a mantra, if you will stop smoking." Her mantra, she tells me, was "om a ram a hum madhu ram ham" (or at least she *thinks* that's what it was), and she repeated it while she paddled, all the way home, on the bus ride, on the plane— and she swears it was the mantra that allowed her to quit.

Moving in with them after Christmas of 1975, I could not have felt like more of an outsider, an antisocial freak in this well-to-do beach town of surfer dudes and blonde bikini kittens and all their fake drama. (Pacific Palisades fight: "If you want to be friends with *me*, you can't be friends with *her*." York, PA, fight: "I'm going to beat your ass after school.") Here I am wearing green mascara and Converse sneakers, and these girls were all about no makeup and platform shoes. It was like being on a permanent pot-infused vacation. This place was strange to me, but in the end we were all teenagers growing up in a wild world. The same kinds of parties, did you get invited, would you fit in, do you want to smoke or drink? Do you want to be with that boy?

I don't think I can overstate the shift in attitudes toward sex in the mid- to late-1970s versus ten or even five years before. *The Joy of Sex*, published in 1972, held a place of honor in my mother's bedroom. (She never knew I read it, but naturally I did, cover to cover.) Young girls are eroticized to some extent in every culture, and at this point in time in our own culture that eroticization had become almost mainstream. Brooke Shields had posed nude for pictures when she was ten, and then, at twelve, she was starring in *Pretty Baby*, a movie about a child prostitute that probably couldn't be made today. Just one year before, Jodie Foster had raised eyebrows with her portrayal of a teenage prostitute in Martin Scorsese's *Taxi Driver*. *Manhattan* was Woody Allen's homage not just to New York City, but to a middle-aged man's longing for a young teenager. And, of course, there was that famous 1974 film where a young girl has an incestuous relationship with her father. That was *Chinatown*, directed by Roman Polanski.

I had been deeply relieved when we relocated to the San Fernando Valley, a grittier place where actual people with actual jobs lived. The Valley had its celebrities, of course—in the 1940s and 50s Lucille Ball and Desi Arnaz lived out there, and Clark Gable and Carole Lombard had a love nest—but it was never known for its glamour. It was more like the prototypical sparkling suburb. The Brady Bunch allegedly lived there. And later, the Kardashians. It would be a few years before the Valley Girl would become the iconic American symbol for girls addicted to shopping, long nails, and fame.

The bathrooms of junior high school were filled with cigarette smoke. Smoking pot and having sex was almost the norm for a teenager. When we visited the homes of our friends, their parents would offer us beer or wine. Everything was treated casually, by our parents, on TV, and in the movies, just shy of "anything goes." Cocaine was just beginning to become popular, but, really, that wasn't yet the drug for the kicked-back Los Angeles vibe. There was a saying "speed kills," but nobody said there was anything wrong with tripping— mushrooms or acid were the preferred buzz. Like the Eagles were telling us, it was all about taking it easy, not letting the sound of our own voices drive us crazy.

Gradually I'd become more interested in acting: when you're a kid living in Los Angeles, being an actor seems like a perfectly reasonable career goal, shared by half the people you know. My little room was papered with posters of Marilyn Monroe (plan A) and Bette Midler (plan B). At home in York, my father's influence prevailed, and I was going to be a brainiac of some sort, perhaps an attorney. Here in Southern California, none of that mattered much. I was cute. I had the head shots. I was going out on auditions and some callbacks and even a commercial. My mother drove me east on the 101 to an office building in West Hollywood. A casting agent would ask me to give off a look—perky! fresh!—and I'd try to oblige. (Carroll O'Connor from *All in the Family* noticed me in a hallway one day wearing a short top. He poked me in my middle and teased, "Nice belly button.") My classmate auditioned as well and got the role that day. California normal.

I wanted to be cheerful about the auditions and the acting classes and all the *work* that seemed to go into chasing the brass ring. But I was still quite unhappy. I felt entirely unmoored. My parents let me entertain the illusion that I was in control of my life, when in fact I controlled nothing. I was just marking time at Hughes Junior High in Woodland Hills. When I wasn't gathered with my girlfriends trying to suss out which teachers were drunk or high ("Did you smell his breath?" "Did you see her eyes?") I'd be daydreaming about change: that Mom would land a big part, or that all the acting and gym and dance classes she drove me to in our big ol' ugly brown Nissan Maxima would lead somewhere. Did I have what it takes to make it in show business? Probably not. I liked the idea of fame much more than the idea of work.

So I was not a pleasant teen. I mean, I tried, I really did. But the message I conveyed to my family in every look and deed was "why did you make me come here? I hate this place, and I hate you." On the other hand—well, the writer J. B. Priestley had a good point: "Like its politicians and its wars, society has the teenagers it deserves."

One day, Roman Polanski appeared at our door. Okay, it wasn't exactly like that. But close. What really happened was this: my sister, Kim, was dating a guy named Henri Sera, a minor film producer who'd visited the house a few times. He knew my mother was in the business, and invited her to a party at Top of the Rocks, a watering hole on Sunset Boulevard. It was an impressive gathering: Diana Ross was there, and Warren Beatty. Mom said hello to Roman, chatted a bit; he made a slightly off-color joke involving sex and tiger balm, and she laughed politely. That was it.

A few weeks later, Henri called to say Roman was interviewing young American girls for a photo shoot that he was in the process of doing for *Vogue Paris*. He asked Mom if he could come over to meet me, and, of course, the answer was yes. I never thought about dressing up, and my mom didn't make me, maybe she was thinking "young", so keep it simple. I was in jeans, sneakers, an unmemorable shirt, and a baseball cap—with my pet cockatiel perched on it. That was his favorite spot.

In a few years, I would get to know a great deal more than I ever wanted to about this man. There was, of course, his horrific childhood. He was born Rajmund Roman Thierry Polanski, in Paris in 1933 to Polish Jews, and in 1937 his parents made the tragic mistake of moving back to Poland, shortly before World War II began. When Germany invaded Poland in 1939, the Polanskis were sent to the Krakow ghetto, and Roman's parents were ultimately sent to concentration camps— his mother to Auschwitz, where she was killed, and his father to Mauthausen-Gusen in Austria, where he survived. Roman saw his father captured and marched off to the camp. When he was twelve, he was miraculously reunited with his father after the war.

But then, the extraordinary trajectory of success. He eventually got into acting as a teenager, and made his first movie—*Knife in the Water*—in Poland in 1962. It was a deeply uncomfortable film about the sexual tension between a bored married couple and a hitchhiker they pick up, and was nominated for Best Foreign Language Film that year. He moved to the United States and went on to direct some of the darkest, most extraordinary movies of our time: *Rosemary's Baby, Repulsion, Macbeth,* and, a few years before we met, the movie that was to be nominated for eleven Academy Awards, *Chinatown.* But even his post-Holocaust life as a celebrated director was marred by the most unspeakable of tragedies: in 1969, his pregnant wife, Sharon Tate—allegedly the first woman he had a real, lasting, fulfilling relationship with—was brutally murdered in their home, along with four others, in the most infamous of the Charles Manson killings.

When I met him in February 1977, I knew nothing of this. I had seen *Chinatown* and didn't really like it. I thought it was both brutal and boring. If I had known he'd directed and starred in one of my favorite movies at the time, *The Fearless Vampire Killers,* I would have been starry-eyed. I was nothing, if not incredibly odd for a girl my age. And my mother and Bob, despite being in the business, weren't exactly film historians. They knew about the Tate murders, so that an air of tragedy hung over him always. They also knew he was powerful and famous and could do things for all of us. In other words, they were pretty much like every other unsophisticated aspiring actor in Hollywood. This was a once in a lifetime opportunity for me and they knew it.

***

POLANSKI SAT DOWN IN the living room and explained what he wanted to do. A French edition of *Vogue* magazine was looking to do a story on the differences between American girls and French girls— exactly why is a little vague, but it seemed perfectly plausible at the time—and he needed to find the right American girls. He showed my mother and Bob a beautiful spread he'd done with Nastassja Kinski in the Seychelles for a summer issue of *Vogue Paris*. The theme was "pirates" and it involved the beach, swords, buried treasure, and Kinski as the captured princess in some kind of medieval golden dress. Whether or not he was having a sexual relationship with Kinski then, when she was still fourteen, is a matter open to debate, but he did shortly thereafter. What isn't debatable is that she was so exquisite in the photos she took your breath away. She also seemed so exotic, so sultry, so knowingly sexual. In a few years Richard Avedon would make the famous image of her wrapped in a boa constrictor.

Anyway, there were these extraordinary images of an international beauty. And then there was me, a teenage girl in jeans and sneakers, barely developed, wearing a bird. I was by all accounts, including my own, a very pleasant but unexceptional-looking girl. My eyes suggested no particular mystery—they were bright, but that was all. I had a roundish face, a slightly pug nose, lips that were cherry red without the benefit of Bonne Bell Lip Smackers. My hair was short, and I wasn't quite pulling off the feathered Valley Girl cut. My voice was surprisingly husky—not Cathy Moriarty sexy, just husky. No one could ever say I slinked into a room. I sort of galumphed.

Looking back on it, I still marvel that he didn't turn on his heel and walk out the door. Was he really looking for prepubescent girls for a photo shoot, or was the photo shoot a good excuse? Maybe he was just tempting fate. After all, Roman Polanski didn't have to work hard to get beautiful women. But maybe beauty wasn't always the point. Maybe for a man who had lived through what no one should ever have to live through, and survived, maybe extreme youth was some sort of life force. And maybe he felt he needed it.

Of course, at that moment, I was thinking nothing like this. Mostly I was thinking: *Great, another adult to deal with. Here's this guy who's like my size and sort of looks like a ferret. But he's super-powerful and he wants to photograph me.* Me! *And look how happy Mom and Bob look.* They were sitting upright, leaning in to him a little, listening happily.

As he showed these photos of jaw-dropping beauties in *Vogue*— girls on beaches, in fields, dressed in backless evening gowns—and explained his American-teenager-versus-French-teenager storyline, I don't know how I stopped myself from laughing out loud. I really didn't have any sense that he was checking me out either, although certainly he must have been making *some* sort of calculation. Could I be one of those girls? This was boring. I wanted out.

I introduced Roman to my cockatiel, which failed to charm, and then exited to my room, my record player, and the over-the-top theatricality of Aerosmith:

> *Leaving the things that are real behind*
> *Leaving the things that you love from mind*

How could anyone have anticipated what was to come…

From The Girl: A Life in the Shadow of Roman Polanski *by Samantha Geimer. Copyright © 2013 by Samantha Geimer. Afterword copyright © 2013 by Lawrence Silver. Reprinted by permission of Atria Books, a Division of Simon & Schuster, Inc.*

Samantha Geimer *is the author of* The Girl, *which was published in 2013 by Simon & Schuster. She was raised in Pennsylvania, but spent the glorious seventies in Los Angeles. She is married and has been living on Kauai for most of the last thirty years where she raised three sons. She is currently all about being a grandma, but is always available to lend a hand to any cause for the empowerment and rights of victims of sexual assault and the justice system.*

JOHNNY WADD: ORIGINS

by Bob Chinn

THE FICTIONAL CHARACTER JOHNNY Wadd was created purely by chance one winter day toward the end of 1970. A tall, skinny fellow named John Curtis Holmes walked into my office looking for a job. At that time, I was only a few years out of film school and was working in the only field of the motion picture industry that had opened up to me: the adult film business, which would later evolve into what would be known as the porn industry. I was working as a producer and a director, churning out extremely low-budget feature films that played the theaters that had the courage to play them as well as the numerous storefront mini-theaters that had begun to pop up across the country.

By now, these films were cheap productions, shot on sixteen-millimeter film in a single day with a total production budget of $750. We had only recently begun to push the envelope with what we could show in regard to hard-core sex, and we were doing so with the belief that we should be protected by the First Amendment to the Constitution.

This was a moot point, however, because the local authorities were intent on shutting us down one way or another, primarily relying on outdated laws and ordinances. So we were forced to do what we were doing under constant threat of arrest and imprisonment. It was a hell of a way to make a living, but other than the need to eat and put a roof over my head, I really did get off on striking my own little blow against censorship.

I was busy editing the trailer for our latest film that day when John walked in for an interview. We all went into the office and John informed us that he had worked as a gaffer and was looking for a job on our film crew. We told him that we didn't need—and really couldn't afford to hire—anyone else. Then John hemmed and hawed for a moment before he casually informed us that he was also an actor.

I took one look at this tall, skinny white guy sporting an unruly Afro hairdo and didn't see a whole lot of potential there. Alain saw me raise my eyebrows, so he said he'd take Holmes' application and give him an interview while I went back to the front room to continue editing the trailer that had to be finished before the end of the day.

A few minutes later, Alain came in to the room where I was busy editing and said: "Bob, you got to take a look at this guy's cock."

"Alain, there are a lot of things I don't want to do right now, but first among them is going in to the office and looking at some skinny guy's cock."

But Alain was adamant, so I went in to have a look at it. John had pulled his pants back up and when we entered the office, Alain said, "Show him."

John lowered his pants to reveal what was undoubtedly the biggest cock I had ever seen in my life. I immediately saw the potential there. I had always wanted to make a movie with a film noir theme—a private dick with a big dick—and I figured Providence had spoken, loud and clear.

"Maybe we can fit you in to the shoot this weekend," I told him. "You free on Sunday?"

He smiled. "Sure, I'm available. But I'm never free."

"We pay the talent fifty dollars a day."

"I get seventy-five."

"No way."

"That's what everybody pays me. I won't work for less," John said adamantly. "Look, I can do four sex scenes in a day."

I looked at Alain. He shrugged. I thought it over for a moment, then, said, "Okay, seventy-five it is—but the Afro's got to go. Buy some

Brilliantine and take that thing down a few notches. I'm going to have you play a private detective."

The extra twenty-five dollars a day John had insisted on put a dent in a production budget whose total for the entire shoot was all of $750. But if John could do four sex scenes a day, we would need to hire only one male actor instead of two, which actually meant we'd come out twenty-five bucks ahead. I got out my pen and knocked out a quick script on the back of a legal-size envelope. I finished the basic plot of the thing in no time, but was still having trouble coming up with a name for our big, swinging private dick detective.

Alain and I had been talking about how much we disliked shooting those pull-out-and-shoot climax scenes theater owners insisted on. Then we began discussing the guy we had just hired and Alain casually remarked, "Man, the wad that guy must be able to shoot with a cock like that."

Right there and then I knew we had it.

"Johnny Wadd," I said. "With two Ds." Sam Spade it wasn't, but it certainly fit our less-than-aspirational needs.

"I like it," said Alain. "Rolls right off the tongue." So to speak.

John showed up on the set wearing the only suit he owned at the time with a matching blue shirt and a hat. Just as I'd asked, he had slicked back his hair and had even trimmed it a bit. He still didn't look like my idea of a private detective but he was prompt and polite and ready to shoot in more ways than one.

The Johnny Wadd I'd envisioned was a hard-boiled, hard drinking private detective right out of Chandler, with a touch of Spillane. I told John that for the first scene he would go over to the bar, pour himself a stiff drink, and take a healthy slug just before the telephone rang. We quickly set up the shot and John took his position at the bar. He picked up the bottle of bourbon, unscrewed the cap, then he took a sniff and grimaced.

"This is real whiskey!" he spluttered.

"So?" I asked.

"I don't drink alcohol."

I took the bottle from him and poured its contents into a large pitcher. As I rinsed the bottle out, Alain, who'd sensed the situation, started boiling three bags of Lipton tea.

"You can drink tea, can't you?" asked Alain, doing his best not to sound too contemptuous, but failing in the way French people tend to whenever they have to deal with what they perceive as American culinary or cultural shortcomings.

"Tea I can drink," responded John. "Just don't make it too strong," Filming went off pretty much as planned, with a couple of notable exceptions. The agent had sent over a last-minute replacement for the no-show middle-aged actress scheduled to play the mother. No-shows were one of the primary monkey wrenches of this business. For any one of a number of reasons, many of the people who performed in these films weren't the most dependable types: they'd be hungover, or get evicted, or just flat-out chicken out. Unfortunately, in this case, a lateral switch wasn't in the cards; the agent either took "middle" to mean "old" age, was working with slim pickings, or just plainly didn't care, because the replacement mother was more like a replacement grandmother. My jaw—and Holmes' otherwise perpetual erection—dropped when I saw her walk through the door. But unfortunately I had no other choice than to go on with the shoot.

John, who had been sitting off in a corner smoking a cigarette, hesitantly got up and walked over to me.

"Uh, Mr. Chinn? Is she the one playing the mother?"

I knew where this was going. Suffice it to say, he wasn't the only one worried about him coming.

"That's her."

"And I'm supposed to…do her?"

"It was scripted that way" I replied, although in my head I was already working out a few revisions.

"I'm not sure I'd be able to…you know…get it up for her." It's important to remember we were at the very dawn of pornographic filmmaking. Nowadays, there's every kind of fetish film imaginable, including a series called "Fossil Fuckers" that would have fit our situation that day. But back then, it was still more or less straight sex, done with young, attractive actors.

"That wouldn't surprise me."

"Just thought I should let you know." He sounded almost apologetic, and I was beginning to feel sorry for the poor guy.

"Don't worry, John. We'll work something out. I hear you."

For the first and only time in his career John had met a woman who he really didn't want to have sex with. But in his mind, the main wrinkle was that he wasn't really the studly, come-at-all-costs professional that he thought he was, and had told us he was. His work ethic and inherent decency were actually kind of endearing.

After we finished the final shot of the day, one of the girls in the cast pulled a joint out of her purse and lit up. She took a heavy toke and handed the joint to John. He raised his right hand and shook it in refusal.

"I don't do marijuana," he said. "It's bad for you."

He then nodded at the bourbon I was quietly enjoying. "I don't drink either. My stepfather was a drunk who constantly beat me and abused my mother."

"You don't drink and you don't do grass," I said. "So what are your vices?"

"Well, I do smoke cigarettes," he replied as he lit one up. I noticed that he had gone through just about an entire pack during the course of the shoot.

"Cigarettes are bad for you, too," I told him as I lit one up myself.

"Got to die of something, right?" he said with a wry smile.

We released the film without any fanfare. It sold to all of our accounts just as all of the rest of them had, and we quickly reinvested the money we received from it into the next project and continued to turn out product.

A month or so passed before one of the theater owners called Linda up and asked, "Hey, when are you going to send us another one of those Johnny Wadd movies?"

Linda dealt with all of our accounts so she had her finger on the pulse of this business that we were engaged in. This time she read that pulse correctly.

I was listening to an imported LP of Stanislav Richter playing Tchaikovsky's "Piano Concerto No. 1 in B-Flat" when Linda came into the room and said, "I think we ought to make another film about that guy with the big dick."

"Why?"

"Murray Offen in New York just called to ask me when the next Johnny Wadd movie would be coming out." New York was perhaps our most profitable account, and Murray's Avon Theatres had bought everything we'd ever made, so we certainly didn't want to disappoint him.

As I was mulling over the logistics, another theater owner called with the same request, and then another. Though I wasn't a marketing whiz, and society was decades away from colloquially throwing around terms like "franchise" and "brand," I realized that in Johnny Wadd, we might actually have an enduring character here.

I decided that the next Johnny Wadd flick should involve a slightly more mysterious and exotic theme. And like many filmmakers, I was quietly wondering if my own background might come into play. One of my grandfathers had been a Transcontinental Railroad worker who'd opened up a restaurant in Chinatown with his savings, so I thought we'd make that our next setting—keeping, of course, within the strict limits of our $750 budget. Our Chinatown adventure might not have exactly been J. J. Gittes–worthy, but I was actually starting to get excited about it.

The second Johnny Wadd film was titled *Flesh of the Lotus*. Despite my best attempts to work in the exotic angle, it didn't have much of a story; what little there was in that capacity was centered around Johnny, hot on the trail of the people who had brutally murdered a former girlfriend. That trail eventually led to Chinatown, where he confronted the killer while, of course, having lots and lots of sex along the way.

To save the cost of hiring an extra actor I decided to appear in it, in a nonsexual role, as the villain. I would even end up having a fight scene with John. To save even more money, we shot in and around the apartment of one of our actors, Alex Eliot. Then again, the term "actors" in this context was a bit of a stretch; our standard deal was that anyone who'd let us use their apartment got a job in the film.

Alex, whose actual surname was Elias, was a nice young man of Hungarian descent. From his outward appearance he looked like an office worker or accountant. Which he might have been, for all I knew, but whenever I offered him a film, he dropped his day job to make an appearance. He was always anxious, willing, and able. He would even eagerly pitch in as a crew member, even though he didn't really have to.

One day, out of curiosity, I asked him why he liked doing these films so much. "Are you kidding?" he replied incredulously. "Acting in these films is the only time I ever get laid."

After a shoot ended, I generally liked to wind down with a couple of drinks. I had brought a half pint of J&B Scotch and was just about to take a nip from it when John walked over to me.

"Could I have some of that?"

"I thought you didn't drink."

"I've taken it up since then. I still don't smoke grass, though."

I handed him the bottle and he took a large sip, savoring it in his mouth like a connoisseur would fine cognac.

"This is good," he said after he swallowed it. "What is it?"

"Scotch," I informed him.

"Scotch," he said, smacking his lips. And he nodded and took another sip.

Flesh of the Lotus was just another routine one-day grind. It wasn't exactly *The Godfather Part II* where sequels were concerned, and I figured it would be the end of the demand for any future Johnny Wadd movies.

I was wrong. The picture ended up being an enormous success, no doubt because of the still-relative novelty of John's own enormity, and the theater owners clamored for more.

The third Johnny Wadd movie, *Blonde in Black Lace,* followed in rapid succession. The plot this time involved blackmail, infidelity, and murder. I had really begun to enjoy doing my little porno-noirs. They provided a well-needed break from the cookie-cutter stuff our assembly line had been grinding out to make money.

For this shoot, John decided that he wanted a hundred dollars instead of the seventy-five dollars we had been paying him. We had already made the initial exception to pay him twenty-five more than we paid any other male actor and at this point we seriously considered terminating the Johnny Wadd series. But the franchise was turning out to be more profitable on a per-film basis than any of our standard features, so we knew we would eventually have to capitulate.

I got hold of John, but before I could get a word out, he said, "Bob, I've got to talk in-person." I figured John wanted to discuss money, so I went to the meeting prepared. Or so I thought.

When I arrived, John told me, "Bob, somebody with an inside line to the vice cops told me that there's going to be some major busts—and from what I heard, your name is near the top of the list. If I were you, I'd cool it right now."

"You're shitting me."

"I wish I was."

"Who told you this?"

"I can't reveal her name, but believe me, she knows what she's talking about."

Sure enough, the police suddenly began cracking down on porno shoots and we quickly decided that if we were going to do that next Wadd movie, it would have to be out of town. It was long past time for a vacation so we unanimously decided to go to Hawaii, where I figured I could improvise the fourth Johnny Wadd movie, *Tropic of Passion*.

I'd grown up in Hawaii, and the islands had always held a special allure for me. My childhood, while not perfect by any means, was replete with idyllic memories of long, improvised play with my friends, gorgeous days at the beach, and the fragrance of indigenous flowers everywhere. It was where I'd first decided I wanted to become a filmmaker, and coming back in that very capacity—if not quite on the same terms I'd envisioned for myself back then—excited me to no end.

In order to circumvent any law that might possibly address bringing someone across state lines for any kind of "immoral" purpose, we simply just mentioned to John that we were going to take a trip to Hawaii and hey, if he just happened to be there, maybe we would make a film.

"Cool," he said. "What flight are you going to be on?"

So John bought his own plane ticket and, lo and behold, he just happened to be on the very same plane that we were on. We even managed to grab a quick shot—which we later incorporated into the film—of John on the plane looking out through the window as it landed at the Honolulu International Airport. And as far as we could determine, legally we were completely in the clear.

We'd rented a nice and somewhat luxurious two-bedroom condo in Waikiki for a week which would serve not only as our housing accommodations for the duration of our stay but also as our primary interior location set. Our room was near the top of the high-rise building and it had a large balcony with a glass-topped patio table and chairs that looked out over Waikiki. Linda and I shared one of the bedrooms, Alain had the other bedroom, and John slept on the pull-out sofa-bed in the living room.

A couple of the girls had never worked with John before, and they were totally unfamiliar with his sole claim to fame. It was always interesting to see the big-eyed reactions of the girls when they first got a look at John's oversized member. They rarely said anything, but you could read it in their reactions, some of which we were actually able to capture in the films as they went down in real time.

Since this was essentially a working vacation, production on the project progressed somewhat lazily, without any set schedule, as we enjoyed what was doubling as an impromptu vacation. Aside from the sex scene and the scene shot at the strip club, everything was improvised on the spot. Alain and I alternated doing the camera work. We drove around the island and managed to grab a lot of interesting location footage, and whenever we saw something that looked like it might work we'd jump out of the car, quickly think of something to film around it, and then go ahead and film it.

We even grabbed a spur-of-the-moment running shot when we saw one of the tourist charter helicopters getting ready to take off near the Marina. It would be a simple matter to integrate this shot into one of the chase scenes, so we rushed over there and quickly shot it. Anything to give the illusion of some kind of action happening within the flimsy plot with which we were working. At any rate, we were all having a great time and it wasn't long before we ended up shooting much more footage than we could feasibly use in the film. In some ways, it was like being in film school all over again.

One day, we were working on our tans while tossing down drinks from the hotel's beachside bar when Alain met this cute, very shy Japanese tourist girl. Even though they could barely communicate with each other they managed to arrange a dinner date for that night.

Even though Alain was the one who had the date, John was beside himself with excitement. He rushed to the hotel gift shop and purchased some nice little souvenirs of Hawaii which he had wrapped as gifts. He insisted that Alain give his date one of them at dinner and the others would be waiting for her when he brought her back to the condo.

Alain would never have thought of doing any of this, and as it turned out, those little presents made that girl very happy. John even rushed back to our condo, straightened it up, and set the stage for a romantic after-dinner setting with flowers, candles, a bottle of wine, and the other little presents. Naturally we all stayed out very late that night so that Alain and his date could have the place to themselves.

In spite of his numerous shortcomings, John was capable of doing some very caring and selfless things for other people. I know that most people who knew him only later in his life would find this hard to believe. The John Holmes about whom people would talk—and about whom movies would ultimately be made in the future, in particular *Wonderland*, which depicted the gruesome murders of four people in the drug world with whom John was in cahoots—was nothing like the John Holmes I knew during this period. As obnoxious and insecure as he could be at times, back then he was basically a decent guy who helped turn a working trip to my childhood Hawaiian home into an enjoyable, even romantic, time for us all.

When we got home, however, John seemed to awaken overnight to the fact that he was rapidly becoming an adult film star, and he adjusted his attitude accordingly. While he was grateful for how the Johnny Wadd series had raised his profile considerably, he was beginning to demand a much higher salary than what we had been paying him. He let us know in no uncertain terms that other producers were paying him $250 a day, and he didn't feel he had to work for less, allegiance be damned. That amount, true or not, was a third of our budgets, and there was no way we were going to pay him that much. Not only was he starting to act like a prima donna, he was also pricing himself out of our league.

"I suppose this'll be the last Johnny Wadd film for you, then," I said, deciding to call his bluff. I also clearly implied that I was keeping my options open with regard to replacing him with someone more affordable in the event that I did decide to continue with the series.

"Well," he hedged. "Give me a call when you want to do another one and we'll work something out."

"Sure," I answered, but at the same time I steadfastly promised myself that I was finished making any more Johnny Wadd movies with an ungrateful John Holmes.

Little did I realize that, in the near future, events would conspire that would lead me to break that steadfast promise.

Bob Chinn *is the director and producer of hundreds of adult films. He is best known for creating John Holmes' alter ego, "Johnny Wadd."*

THE SNAKE AND BAKE MURDER

by Steve Hodel

THE FOLLOWING IS AN actual murder investigation. It is just one of the approximately three hundred that I investigated during my seventeen-year assignment in homicide.

The facts are true. Only the names have been changed and the dates slightly modified, to protect the children and the grandchildren of the guilty.

THE CALL-IN

IT WAS A SATURDAY night in early June, 1974. I was home, in my apartment in East Hollywood. Girlfriend and I were on our third Scotch when the phone rang. It was my D3, Paul O'Steen. An old schooler's old schooler.

"Steve, we got one. Total clusterfuck, and from the briefing I just got from the Watch Commander, I mean that literally. One wit and three suspects at the station. Get your ass in. It's a mess."

Forty-five minutes from call-in to the red zone in front of Hollywood station. I prided myself on getting there in under an hour. O'Steen was sitting at his desk talking to a female with long red hair. Her back was to me.

As I crossed the squad room, I noticed four uniformed coppers, coffee cups in hands, standing and talking at the nearby auto theft table. All four kept stealing furtive glances at Paul and the woman with the red hair.

Paul stood up at my approach. The woman remained seated but turned in my direction. "Steve, this is Mrs. Brandy Dawson. She and her husband were kidnapped from their home in Laurel Canyon. She's also a witness to his murder. We have the three suspects in custody in lockup. She'll give you the full story. Better use the interrogation room. You will want to tape this one." He glanced over at the blue suiters. "I'm taking uniform with me up to their residence. Need to secure it. The crime started there."

"Started? I asked. "Is the husband's body at the house?

Paul shook his head as he walked toward the blue suits, "No. His body's buried somewhere in Arizona. She'll fill you in."

I turned to Brandy, "Arizona?"

She gave me a nervous smile, "It's a long story. I could sure use some whiskey. Is that possible?"

"Only in the movies. How about some coffee?"

THE INTERVIEW

I ESCORTED HER TO the tape room, handed her a cup of coffee, and, for the first time, gave her a complete once over. She was absolutely stunning. Probably in her late twenties, but had a much younger, almost hippie-teen look. Tall, about five seven, trim, and was wearing cut-off Levi's shorts, brown leather sandals, and a see-through peasant blouse that revealed an ample pair of breasts.

I noticed she had a number of fresh scratches and bruises on her arms and both legs, and her clothing was heavily soiled with what looked like dark black oil stains. Not to mention her perfume was quite unusual—eau de gasoline.

I turned on the recorder. "Would you state your full name, date of birth, and home address?"

"Yes, my name is Brandy Elizabeth Dawson. I am twenty-six. I was born on October thirtieth, nineteen-forty-seven. I live at eight-three-four-four Weepah Way, in Laurel Canyon."

"Brandy, it is my understanding that you and your husband were kidnapped and he was murdered, but you survived. Is that correct?"

"Yes."

"What I would like you to do is to start from the very beginning and tell me in detail exactly what happened. Can you do that?"

For the next two hours, intermittently between tears and laughter, and four refills of coffee, Brandy Dawson told me her story. Working "Hollyweird" for the previous eight years, I thought I had heard it all.

I was wrong.

Brandy had been living with David Dawson, who was ten years older than she was, for the past four years and considered him her "common law" husband. (In 1974, the State of California required a minimum of seven years for legal status.) They had met at a beach party in Malibu in 1970.

Six months prior, on January 1, the couple had signed a two-year lease on a large private residence in the Hollywood Hills. She described the home as having four large bedrooms, a private backyard with a swimming pool and a long private driveway with off-street parking. In February, the couple opened up what Brandy described as "a private social club." The rules were simple: membership was free, and club meetings were held on both Friday and Saturday nights at the Dawsons' Laurel Canyon home. The minimum age requirement was twenty-one. Free drinks were provided, and admittance was by invitation only and required each adult to present his or her private membership identification card at the door. Each member was allowed to bring one guest. Drinks, food, and "entertainment" were also provided at no charge. But a fifty-dollar "club contribution" was required per couple each visit, to help cover the overhead.

Brandy went on to explain that their home was in effect "a swing pad," a place where consenting adults could come and realize their sexual fantasies. Members brought a partner and freely engaged in-group sex with other members. Twosomes, threesomes, foursomes, gay, straight, bi; all were welcome as long as they followed the rules:

no drugs and no violence. Entertainment was provided by Brandy and David, who, on Friday and Saturday nights, performed a thirty-minute warm up for the members' viewing pleasure. Enjoying the fact that I had become visibly embarrassed, she went on to inform me that their routine was broken into three distinct ten-minute acts. "Oral, then regular sex, then, you know, the other kind."

Brandy described David as "a John Holmes lookalike in every respect." (Holmes, aka "Johnny Wadd," a rising—pun intended—porn star in the seventies, became known as the "Sultan of Smut." At the peak of his film career, Holmes reportedly insured his manhood with Lloyd's of London for $14 million, claiming he arrived at that number by calculating it at $1 million per inch.) After the Brandy and David show, the members would generally engage in a social hour where they could make their preferences known and choose their partner(s). Three of the four bedrooms had wall-to-wall beds in addition to a half-dozen chaise lounges poolside for the warm summer nights.

As she continued her story, it was clear that Brandy saw providing a private place where consenting adults could come and freely engage in group sex as a community service. I challenged her view by asking "How much money were the two of you making off the club?"

My questioning flipped Brandy's demeanor from free love to free for all. "Fuck you!" she said, as her eyes flashed. Clearly she had some issues with what she sensed was a Puritanical assault on her right to be a sexually open woman of the times.

I shifted gears. "Okay, how many members typically showed up per night?"

"Usually about twenty-five."

I quickly did the math in my head: fifty dollars per couple equaled $600 a night, times eight nights, which equaled $4,800 a month, or $25,000 a month in today's dollars. That was a whole lot of beer, wine, and bologna sandwiches.

As if sensing the financial wheels turning in my head, she continued: "We had a lot of expenses. We paid for the beer and wine and food. A maid came twice a week. But *no*, it was not prostitution. Nobody ever charged anybody for sex. Maybe you pay for it, detective, but with us it was all *free love*."

She might have perceived my line of questioning as judgment on my part. But it wasn't. Whenever that kind of cash was involved, free love or not, there was motive. And where there was motive, the only kind of judgment was the kind of judgment day that David and Brandy Dawson were about to realize had finally come to their doorstep that night.

THE CRIME

BRANDY IDENTIFIED THE THREE suspects we had in custody as her employees. She had hired the Alvarez brothers (Ernesto, twenty-two, and Juan, twenty-five), as security. After a month of club meetings, she found that occasionally one of the members would have too much to drink and start an argument. Disputes sometimes arose over who was going to do what with whom, and the presence of two ostensible peacemakers had, in recent months, all-but-eliminated the problem. The third suspect was Dominick "Nick" Vicente. He was thirty-one. Not a lot upstairs, but great with his hands. He worked as the Dawsons' general handyman and gofer.

Early Saturday morning, June 1 at about 1:45 a.m., the last couple left the house. Rules required all members to be out the door by 2:00 a.m. David and Brandy were having a cold beer poolside. Both heard Juan call out from the living room, "Mr. Dawson, I have a question."

David called back, "Yes, Juan. What is it?"

Juan approached the couple with a four-inch blue steel revolver in hand. "Do you want me to shoot you here and now, or do you want to come with us quietly and maybe live?"

His brother, Ernesto, and Nick, the handyman, were right behind him. Nick was holding a large roll of duct tape, and Ernesto had two pairs of handcuffs. Brandy and David were handcuffed and gagged with duct tape, then ordered to walk out the front door. Ernesto opened the trunk to his 1965 Cadillac Coupe DeVille and David was ordered to climb inside. Brandy watched as David complied and Nick skillfully hogtied him with rope as though he were a rodeo steer taken to the ground.

Next it was Brandy's turn. Nick opened the trunk to his '67 Ford Galaxie, which had been parked next to the Alvarez brothers' Caddie. Brandy, too, was forced to get inside and bound in like fashion.

Brandy described the next seven hours as "pure hell." Her whole body began shaking, and tears flowed as she spoke. "They killed him. They said they would let him live if he cooperated, but they killed him anyway."

I turned off the tape and tried to calm her. "Let's take a short break, Brandy. Would you like a Coca-Cola?"

"Yes, please. Do you have aspirin?"

"Yes, be right back." I dropped a quarter in the machine for a large cookie, and another for the can of Coke. I walked to my desk, unlocked the drawer, and removed my bottle of Johnny Walker Red, took a large swig, and poured a double into a Styrofoam cup, then topped it off with some Coca-Cola. I opened my tin of aspirin and grabbed two tablets and returned to the interview room.

I placed the cup of Coke on the table and handed her the aspirin. "Here, this should help."

Her eyes widened with amazement as she swigged the drink. "I thought you said…"

"Only in extreme medical emergencies. You qualify."

Brandy went on to describe the seven-hour ride in the trunk. She could only breathe through her nose and could barely move an inch in either direction. Ten minutes into the drive, she heard the noise. It was close. A slow clicking sound that increased rapidly to what sounded like an electric buzzing.

As a child, growing up in a rural section of Clark County, Nevada, she had heard that sound a hundred times. It was unmistakable. She knew that somewhere in the darkness inside the trunk of the vehicle, just a few feet from her head, was a rattlesnake. The snake, sensing a predator was nearby, was shaking its tail as a warning that it was ready to strike. She remained frozen, fearing the slightest movement might cause the snake to attack her.

Three hours more of driving, with daylight breaking, she came face-to-face with her worst fear. Not three feet away was a glass aquarium with a wire mesh covering the top. Inside it was a three-foot

Western diamondback rattlesnake, a pit viper, known to be one of the deadliest snakes of its species.

Brandy went on to relate that she had lost all sense of time but recalled the car stopped on at least three separate occasions, each lasting no more than about ten minutes. The second stop was to gas up, and she recalled that the fumes were so overpowering she was afraid she might vomit and choke to death. On the fourth stop, they opened the trunk and the morning sun flooded in and temporarily blinded her. Both Alvarez brothers grabbed and lifted her out and dropped her on the ground. It was sand. She looked around and could see nothing but small dunes. They were somewhere in the desert.

The two brothers untied her feet, unlocked her handcuffs, and removed the duct tape from her mouth. They roughly pulled her to her feet and walked her about a hundred feet from the vehicle. She looked down and saw David lying motionless on the ground. He was still tied and handcuffed, and a plastic bag had been placed over his head and tied tightly around his neck. He wasn't breathing.

Juan handed her a shovel and ordered her to dig. "First you dig your husband's grave. Then your own."

She refused. He slapped her, removed the blue steel revolver from his waistband, pointed it at her head, and again said, "Dig."

Nick joined the two men, and the three began laughing as they took long swigs of tequila from the half-filled bottle.

She started digging, but couldn't resist asking them, "Why are you doing this? David and I were your friends. We gave you jobs and money."

They told her that was exactly why they did it. For the money. They told her they knew exactly how much money was coming in each month, and they wanted it. All of it. They were taking over the business. The house, the running of the club, everything. Their plan was simple. They would tell everyone that the Dawsons decided to move to Mexico and left the three of them in charge. Nothing would change; everything would stay the same, just under new management.

Brandy finished digging the hole and Nick and Juan picked up David's body and threw it into the shallow grave. She then saw Ernesto approach the grave carrying a large, heavy bag. He poured the contents, a white powder, into the hole and completely covered the body.

Brandy was ordered to fill the hole with sand. They told her that they had bought some lime, and it would dissolve the body so nobody would be able to recognize who he was.

The men then ordered her to start digging a second grave, "This one's for you."

At this point in the interview, Brandy's whole persona changed. She was back to the woman I had met a few hours earlier. More self-assured and confident. No tears, no fear. Even her voice became more animated. Her demeanor became almost excited, as if she was actually reliving the moments. Working in Hollywood all these years, I now wondered if I'd come face-to-face with a bona fide femme fatale—the kind of woman who could shift on a dime, whose beauty masked a dubious morality—or if I was just dealing with someone whose circumstances were such that she'd had to compartmentalize what had happened to her.

"When they told me their plan, I knew it was a do or die moment for me. I knew that if I couldn't persuade them—then I would be dead in just a few more minutes."

I didn't understand what she was saying. "Persuade them of what?"

She stared directly into my eyes as she spoke the words, "Persuade them that I wanted him dead."

I looked at her in disbelief. "What?"

"Don't you see detective? I *had* to convince them and I did! That's the only reason I am alive."

"How? What did you say?"

Brandy picked up the foam cup and downed the rest of her Johnny Walker and Coke.

"I told them that they had done me a favor, and I was glad David was dead. I told them that he was a sadist and had beaten me for years, that I hated his guts and secretly dreamt that he would be killed in a car accident. They didn't believe me. So, I said, 'Well, you can believe this.' And I walked over to where David was buried, took off my shorts and underpants, and I pissed on him. I said, 'There, David.

That's my payback and your karma for being such a bastard to me all these years.' I literally pissed on his grave."

I had never heard or seen anything like this woman. I tried to conceal my shock as I asked her, "Was he?"

She stared back blankly. "Was he what?"

"Was he a sadist? Had he beaten you for years?"

She shook her head. "Hell no. He was loving and caring and the sweetest man I've ever known. He only brought me pleasure. He was the best lover a woman could ever want."

Brandy told the three that they would all be equal partners and pointed out that if they killed her, they would lose the house; the lease was in her name, and the owner would evict them from the property, then raise the rent. Only Brandy could keep it locked in at the present rate for the next two years. She told them that with their help she could increase the club's activity from two to four nights a week. That would double the income from five to ten thousand a month which, split four ways, was $2,500 a month for each of them…tax-free, no less!

She could tell all three men were high from drinking booze and popping uppers. She almost had them convinced. She again looked directly at me and, with unmistakable pride, said, "I closed the deal by pulling off my blouse and telling them again how thankful I was for what they had done…then I asked them to fuck me right here next to his grave."

I had never met this breed of cat before and didn't know what to think of her. She had the beauty of a Persian, but her speech and actions were pure feral. Wild and dangerous. I was simultaneously attracted to and repulsed by her. "And did they?"

She smiled. "Fuck me? No, I called their bluff and all three folded. Juan was a big man with a big gun in his hand, but I could tell he was afraid of me. No real huevos. All they could think of was how much money they were going to be making."

We had passed the two-hour mark in the interview. I was exhausted, just listening to her, but Brandy seemed to thrive and grow stronger as she retold the horrors.

"What happened next?"

"I told them we should drive back to the Laurel Canyon house and make a plan. They agreed. I rode with Nick in his Ford, and Juan and Ernesto followed us in their Caddie. I asked Nick where we were, and he told me we were near Yuma, Arizona, about a mile off the main highway. Nick also pointed to a hardware store right on the main highway as we drove past it and said that that was where they stopped and bought a shovel and the two bags of lime to put over our bodies."

"Wait—did you say 'lime'?"

"Yes, why?"

My lips curled into a smile. I sensed that maybe we'd just gotten our first break in the case.

THE ARREST

"TELL ME ABOUT TONIGHT'S arrest."

"It was at Ben Frank's on the strip. We got back from the long drive from the desert at about eight o'clock and they wanted to stop for a hamburger before going back up to the house. We all went inside, and I told them I had to use the bathroom."

"I went to the back and called Sergeant Kenny Bell at West Hollywood Sheriff's Vice. I told him I was at Ben Frank's, that my husband had been murdered, and the three guys that did it were with me."

"He and his partners were there in five minutes. They walked in and put their guns on all three and arrested them. I was taken to West Hollywood, and then two LAPD uniformed officers came and brought me here."

"How do you know Sergeant Bell?"

"We met four years ago at the Troubadour on Santa Monica at a Neil Diamond concert. Kenny thought I was drinking underage, but when I showed him my ID everything was cool, and we became friends."

"Like boyfriend/girlfriend friends?"

"Yeah, I guess. David didn't mind; he did it too."

I looked at my watch; it was almost 1:00 a.m. "I'm going to have to go out in the field and do some work and then go up to your house and get some photographs of the inside. It's part of the crime scene. Do you have a friend that you can stay with for a few days? Someone I could drop you off with?"

"Yes, Bonnie Wilson in Los Feliz; she's a good friend."

Brandy called and woke Bonnie, who said for her to come right over. I dropped her off and told her I would call her mid-morning and that she should be ready for another ride out to Yuma.

She stood up. Those emerald green eyes dissolved into a pool of water. "Do you think David will ever forgive me for what I did?"

I nodded, "He'll forgive you. You're a survivor, Brandy, and that's what he would have wanted."

THE EVIDENCE

IN THE SEVENTIES, BEN Frank's (now Mel's Drive-In) was one of Hollywood's hippest coffee shops. Everyone who was anyone and who was no one went there. First they went cruising, boozing, and schmoozing at the Whisky, Pandora's Box, and the Troubadour, and the rest of the nightclubs along the strip. Then it was tradition to end the night with a hamburger and fries at Ben's.

Two patrol officers were standing next to the suspects' vehicles as I pulled into the lot. The Ford and the Caddie were clearly what we typically referred to as "beaters." Just what you'd expect from the kind of men that Brandy had been describing for the past three hours.

The younger rookie officer shined his flashlight on the trunk of the Ford. "We just relieved the night watch guys who had been here for like three hours. They told us there's a dead body in the trunk. Is that true?"

"No body, probably just a live rattlesnake."

He instantly backed up a few steps, "Holy shit."

The Hollywood Tow Truck, our official police impound, arrived. I had known the driver, Dennis Effle, for six years. "Dennis, you're going to love this one. I think we're going to find a live rattlesnake in the trunk."

"Fuck that, Steve. That shit is above my pay grade. I ain't messing with it."

"It's okay, the snake's locked in a glass cage. Or at least it was. Once we confirm it's in there, I'll have to get Animal Regulation out here to remove it. You won't have to go near it."

Dennis shook his head in disbelief. "Fucking Hollywood. Nothing but fruits and nuts. You got the trunk keys?"

"No, you'll have to pop the trunk. I consider this—what's the term I'm looking for…'exigent circumstances' so we won't need a search warrant."

Dennis went to his tool kit, removed a hammer and punch, and had it open in thirty seconds. The officers, who by now were standing a good fifteen feet away, shined their flashlights into the darkness. There it was. One very mean, very pissed off–looking snake. It stared up at the four of us from inside its glass cage and shook its rattle as if to say, "stay away, motherfuckers."

I told the uniform guys to make out the impound forms, but not to touch anything inside either vehicle. "Nobody touches anything," I said. "This is a Murder One investigation." I also directed them to go inside Ben Frank's and use a landline to call Communications Division to get animal regulation to impound the snake. Otherwise, the press would pick up the unit's police broadcast and be there taking pictures before they could say, "Roger that." I needed another twenty-four-hour lead before the press got wind of what we had.

It was a ten minute drive to the Dawson house north of the Strip. The sixties might have technically been over by 1974, but you would never have known from a jaunt into Laurel Canyon, which was still filled with actors, writers, and musicians, all clinging to the counterculture. And yet, for all its "peace, love, and granola" rhetoric, the counterculture—especially the music-based one in Laurel Canyon—was not exactly known for being big on women's rights. It was okay for women to be singers, or groupies, but not much else. The Dawsons' house was an exception: it was not only the perfect locale for a swing pad, but Brandy was clearly more than just a perfect domestic hostess: she was a proprietress on equal footing with David.

Sergeant O'Steen and two of the four officers were still at the house. Paul had obtained overall photos of the interior as well as the front entrance and driveway. I did a quick walkthrough. The place was tastefully decorated. A modern look, with large cushions in the living room. Queen-size beds in two of four bedrooms and two large water beds in the third. The fourth master bedroom had a king-size four-poster bed with a large mirror overhead. Surrounding it on the walls were large framed drawings of East Indian couples, engaged in sex, leaving nothing to the imagination. *Kama Sutra* 101, which was perfect given the place's proximity to the famed highway with which it shared that number.

Paul motioned for me to follow him. We walked down the hallway which opened into a small room containing a large glass jewelry display case. The sign on top read, *20 percent Discount to all Club Members.* Inside were adult toys of every size, shape, and color. Next to them were leather restraints and handcuffs. On the second shelf were French ticklers, his 'n' hers vibrators, ginseng lubricants, and an assortment of condoms. A toy box with everything a swinging social clubber could hope for—and better yet, they were offered at a twenty percent discount!

Paul and I agreed that having an SID (Scientific Investigation Division) print man out to the house was pointless. Since all three suspects were employees and had free run of the place, the presence of their prints was meaningless. We secured the residence and headed back to Hollywood Station.

THE SUSPECTS

First Ernesto, then Nick, then Juan were brought into the interrogation room. I took a few Polaroids of each man and started the tape recorder.

All three refused to offer any statement and asked that they be provided an attorney. That effectively ended my contact with them. They were formally booked, mugged, and fingerprinted and charged with 187 PC (Murder)—No Bail.

By the time I finished writing the arrest reports, it was 9:00 a.m. Sunday morning. My plan was to borrow a policewoman partner from Juvenile or the Sex Team, pick up Brandy, and drive to Yuma where we'd stay the night and search for the body early Monday morning. I called Sergeant Audrey Fletcher at home. She would be perfect. A veteran cop, smart as a whip, and totally nonjudgmental. A definite requirement when it came to being around Brandy Dawson.

She picked up on the first ring. I briefed her on what I had. "God, yes, Steve. Love to get out of town for a few days."

"Can you be ready to go in two hours? I can pick you up. You still living at the house on Beachwood Drive?"

"I'll be packed and ready to go. Yes, been here since fifty-two. I'll probably die here."

Tragically, she was correct. She was still living at that home when, one cold, winter evening, she drove to the beach, walked out on the sand, put her service revolver to her head, and pulled the trigger. She was my first detective partner, possessed an uncanny ability to read people rightly, and was one of the smartest women I had ever met. During those years, the highest rank a woman could get promoted to was Sergeant. Had Sergeant Fletcher been a man, she would likely have made Chief.

YUMA REVISITED

I GRABBED A QUICK breakfast and picked up Audrey, then Brandy. She had borrowed her girlfriend's The Who T-shirt, and again was wearing clean jeans, brown sandals, and no bra. The grease and sand were gone. Clean and freshly showered, with her long red hair pinned back in a ponytail, she looked like a young Hollywood starlet. An absolute knockout. As I smiled at her, I was forced to admit to myself that, above my every moral and professional leaning, I was enchanted and had developed a very strong crush on this witness/victim.

We made the three-hundred-mile drive in about five hours and checked in to adjacent rooms at a cheap motel on Interstate 8, just east of town.

I had called the local sheriff before leaving Hollywood and given him a quick summary of the crime and our reason for coming to town. He said he would have his detectives ready to assist on Monday morning and suggested we meet at the Yuma Sheriff's Office at 0900.

There would be no disco dancing in Yuma, but the three of us had one of the best Mexican dinners I've ever had, which we washed down with four Carta Blanca cervezas before heading off to an early bedtime. Peaceful as could be.

Which was good, because the next morning I found myself in a freaking convoy.

We were the lead car, followed by Yuma sheriff's detectives, who were in turn followed by Yuma PD, a two-man team from the FBI, a medical examiner, and the Yuma County coroner. Four cars and a Coroner's wagon headed down Highway 8 in search of a body buried somewhere in the middle of the desert.

Brandy, true to her word, had an excellent sense of direction. "There it is!" she yelled. "That's the store where Nick said they bought the shovel at."

She was right. The owner himself had made the sale and remembered the shovel and two forty-pound bags of lime.

I showed him the three separate six-man photos. He looked at all three, then put his finger on the photo of Juan Alvarez, "I'm sure he was the one that bought the shovel, but can't say about the other two. I think one of them waited in the car, so I never did see him."

With a positive ID in pocket we hit the road again, followed by Yuma Five O, the Feds, and a Quincy MD lookalike. Brandy was now in her full-detective mode, "I think it was about ten minutes from the store to where they drove off the road. I could feel it changed from cement to driving on sand, and I could feel the wheels spin a little."

The next hour was frustrating. We tried four dirt roads, but found nothing. All the sand dunes looked alike. It was getting hot, and the uniformed Yuma PD officers gave up and headed back to town. We were seriously thinking about following them when all of a sudden Brandy yelled, "There! Over there! That's it!"

I looked at the side road, which was identical to all the others we had tried.

"How do you know? It's the same as all the others."

"No, it isn't. I remember cause when I saw that cactus, it reminded me of David."

Audrey was the first to get it. She started laughing hysterically at the sight. Because standing tall and fully erect at the entrance to the turnoff was a giant saguaro cactus. At its base, one on each side, were two enormous, round, barrel cacti. If I'd been more supernaturally inclined, I would have sworn it was David, the "Johnny Wadd" look-alike, calling out from the grave, his giant penis pointing the way to his final resting place.

The body was still remarkably preserved given the heat and circumstances. The Coroner, who had taken charge of the removal, suspected that the suspects had wanted "lye," but had asked for "lime." Ironically, as I'd initially suspected, their mistake could well have acted more to help preserve the body than to speed up the decomposition.

THE TRIAL

THE PRELIMINARY HEARING FOR the State of California v. Juan and Ernesto Alvarez and Dominick Vicente was scheduled for June 16, 1974.

Even without admissions or a cop out, my case was airtight. I had a percipient witness and actual surviving victim of the crimes who witnessed the killing. Fingerprints of all three defendants were found on the plastic bag used to suffocate David Dawson. Samples of the victim's blood type (AB Negative, very rare) were found inside the trunk of the Alvarez brothers' Cadillac. (DNA would not be discovered for another decade.) I had a witness to the purchase of the shovel and lime that were used in the commission of the crime, and his identification of one of the defendants as purchasing it from him at his store. A third living witness, the Western Diamondback rattlesnake, would be brought to court and offered in evidence. (Brandy later informed me, pretrial, that the reason for the snake was that the brothers originally planned to turn him loose inside the trunk of the car and have him bite and kill her. But her fast-talking changed that and put the snake out of a job as well as saving her from a horrible and painful death.)

In California, a preliminary hearing is not a full trial. It is held to "show cause" that enough evidence exists to bind the defendant(s) over to a full trial in Superior Court. Guilt beyond a reasonable doubt is not required. It is procedural, and usually only a small part of the evidence is presented. Just the bare minimum. Just enough to "hold them to answer."

The Deputy DA's plan was to call and have Brandy Dawson testify to some of the main facts and her observations, then have the LAPD print man testify to having found all three defendants' fingerprints on the person of the victim, David Dawson. Both Alvarez brothers were represented by a Deputy Public Defender and Nick Vicente had a court-appointed lawyer.

What followed was an absolute nightmare.

Working so many years in Hollywood, as well as seeing my fair share of film noir, I was intimately familiar with the brassily tough makeup of the classic femme fatale. I'd seen firsthand the Barbara Stanwyck–esque fast-thinking resourcefulness that had been Brandy's salvation. But in my admiration for her, mixed in with something a little bit stronger than that, and in my haste to identify a trope so readily present in both celluloid and real-life Hollywood crime, I'd overlooked the undeniable chink in the femme fatale's armor, the stain on her character left by a streak of tear-streamed mascara: namely, the self-destructive behavior that, in life as in film, would inevitably be her undoing.

Brandy was nervous and forgetful. She was unrecognizable from the self-assured, articulate woman I had interviewed in the detective bureau just two weeks before. She became defensive and angry on cross-examination by the defense lawyers and started trash talking, even using occasional profanity. The judge quickly became hostile toward her, which made conditions worse.

He threatened to hold her in contempt, to which she responded, "That's fine with me. I don't care. Fuck it all."

The judge called for a fifteen-minute recess and told the prosecutor to "get your witness under control, or she will be going to lockup."

"Yes, your honor. I'm sorry. She's been distraught since the death of her husband."

Brandy, still on the witness stand, yelled out, "Not death, it was murder. They murdered him."

During the court time out I huddled with the prosecutor, and we decided that we needed to get her off the stand and replace her with me testifying to the finding and recovery of the body and then put the print man on and end it there. The hearing resumed with Brandy still on the witness stand.

The prosecutor immediately thanked Brandy for her testimony and said, "No further questions."

Nick Vicente's attorney spoke out. "Just a few more questions, Your Honor." Because this was a prelim and not the actual trial, he was severely limited to what he could pursue, but nevertheless he was able to get a fact on the record that I feared just might torpedo the entire case.

With the judge still steaming from what he considered was the witness's "attitude problem," the defense attorney asked, "Mrs. Dawson, we learned earlier that my client was in your employ as a handyman at your adult social club, correct?"

Brandy responded, "Yes, he did odd jobs."

"Odd jobs, yes. Speaking of odd, can you confirm for us that you have a piercing? A piercing of a metal ring through your clitoris?"

The entire courtroom looked up at the witness in stunned silence.

The judge was the first to speak. "What did you just say?" He ordered the court reporter to read back the statement.

The court reporter, an older woman of about fifty, turned beet red as she read back the question.

"'Odd jobs, yes. Speaking of odd, can you confirm for us that you have a piercing? A piercing of a metal ring through your clitoris?'"

The prosecutor jumped to his feet. "Objection, Your Honor. This is totally irrelevant and immaterial. Mrs. Dawson's personal tastes have absolutely no bearing on the facts of this case."

"Objection is overruled. The witness will answer the question."

Brandy now in full-defiance answered, "Yes I do. For five years, I've had it. Do you have a problem with that?"

Nick's lawyer smiled at her, "Thank you, Mrs. Dawson. No further questions at this time."

In what I can only conceive of as being his own personal prurient interests, certainly there was no legal basis for it, the judge again held a recess, ordering that Brandy Dawson be subjected to a "full body search" by a female deputy to determine if, in fact, she had a metal ring piercing her clitoris.

The deputy dutifully performed the search and confirmed that Mrs. Dawson did, indeed, have a ring in said clitoris.

I was called as the second witness and testified to driving to Yuma, recovering the body, and submitting the Coroner's protocol which established the cause of death. The SID print man identified all three defendants' fingerprints as being on the plastic bag which had been placed over the victim's head and caused him to suffocate. The judge, despite his obvious personal hostility and disgust for our star witness, bound all three defendants over for trial in Superior Court.

Two months later, I received a call from the prosecutor who had conducted the preliminary hearing. He informed me that there would be no trial. His office had come to a plea bargain agreement with all three defendants through their attorneys. They were pleading to second-degree murder, and he expected they would serve about twelve years.

I was enraged. "Twelve less a third off for good behavior—that means they won't do more than eight years, counselor. Eight years for what should be a capital case? How do you justify that? We can win it. What's the problem?"

There was a long pause, and he finally responded. "Brandy Dawson. Brandy's the problem, Detective. Their defense would have been that she was the ringleader and mastermind. Planned the whole thing herself. They were just good soldiers, following her orders." He hung up the phone.

I was angry, of course, but understood that they'd go with what had worked for so many other cases, especially those involving women: blame the victim. So much for all the so-called advances in women's rights. But I also knew he was right. A full trial would have been a disaster. At best it would have probably resulted in the same outcome—at worst a hung jury.

As I pondered the near–femme fatale whose case I'd just helped close, my mind reflected on some of my department's more film noir–worthy murders, ones we gave names, like the "White Gardenia Murder," the "Red Lipstick Murder," and, of course, the "Black Dahlia Murder." This forty-year-old case was one of my most unusual call-outs. I thought it would only be right to name it for a popular domestic product of the day, given the case's literal and figurative reptilian elements, as well as the fact that it had originated in a home—if not exactly homey—environment, one in which David Dawson's female partner had enjoyed full partnership status, but in the end had been relegated to just another female victim.

It's known to this day as the "Snake and Bake Murder."

Steve Hodel *is a* New York Times *bestselling author. He spent twenty-four years with the LAPD, where, as a homicide detective, he worked on more than three hundred murder cases and achieved one of the highest "solve rates" in the force. He is a licensed PI and author and his first book,* Black Dahlia Avenger: A Genius for Murder *was a* New York Times *bestseller and was nominated for an MWA Edgar Award in the Best Fact category. Steve has written three additional books:* Most Evil, *a* Los Angeles Times *bestseller,* Black Dahlia Avenger II, *a sequel and an eight-year follow-up to his true-crime investigations, and the recently published* Most Evil II *(Rare Bird Books, 2015). His investigations, now in their sixteenth year, have been featured on* NBC Dateline, CBS 48-Hours, Court TV, A&E Bill Kurtis, Cold Case Files, CNN Anderson Cooper, *and the Discovery Channel. Steve resides in his hometown of Los Angeles.*

A FEW, MOSTLY TRUE, THINGS ABOUT LA

by Jim Natal

S AFE, WARM, IF, LA…

Event horizon
No one here gets out alive
Memory's black hole

   Tall ships, two hundred years of America, palm trees and independence shimmering in the heat. My first summer in Los Angeles, crashed unscripted in the guest room of a couple I barely knew at the farthest margin of Santa Monica, where a ripple from a stone thrown into the bay would widen to the east until it backwashed against the breakwater of Interstate 10—a freeway not an expressway—rush hour traffic jams outside the kitchen window. Every acquaintance since has branched from there like capillaries and canyon roads, like backward brackets in a tournament chart. LA was brazen that bicentennial July, a wide and garish necktie that didn't quite make it down to the beltline, a Zen riddle whose only answer was "What's so funny?" if you laughed too.

   Rain, snowcaps, mudslides
   Then it doesn't rain for years
   Fountain of sorrow

Beater '66 VW bus, New Mexico plates, every lane a slow lane
with a horizontal steering wheel and the turning radius of a tramp
freighter. Immediate pilgrimage to 77 Sunset Strip, the 1960s show
that had set the California hook. Except it wasn't there; no door beside
Dino's Lodge where the investigations office should have been and the
address had four numbers instead of double lucky sevens. LA illusion/
disillusion. Should have known things are not necessarily what they
appear to be; art and artifice, fiction and nonfiction intertwined,
sometimes interchangeable. Bedside Raymond Chandler had it
right—that saffron-filtered afternoon light turns harsh in an instant,
shows all the creases and scars, the bus ticket disappointments. Wasn't
that what kept the private eyes in business? Not so apparent then that
LA was the city the future relied upon, a destiny cast from character
actors, drugstore counters, and reinvention. You are who you say you
are until proven otherwise.

Next revolution
This old world keeps spinnin' 'round
The pier carousel

Mornings. Crows squawking, hummingbirds zipping, parrots
in the fronds, and noisy little finches flocking like extras, promoting
themselves. Even plants were Birds of Paradise. The weather always
sunny side up, barely two minutes of the local newscast, floral days
following one after another like Rose Bowl floats. People told me
they missed having seasons. All this Chicago boy cared about was
that one season had gone missing, was presumed dead. I asked where
all the "fruits and nuts" were, staple fodder for the LA jokes on the
New York late night talk shows (before the hosts relocated West).
"You want that?" a new friend shrugged. "Just go down to Hollywood
Boulevard." Went once, no need to go back. Bought into the dream,
didn't want to undream it.

Shoreline silver coins
Tide checks out but never leaves
Midnight grunion run

Academy Awards rehearsal. Exit through the artist's door, blinding sidewalk glare, dozens of cameras raised then dropped, Doppler murmur surfing through the crowd—"It's nobody… nobody…nobody." Hit me like a commuter train except there weren't any, ego pulped in a blender, wondered if I'd made a mistake, should have tried San Francisco instead, worn flowers in my hair ten years too late. Scenes and scenery more oppressive than over-whitened teeth, ostentatious displays of wealth, unaffordable, unattainable even in my gold chain screenwriter fantasies. The Porsche convertibles. Cantilevered canyon houses and Malibu poolside parties. The beautiful women in restaurants with even more beautiful men. My friend laughed, took pity, divulged the secret combination: "They don't actually own any of it. Everyone's in hock up to their eyeballs."

> *Unfettered, alive*
> *The only faultlines are yours*
> *Lost maps to the stars*

Jim Natal's *most recent poetry collection,* 52 Views: The Haibun Variations, *was published by Tebot Bach in April 2013. He is the author of three previous collections:* Memory and Rain, Talking Back to the Rocks, *and* In the Bee Trees, *which was a finalist for the 2000 Pen Center USA and Publisher's Marketing Association Ben Franklin Awards. He also is the author of three chapbooks (*Explaining Water With Water, Oil on Paper, *and* The Landscape from Behind*) and two limited-edition chapbooks (*A Collector of Infinity *and* Rain in L.A.*). A multi-year Pushcart Prize nominee (including 2012), his poetry has been published or reviewed in* Bellingham Review, Runes, Spillway, Pool, Reed, The Paterson Literary Review, Poetry International, *and* The Los Angeles Review, *among other print and online journals.*

WHEN REALITY WAS A JOKE: THE MAKING OF ALBERT BROOKS' *REAL LIFE* (1979)

by Tom Teicholz

TODAY, REALITY TV IS a genre for which they award Emmys, from which careers are born, love is found, and fortunes are made. Reality TV represents a huge share of the TV industry, and we accept that these shows are cast, produced, and edited to enhance their drama. Yet if we see humor in the self-seriousness of the participants and delight in the outrageousness of their antics, if we see the irony in the genre's ability to produce stars (and even presidential candidates!) and acknowledge it as part of "show business"—these insights were already abundantly elucidated in Albert Brooks' prescient 1979 debut feature film, *Real Life*.

Brooks realized, long before anyone else, that cameras filming real people's lives would not only affect and change the subjects, it would affect those making the film. Brooks understood that in the end, any production was inevitably showbiz, and that showbiz is a beast that must be fed and whose gravity, like a black hole, sucks up every imaginable cliché and past convention. In other words, a subject ripe for the comic intervention of Brooks, whose style was avant-garde and cerebral and rooted in the deconstruction of the creative process and exploding classic comedic tropes (Brooks was meta before meta was cool), all framed by his ongoing existential crisis. *Real Life* made clear what has now become fact: that people in Hollywood have no conception of reality, but every confidence that they know how to deliver a fake version of it.

The son of comedian Harry Einstein (who performed as Parkyakarkus) and actress/singer Thelma Leeds, Brooks grew up in a Beverly Hills steeped in showbiz—his father died when Albert was eleven, after appearing at a Friars Club Roast for Lucille Ball and Desi Arnaz. By his twenties, Brooks had established himself as a comic performer in his own right, appearing on TV variety programs from *Dean Martin* and *Ed Sullivan* to *The Tonight Show with Johnny Carson*. Brooks didn't tell jokes; he did bits that were originated for the appearances and didn't repeat, such as a mime who couldn't stop talking, an inept ventriloquist, or a comedian who has run out of material and won't debase himself by doing all the things that would get an easy laugh (pulling down his pants, getting a pie in the face), which Brooks did even as he said he wouldn't. He even did a stand-up comedy tour opening for rock acts.

In 1971, *Esquire* featured Brooks' humor piece, "Albert Brooks' Famous School for Comedians" that was, in and of itself, predictive of comedy schools like The Groundlings and the Upright Citizens Brigade that would soon arise, sending up the notion that comedy can be taught. As Brooks recently recalled, "The scary thing about that is they got maybe five thousand replies. People just had no idea that this was a joke."

The producer of PBS's *The Great American Dream Machine* asked him to turn his *Esquire* piece into a short film that was "like an infomercial," Brooks said. "That was the first time I ever picked up a camera and I thought, *If I point it here and I say that, it should be funny,* and it worked. It was a very successful film for them."

In the meantime, Dick Ebersol, then-director of weekend late night programming at NBC, and Lorne Michaels, a Canadian-born comedian who had written for *Laugh-In,* approached Brooks about doing a comedy

program, which would be called *The Albert Brooks Show* and would air
live from New York at 11:30 p.m. on Saturday nights.

Brooks wasn't interested. He didn't believe live would be funnier
than taped, and to him there was no novelty in it, as Johnny Carson
and Ed Sullivan had been doing live for a long time. Also, Brooks had
no desire to leave his native Los Angeles for New York, or to work on
a show that first began at the late hour of 11:30 p.m. As he told Bill
Zehme in an interview for *Playboy* in 1999, "I was just too wiped out as
a performer to put myself through that live stress. I didn't really even
consider moving to New York to go through all that rigamarole. They
came back to me three times and, finally—to chicken out, actually—I
said, 'You shouldn't have a permanent host, anyway. Every show has
one host; you should get a different host every week.'

Still, although Ebersol and Michaels would go on to hire a young
cast of Second City performers, many of whom had appeared in
National Lampoon's Lemmings and the *National Lampoon Radio Hour*,
none had Brooks' name recognition. So in order to secure Brooks'
participation, Ebersol and Michaels agreed to let him make six short
films from Los Angeles, giving him not only complete editorial
control but ownership of the films as well.

Brooks told *Playboy*, "Because they didn't have anyone, talent-
wise, attached to the show yet, they still wanted to get me on board. So
I suggested the short films. I served a purpose for them and even did
their first publicity. Back in May of 1975, before the show debuted in
October, before any cast was hired, Lorne Michaels and I did the press
junket at Universal Studios. Writers were asking, 'So, Albert, what's
this show going to be?' And I said, 'I have no idea. Lorne?' And he
wasn't sure either. Nobody knew."

Michaels asked Los Angeles–based producer Penelope Spheeris,
who had founded Rock 'N Reel, the first music video production
company, to work with Brooks. Spheeris recalled that the first time
they met, Brooks came to her Hollywood office in the landmark
Sunset Boulevard "Crossroads of the World" development. "He
looked around and said, 'Crossroads of the entire world? I love it.'"

Each of the six short films Brooks wrote and directed was brilliant
in its own way, with Brooks appearing in most. There was a film about

Brooks performing heart surgery (but forgetting that anesthesia needed to be supplied). There was a "Fall Preview" of three fictitious forthcoming TV programs: *Medical Season*, *The Three of Us*, and *Black Vet*. *Black Vet* was a show about an African-American veterinarian who was a Vietnam War veteran; *The Three of Us* was a sitcom about a couple who lived with the wife's best friend—with Brooks constantly pleading for a polyamorous relationship (which looked all the more prognostic in retrospect when ABC debuted *Three's Company* just a few years later); and *Medical Season* was a reality show that promised, "Real stories, real people, real action, and reality was never like this!" and demonstrated that in 1975 Brooks was already thinking about the comedy inherent in a reality show. Another of the shorts was entitled "The National Audience Research Institute," which aired on January 10, 1976, wherein Brooks visited the Institute to figure out what people didn't like about him and how he could improve himself.

Brooks recalled, "We did it down and dirty. When we needed a hospital, we went, we begged. We got to go into the Cedars operating room. That was my filmmaking college."

Michaels wanted each of Brooks' films to be five minutes long. Brooks made them at whatever length he thought worked best…and, because of the terms of his deal, he could. Brooks: "I just became a pain in the neck. I was resented… It all came down to the fifth film, in which I performed open-heart surgery. It was fourteen minutes long, and Lorne was upset. It only aired because my friend Rob Reiner was hosting and said, 'I went to school with Albert. I'll take his film.' Lorne didn't want the problem anymore. The relationship was symbiotic while it lasted; it helped me, it helped them. I learned my craft and got out."

Around that time, David Geffen, whose record label, Asylum, had produced Brooks' comedy album *A Star is Bought* (and on which Geffen did a cameo), left Asylum for Warner Brothers Motion Pictures. Brooks: "He said, 'Come over and make a movie. I came over, and Monica Johnson and Harry Shearer and I, we got an office.'"

Brooks knew Shearer from *The Credibility Gap* satire radio program on which Brooks appeared regularly, Shearer also cowrote and coproduced *A Star is Bought*. "Harry is brilliant," Brooks said,

"Really a world-class satirist." Johnson, a talented sitcom writer, was the sister of comedy writer Jerry Belson. Johnson had originally been partnered with Marilyn Suzanne Miller, with whom she'd written scripts for *The Mary Tyler Moore Show*. The writing team broke up in 1974, and Miller went on to become one of the original writers at *Saturday Night Live*. Of Johnson, and her importance to writing *Real Life*, Brooks said: "We clicked. She was a very good person to bounce things off of and talk to. A brilliant person who was a giant. She understood what I was doing like nobody else, and that is such a great rarity, and she was funny. She could help me [when] we wrote together." Johnson had a long writing partnership with Brooks that included such Brooks classics as *Modern Romance*, *Lost In America*, *The Scout*, *Mother*, and *The Muse*. She passed away in 2010.

Brooks' original idea was about a self-help guru. "It was a Werner Erhard–type character who would put people to sleep, thousands of people on the floor, it was 'Program Their Dreams'. It was a very interesting movie, but I got more and more panicked because I thought, *This is too much for me to direct. I don't think I know how to direct this.*

Fortunately, Brooks had another idea for a movie. He had seen *An American Family*, the PBS documentary about the Loud family, generally considered the first "reality" television program; and then he read a quote by Margaret Mead about the power of a documentary like *American Family*. Mead called it "as new and significant as the invention of drama or the novel…a new way in which people can learn to look at life, by seeing the real life of others interpreted by the camera."

Brooks brought it to his cowriters and announced, "We're going to do this." They started writing the film and Brooks grew confident that he could direct it, "It had all the elements I knew I could do." Then one day at Warner Brothers, Brooks passed David Geffen in the hall. Brooks recalls Geffen asking, "'How's it going?' Brooks said, 'We're doing another idea but I really like it,' and Geffen said, 'Hurry up.'" What Brooks didn't know was that Geffen was on his way out.

Brooks now had to submit the script to Ted Ashley, a former talent agent, who was Warner Brothers' CEO.

"I wish you could've been there when I went into Warner's when I finished [the script of] *Real Life*," Brooks said. "I pitched this idea to Ashley to get the financing and he looked at me like, 'How did you get on this lot? What are you talking about?' We were gone."

Brooks had a script, but he needed to find the money to make the movie. Norman Epstein, who was Linda Ronstadt's manager at the time, suggested Jonathan Kovler, then owner of the Chicago Bulls, who was Epstein's cousin.

"I had a meeting with him," Brooks recounted. "He was at LaCosta, and I actually sat with him in a steam room and pitched him." Kovler agreed to finance the film for $500,000 on the condition that Brooks pay any overages. "Believe me," Brooks said, "the movie would've ended at whatever scene the five hundred thousand dollars [ran out]."

Real Life opens with Brooks attending a community meeting in Phoenix to announce his project. Brooks plays a Hollywood entertainer and filmmaker named Albert Brooks, whose narcissism is matched only by his optimism, and who imagines he can get anyone to do his bidding—all to his own self-aggrandizement. "It's a Hollywood Albert Brooks," Brooks explained. "It's Albert Brooks, the celebrity. It's the same Albert Brooks I did on *A Star Is Bought*, the comedy album. It's the Hollywood guy."

Brooks is dressed in a bright red Western-style shirt with a red neckerchief—a visual gag of how a person in Hollywood might think people in Arizona dress and which, in fact, looks more Hollywood than Arizona. Brooks explained that his character was "this Hollywood phony" who imagined that wearing such outlandish western garb would make the folks in Phoenix like him. (As a side note, Brooks no longer remembers whether or not the shirt was made by the Hollywood country and western tailor Nudie Cohn, born Nuta Kotlyarenko, who has a small cameo in the film.)

Brooks was the first of his contemporary comedians to play a lead character who went by his real name. Since then, a number of actors and celebrities such as Kareem Abdul Jabbar in *Airplane!* or Neil Patrick Harris in the *Harold and Kumar* series have played themselves, and a generation of stand-ups such as Gary Shandling, Jerry Seinfeld, Larry David, and more recently, Amy Schumer, Abbi

Jacobson, and Ilana Glazer play versions of themselves onscreen, but Brooks was there first.

In the opening, Brooks touts the ensuing one-year project's affiliation with a think tank, "The National Institute of Human Behavior in Boulder, Colorado," which harks back to his SNL "Audience Research Institute" short. Brooks discusses the selection of the family—which, although claiming to be scientific, he reveals was determined by Brooks not wanting to spend the winter in Wisconsin. Here too, using science to validate inane notions, Brooks was ahead of his time. Or as he put it recently: "that certainly has become way more popular: fake validity."

In the film, Brooks has high ambitions for the reality film project. As he later brags to the family, "You're going to be on Jonas Salk's coffee table." This notion of Brooks' comedy having altruistic goals which could lead to a Nobel Prize for him is a notion he would return to and elaborate on many years later, in his 2005 film *Looking for Comedy in the Muslim World*.

At the meeting Brooks breaks into song, backed by Mort Lindsay and the *Merv Griffin Show* orchestra, further evidence of Brooks' being a creature of Hollywood invention. Brooks then rushes off to the airport to meet the family, at which point we learn that Brooks has sent them on an all-expenses-paid week's vacation to Hawaii. He and his attendant camera crew greet them at the airport with leis, as though they had landed in Honolulu instead of Phoenix. It is only a few minutes into Brooks' filming of 'reality,' but already everything is staged. As Brooks explained recently, "As soon as you let cameras into people's lives, there's no more reality. It doesn't exist. That's the whole point of the movie." A point which is underscored further when the family arrives at their home, to be welcomed by the assembled crew who cheer, a scene that today has become a staple of reality shows from *Extreme Home Makeover* to *The Bachelor* and *Bachelorette*.

Brooks is similarly spot-on about the role technology will play in filming reality programs. He explains that he has outfitted the rooms with Japanese wall cameras which are activated by body heat, as well as portable filming units (which look like diving bell helmets) called the Ettinauer 226XL. In one of the film's most quoted lines, Brooks says about the cameras: "we have four of those." The multiple cameras in the rooms and the camera angles are very much the stuff of today's reality television, while the Ettinauer cameras look very much like the ones James Cameron invented to film underwater.

Charles Grodin's performance as Warren Yeager, the family patriarch, is pitch perfect. Brooks chose Grodin based on watching him in an early—and similarly notorious—reality-based program. "I remember watching Charles Grodin on *Candid Camera*," Brooks said, "and he was the most natural guy in the world. He could fool those people. What professional could pass for a natural guy?"

Yeager is a veterinarian who is eager to make the film to promote his practice. However, as Brooks films him in his surgery, Yeager kills a horse by over-sedating it.

"I loved that scene," Brooks said. "We were able to get a horse. It was not a show horse; it was a very old horse. The horse was fine, but they put him out. There was only one person, a real vet, who could do that in California, and he was in the scene. He was that old guy behind the mask, and he allowed it and did it. It still makes me laugh."

Yeager tells Brooks he doesn't want that scene to be in the film and Brooks tries to convince him that it shows him in a favorable light. Brooks tells him, "You did great... People make mistakes all the time... To err is human, to film divine." In a subsequent scene Yeager says, "What's going to happen when the kids go to school and their friends say 'Did your Dad really kill that horse?'" Phony is as phony does.

Brooks' comedy was ahead of its time in other important ways. As Brooks films the first family dinner, Yeager's wife, Jeannette, played by Frances Lee McCain, starts talking about her menstrual cramps—which, when addressed onscreen today by writers such as Lena Dunham, Amy Schumer, Tina Fey, Ilana Glazer, Abbi Jacobson, and Caitlin Moran, is considered revolutionary, four decades after Brooks.

Brooks also foresaw the symbiotic relationship that would develop between reality "stars" and the media, and how news would become big business. In *Real Life* a local reporter barges into the Yeager's home because he feels this story could go "national." The media, in a scene that foreshadowed today's codependent relationship between entertainment-oriented on-air personalities and reality stars, follow the family down the street, trying to get reactions from them.

Real Life is filled with great lines, such as when Jeannette is ready to drive off. She tells Brooks, "I need to be alone," to which Brooks responds, "OK. Can I come with you?" Or when Brooks says to one of the academic researchers: "I think we're very much alike. See, that's why we can get into these debates. I think you'd be surprised at how much alike we really are." To which the researcher responds: "I'd be more than surprised. I'd be suicidal." Or when Brooks, at wit's end, exclaims: "Why did I pick reality? I don't know anything about it." Of course! Then there's the phrase from the movie that has become part of our vernacular: "movie jail," an expression Brooks came up with for the scene where he tries to justify manufacturing an ending to his reality film. Brooks says, "There's no law that says we can't start real and end fake. What are they going to do, put me in movie jail?"

As much as anything else, Brooks recalls the pressure he was under. One day, three quarters of the way into shooting, when, convinced he would not be able to finish the film without going over budget, Brooks had to decide "Do you do the movie or do you just give it up?" He was sitting by himself at lunch, trying to decide what to do, when Grodin walked over to him and said, "Albert, I've got to leave at four," which no one can do on a movie set. Brooks thought it was "really funny." And somehow that made the moment pass and Brooks proceeded to finish the movie, under budget. For which he gives credit to Spheeris: "Penelope was great. It was down and dirty and there was no one better at figuring out how to get shortcuts."

And, invariably, life imitated art imitating life as Brooks' character is faced with the film shutting down: the studio is pulling the plug, the consultants are quitting, and the Yeager family are all signing releases, as what was meant to be a year's project has lasted just a few months. Brooks has lost his mind. He decides to save the film by manufacturing an ending, and to ensure its success, he will steal a plot device from a successful film. He first considers *Star Wars*, then *Jaws*—films whose lasting impact on the film industry Brooks could only have guessed. Ultimately, however, he decides to steal from a story that was itself based in reality: the burning of Atlanta in *Gone with the Wind*. Brooks literally and metaphorically burns his house down.

Brooks bought his meta-driven humor to every aspect of *Real Life*. The music for *Real Life* was composed by Mort Lindsay, who appears in the film and was indeed the bandleader on the then popular *Merv Griffin Show*. "There are scenes that never made it into the movie," Brooks said recently. "I filmed a whole scene where it was me and Mort trying to write themes to the people. Mort said: 'What do you think of that?' I said, 'She's much meaner than that, Mort.' So Mort goes: 'What about this?'"

The film also features the voice of Jennings Lang, a well-known Hollywood film and TV executive, as the head of the studio that's financing Brooks' movie. "I always liked the way he talked," Brooks explained. "He's got the best voice in the world. He had the script, but that wasn't going well, so I recorded a conversation. What we did was talk for three hours about the movie business. I'd say, 'Jennings, what about when you first started?' [And he'd answer,] 'Fuck, Albert! Who gives a shit!?' It took me two weeks to edit that conversation. Which I've done many times since."

One of the arguments the movie exec makes is that no couple is going to pay for a babysitter, movie tickets, dinner, and parking to see "reality" without big-name stars. True enough; in the span of time since *Real Life* debuted, the Hollywood business model has increasingly turned to brand name action franchises, with visual effects best seen on a large screen (and preferably in Imax and/or 3D at a premium ticket price). On the other hand, it's hard to imagine that even Brooks could have predicted the extent to which reality stars would become so newsworthy, that reality TV contests would grow to such popularity, or that TV shows would become so binge-worthy that couples would prefer to stay home and watch TV than pay for a babysitter and movie tickets. Then again, maybe that's exactly what happened. Maybe *Real Life* predicted it all.

Once Brooks finished the film, he still had to sell it. They held screenings. "This was so early that you didn't have to do cards," Brooks said, "You would just do screenings... Before the internet, everything

was safe. I would show all my movies up until *The Muse*, I guess. It
never got out."

The screenings were successful. Brooks recounts: "Paramount
offered one million dollars. Everybody was thrilled. This paid back
the investors. It let everybody who had any participation in it get
some profit. It was wonderful. We all went out and rejoiced." Perhaps
a bit too soon.

As Brooks recalled: "Then—and this is one of my profound lessons
in show business—my lawyer, Tom Pollock at the time, called me and
said, 'They changed their mind. They're going to pay eight hundred
and fifty dollars.' I, of course, said, 'They can't do that.' He said, 'Really?
Why is that?' 'Because they promised.' 'You're going to have a hard time
making them.'" They paid $850,000. That allowed Kovler to be repaid at
a profit, and Brooks, Spheeris, and others, after three years work, split
the remainder. As Brooks now says, "It was still great."

Brooks' deal with Paramount was that they couldn't test the film
(to test they would have paid more but Brooks said no). Barry Diller,
who ran Paramount at the time, wanted to open the film in small
cities and lead up to New York. Brooks knew that the film would
succeed or fail based on the New York critics. He convinced Diller to
open the movie there. Brooks promised to do whatever publicity he
could, saying, "I'll go on *Johnny Carson*. Whatever I could pull out of
my hat, which was a small hat."

On March 2, 1979, Janet Maslin reviewed *Real Life* in *The New
York Times*. She called it "very witty." Brooks, she wrote, "is never
without his absolute insincerity and irrational good cheer. *Real Life* is
full of delightful nonsense, a very funny account of one man's crusade
to capture all the truth and wisdom that money can buy." The film was
launched.

Paul Slansky, who, as an editor for *New Times Magazine*, had seen
a preview of the movie, described it as, "one of the funniest brilliant
movies I'd ever seen. It was unlike anything else. I had no idea how
prescient it would be. A seminal movie."

For the week after that review, the movie was deemed a success.
However, as distribution spread beyond New York and Los Angeles,
the movie did not have the same appeal to the general populace. Still,

the movie had a tremendous impact on Brooks' career…and, yes, his own real life. First and foremost, *Real Life* established Brooks as a credible motion picture writer, director, and actor, which led to his subsequent filmic existential comedies, such as *Modern Romance, Lost in America, Defending Your Life,* and *Mother.*

Slansky, who became friends with Brooks, believes *Real Life* established Brooks as a visionary. "He sees things in ways we don't. It's not for nothing that his name is Albert Einstein. There's something almost mathematical about Albert's humor. It's so exactly right. Like this is the way you phrase this to make it funny. He just sees these things."

When Brooks made *Real Life*, reality TV was still a joke. Almost forty years later, *Real Life* is all that much funnier, and Brooks' achievement is all the more gobsmacking because the film's absurdity now has the ring of truth. As scrolling through the day's headlines, or the evening or weekend's onscreen entertainment, makes abundantly clear, what Brooks took as comic has now become our own reality.

It appears the joke's on us.

Tom Teicholz *is a film producer in LA. Everywhere else, he's an award-winning journalist and producer creating print, video, and online content for Intel, Logitech, start-ups, museums, and nonprofits, as well as Forbes.com and* The Huffington Post.